INDIA AND THE UNTHINKABLE

INDIA AND THE UNTHINKABLE

Backwaters Collective on Metaphysics and Politics I

Edited by

VINAY LAL

ROBY RAJAN

OXFORD
UNIVERSITY PRESS

Oxford University Press is a department of the University of Oxford.
It furthers the University's objective of excellence in research, scholarship,
and education by publishing worldwide. Oxford is a registered trademark of
Oxford University Press in the UK and in certain other countries.

Published in India by
Oxford University Press
22 Workspace, 2nd Floor, 1/22 Asaf Ali Road, New Delhi 110002, India

First Edition published in 2016
Third impression 2024

ISBN-13:978-0-19-946686-3
ISBN-10:0-19-946686-6

Typeset in ScalaPro 10/13
by Tranistics Data Technologies, Kolkata 700 091
Printed in India by Manipal Technologies limited, Manipal

CONTENTS

PREFACE

Civilizational Dialogues and the Politics of a Collective

VINAY LAL

I

In May 2009, with the elimination of Velupillai Prabhakaran, the long-time leader of the feared Liberation Tigers of Tamil Eelam (LTTE)—an armed group committed to the creation of a Tamil homeland in Sinhala-dominated Sri Lanka—a civil war noted for the ferocity with which the state and its opponents fought each other appeared finally to have drawn to a close. Much before Prabhakaran's death, the LTTE had been designated by various states as a terrorist organization, though its members and support-ers were of course inclined to characterize the LTTE as a fighting force without any peers and as a pioneer in advancing strategies of guerrilla warfare that have now been embraced by insurrectionary groups around the world, from suicide bombings by female cadres to the skilful deployment of the internet among diasporic support groups for fundraising. Still, to some others, there was something yet more remarkable and sad about one of the most protracted and intractable civil wars of our times, which apparently pitted the adherents of two non-Abrahamic faiths against each other. Hinduism's followers have long claimed that their religion, which is certainly more decentralized than any other faith and presents an anarchic countenance to outside observers, is unusually if not uniquely tolerant; similarly, Buddhism is often represented as the religion that has been least prone to be put into the service of the flag, the nation state, or corporate interests. Insofar as intellectuals who are not predisposed by birth or upbringing towards religious feelings may be said to have a religion, it is seemingly Buddhism towards which they are most likely to gravitate: in the modern West, for instance, it is perhaps not an accident that intellectuals who have moved away from Christianity, Judaism, or a rigid adherence to secularism have been drawn to the somewhat more secularized versions of 'Eastern faiths', among them Zen Buddhism and the relatively more abstract or monistic forms of Vedantic Hinduism.

We need not, at this juncture, concern ourselves at any length with the question of what approximation the self-representations of Hinduism and Buddhism have to reality. Some will, for instance, argue that the very idea of 'Hindu tolerance' is compromised as a species of Orientalism, though a variety of Orientalism that attracts rather than repels some Hindu nationalists. Many more will dismiss outright the idea of 'Hindu tolerance', pointing to the pogroms instigated against Sikhs in north India in the wake of the assassination of Prime Minister Indira Gandhi on 31 October 1984, and against Muslims in Gujarat in 2002, or to the immense disabilities imposed on Dalits for generations. What is less commonly realized is that the idea of 'Hindu tolerance' has come under assault not only from Marxists and Dalits but even from many who are firmly persuaded of the view that the ideal of *Vasudhaiva Kutumbakam*—the entire earth is one family—is the cornerstone of the Hindu world view and carries within it the seeds of traditions of hospitality and ecumenism that have long been the characteristic traits of Indian civilization. Thus, in the Hindutva view, 'Hindu tolerance' was all too real, and constantly made the Hindu vulnerable to depredations from outsiders and invaders who were not similarly hobbled by civic restraint or considerations of hospitality. If to the Indian Left the idea of Hindu tolerance is a chimera, a form of self-flattery to which the Hindu takes frequent resort as if to compensate for centuries of rule under foreigners, to those at the other end of the political spectrum the reasons for jettisoning the idea are equally compelling.[1]

What is true of the idea of 'Hindu tolerance' is much the case with many elements of contemporary discourse. To take one further example, the secularists and the Hindu extremists who waged a battle over the Babri Masjid were doubtless sharply divided over their understanding of the ethical and socio-political obligations that one might owe to minorities in a democracy, but they were nevertheless united in their unstinting allegiance to the idea that the dispute could be resolved on the terrain of 'history'.[2] But, before venturing into a more prolonged discussion of the nature of contemporary intellectual life, some cues may be taken from the origins of the enterprise now known as 'The Backwaters Collective on Metaphysics and Politics'. Not long after the end of the civil war in Sri Lanka, a few friends gathered together to reflect on how best the intellectual, cultural, and spiritual resources of Indian civilization might be deployed to think ethically about contemporary politics and help in seeking solutions to seemingly intractable conflicts. I myself have long thought, for example, that it is distinctly odd that Americans should have become the major brokers of peace in West Asia—or what in the United States is called the Middle East—and most particularly in respect of the conflict over Palestine. Other great powers have, of course, been known to arrogate such rights to themselves, though it is their meddling that more often than not produces such conflicts in the first place. Americans especially seem least calculated to understand the complicated histories that have informed older civilizations. The question of American insincerity as a supposed 'neutral' or third party apart, and there is much that can be summoned to show just what a mockery the American-led 'peace process' has made of the possibilities of enduring peace and justice in Palestine, what does the United States know of relations between Muslims and Jews, or even between Muslims and Christians? The United States has been projecting itself as the 'one indispensable nation', a view openly embraced by three recent American presidents—Bill Clinton, George W. Bush, and now Barack Obama—though its posturing as the global custodian and champion of the values of freedom and democracy has a history that can be dated back at least to its rhetorical adumbration of Wilsonian self-determination. But we can with at least equal plausibility suggest that a nation that is built on the foundations of genocide and slavery, knows no other way of resolving its differences with others than through the naked imposition of its will, and now takes its official and consumerist notion of multiculturalism as a model for the rest of the world to emulate, is scarcely qualified to cast itself as a mediator of political, cultural, and religious conflicts. Civilizations, it must be added, are much richer entities than nation states, allowing—amidst hostility and conflict—for accommodation, cultural pluralism, and even inter-culturality. This is movingly conveyed, to take one illustration, in Mark Mazower's history of Salonica, today a largely Greek orthodox city on the Aegean Sea. For close to five centuries, from 1430 to 1912, Thessaloniki, the other name by which it is known, was under Ottoman rule; in the late fifteenth century, it had an influx of Jews fleeing persecution in Spain. Muslims, Christians, and Jews flourished here; so did Turks, Greeks, Albanians, Bulgarians, Serbs, and others, all cohabiting the same space. The 'silencing of the city's multifarious pasts' was a twentieth century obsession[3]: the fall of the Ottoman empire turned Salonica into a European city, though Western scholars do not generally characterize the exchange of populations—Greece received a million orthodox Christians from Asia Minor, and Turkey in turn took 500,000 Muslims—even as a milder form of 'ethnic cleansing'. One of the more astonishing nuggets from Mazower's grand history concerns the Nazis, whose quest for racial purity and annihilationist impulse could not countenance the fact, as they discovered it, that Salonica had never had a Jewish ghetto. The Nazi commander's disappointment is writ large in his assessment, conveyed to his superiors, that 'for the average Greek there is no Jewish question. He does not see the political danger of world Jewry'.[4] Had the people in this part of the world been properly civilized, akin to the Germans and the French, they would have known how to put the Jew in his place.

The friends who first congregated in Colombo in December 2010, and eventually put together what would become known as the Backwaters Collective on Metaphysics and Politics, were, however, animated by far more than the desire to see how the intellectual or spiritual insights of Indic traditions might be deployed to help resolve conflicts. A number of other impulses were present to varying degrees, which I would like to enumerate before taking up each for discussion at somewhat greater length. Most if not all of us had read widely in Gandhi, though his attraction to us resided not only on account of his radical commitment to non-violence, an idea to which the fashionable postcolonial crowd was largely if not wholly indifferent, or because of his insistence on an ethical life in politics, but also by virtue of his incipient critique of modern knowledge systems. A few of us in this group, Ashis Nandy for longer than anyone else, have been writing about, and probing, the politics of knowledge for some time—and it must be said at once that such a politics of knowledge is attentive to more than just those questions with which we are all familiar, such as questions about who speaks for whom, or the conditions under which knowledge production takes place. Some in our group, however, were also inspired by the figure of Sree Narayana Guru (1854–1928),[5] a radical Advaitin, itinerant philosopher, metaphysician, and reformer from Kerala, who both generated immense social unrest in the state of Travancore and bequeathed a large repository of philosophical writings that have received little scholarly attention. Indeed, though the notion of Kerala as a model Indian state has become an entrenched part of the folklore of 'development' at its best, none of the development economists, professional social scientists, or social commentators have as much as acknowledged the hand of Narayana Guru in enabling this script, even if those well-versed in the history of Kerala before its electoral takeover by the communists were fully cognizant of Narayana Guru's role in shaping modern Kerala.[6]

It is partly as a tribute to Narayana Guru that our small group took a decision at Colombo and over subsequent discussions to convene, if circumstances permitted, in Kerala on an annual basis. The name, 'The Backwaters Collective on Metaphysics and Politics', was proposed around this time. In the tourist literature produced both by the State of Kerala and the Government of India, Kerala is described as 'God's own country'. One might not wish to take such forms of pomposity too seriously, since they are rather keen on this idea in a great many other places as well, such as Texas, Montana, Wyoming—and more broadly the entire United States. Thus American exceptionalism, on which too many words need not be wasted. But in Kerala, 'God's own country' signifies more particularly 'the backwaters', a rather extensive and labyrinthine network of canals, lakes, and rivers that runs nearly half the length of the state. The backwaters have been described as a unique ecosystem, rich in distinct forms of aquatic life: freshwater from the rivers mingles with seawater from the Arabian Sea and the entire landscape is bathed in emerald green. But 'backwaters' in the title seemed very accommodating to us for myriad other reasons. Kerala is one of those places which generate fierce attachments. For those interested in Indian politics, it has been the site of some of the more arresting developments in Indian politics; it is also one of the few places in India—and, considering the evisceration of organized labour in so many parts of the world, around the globe—where one can still witness the power of labour unions. Students of Indian philosophy know the town of Kalady near Cochin—the Collective's favourite haunt, though one meeting was organized at the seaside town of Varkala—as the birthplace of Shankaracharya, and over the last three decades, scholarly attention has turned towards the so-called Kerala School of Mathematics (fourteenth to sixteenth centuries), from where the work of Indian mathematicians on infinite series and calculus may perhaps have been transmitted to Europe. One might go on in this vein, but there were yet weightier considerations in attaching ourselves to the idea of the 'backwaters'. One of the more germane facts is that too often the history of India is reduced to north India, to the comings and goings of kings, warriors, priests, merchants, scholars, and others in the Gangetic plain, and that peninsular India is only remembered as an afterthought. For a variety of reasons, moreover, intellectual life in independent India has gravitated around Delhi, and all of us were keen that we should make a concerted effort to avoid the country's capital.

In the global world of knowledge as it is constituted today, India itself is deemed to be part of the 'backwaters'; if India sits largely on the periphery, occasionally able to make a foray into the portals of knowledge, much of the rest of the global South inhabits the Never Never.[7] The Indian middle classes bemoan the fact that not a single Indian institution of higher education—not even one of the over dozen Indian Institutes of Technology, admission to which is described as much tougher than entrance into Ivy League schools—is ranked within the world's top 200 universities. There are endless discussions about why the only Nobel laureates of Indian origin (other than the recipients of the Nobel Peace Prize) reside overseas, and one of the

pet theories that makes the rounds of polite living room discussions
in upper class homes in India's metropolises is that Indians are never
permitted to succeed in their own country, and that talent is wasted
on account of corruption, red tape, a rigid insistence on rules and
seniority, and so on. None of this is of any concern to members of
the Backwaters Collective, nor are we even remotely tormented by
the concern that 1.25 billion people seem to be unable to bring back
a single gold medal from the Olympics. Even more importantly, the
Collective's members do not construe Harvard, Oxford, and other
elite institutions as torchbearers of standards that must be emulated
by everyone else around the globe. We have certainly heard enough of
'world class institutions' and their dedication to 'excellence': these hollow, rather pathetic, words and phrases are manna to administrators,
educators, and policy-makers, but signify nothing.[8] What cannot be
obscured is a fact that is truly painful, namely that the social sciences
in India and throughout the global South have been borrowed lock,
stock, and barrel from the West. The colonization of the Americas,
Asia, and Africa entailed the evisceration of people's livelihoods, the
decimation of their cultural norms and intellectual traditions, the
desecration of their deities and beliefs, and the wholesale destruction of their landscapes. Such forms of colonization would take, in
the wake of decolonization, more insidious forms. The categories of
knowledge that emerged from the experience and intellectual outlook
of white men were universalized so that they became everyone else's
history, and in course of time were enveloped by the languages of
human rights, multiculturalism, diversity, the right to protect, and
the rest of the paraphernalia that furnishes the arsenal for what are
described as liberal democracies. Our invocation of 'Backwaters' is
a sad acknowledgement of the lowly place of India in the global hierarchy of knowledge; it also, simultaneously, signals our defiance of
the dominant systems of knowledge and our hope that it is still possible to work towards an ecological plurality of knowledges.

II

Mohandas Gandhi and Sree Narayana Guru met only once. Their
meeting, on 12 March 1925, is well recorded even if the narratives
woven around it are partial. The occasion was furnished by what in

the annals of Indian nationalism is known as the Vykom Satyagraha.[9] Some thirty-five kilometres southeast of Cochin, or Kochi, the small town of Vykom hosted a Mahadeva temple administered by the Namboodiris. The lower castes—among them, the Ezhavas (traditionally toddy tappers), Thiyyas (coconut pluckers), and the Pulayas, viewed as the lowest of the low—were forbidden use of the road that ran outside the temple, though converts from the low castes, Christians, Muslims, and dogs and cows had free run of the public thoroughfare. In early 1924, T. K. Madhavan, a devotee of the Guru and an admirer of the Mahatma, who chafed at this injustice, sought the assistance of the local branch of the Indian National Congress in spearheading a campaign of non-violent resistance that would compel the temple authorities to remove the liabilities that prevented the lower castes from the use of a public road and eventually pave the way for their entry into the temple itself. In a rare gesture of what might be termed political involvement, Narayana Guru visited Vykom and expressed his solidarity with the demonstrators. A year after the *satyagraha* had commenced, Gandhi, prompted by various considerations, decided to wade into the struggle with a personal visit to Vykom. He met with the satyagrahis, local Congressmen, and the leader of the Namboodiri community. The details of that last audience are intriguing, to say the least; as one of Gandhi's biographers has put it, though the trained barrister and experienced negotiator had proved to be quite a match for colonial administrators, the Namboodiri Brahmin seemed to have had the upper-hand in his cross-examination of the Mahatma and his allegiance to Hinduism. Gandhi's interlocutor sought to persuade him that the lower castes were merely living out the punishment that was their due for their misdeeds in the past. Most tellingly, we are told, Gandhi himself was turned into something of a pariah: 'Immediately after Gandhi exits through his gate,' his biographer writes, 'the Brahman holds a purification ceremony in the pavilion where the encounter occurred so as to banish any pollution that may have trailed behind the Mahatma.'[10] A Gujarati bania, whatever his reputation in India, was not going to be permitted to get the better of a Namboodiri Brahmin.

It is, however, the meeting of Gandhi and Narayana Guru that compels our attention. It has sometimes been represented as the confluence of the north and the south, the intermingling of two different strands of the rich fabric of Indian spirituality. It has also been comforting to many to think of the event as a meeting of the Saint and the Reformer, but who is the saint and who is the reformer? Should we suppose, as seems quite reasonable, that Narayana Guru is being cast as the saint and Gandhi as the reformer? Gandhi has been assimilated to a long line of social reformers, but General Smuts spoke with enormous relief when, upon Gandhi's departure from South Africa in 1914, he remarked that 'the saint has finally left our shores'. One of the many reasons why Gandhi confounded his opponents was that they did not expect a saint, or at least someone of a saintly disposition, to meddle in politics. Narayana Guru, on the other hand, certainly appears to bear all the marks of a saint on his person, but it has been common to think of him as a social reformer who was critical in uplifting the low-caste Ezhava community into which he was born and bringing the question of caste to the fore.[11] He was known to his followers as rather apolitical; and, yet, he lent his name to the Vykom Satyagraha. In the terms of the present intellectual enterprise, there can be little doubt that Gandhi would ordinarily be cast as the 'politician' and Narayana Guru as the 'metaphysician', but neither term seems wholly satisfactory in capturing either personality.

Gandhi's biographers have often been obsessed with detail and many of the narratives of his life have, in emulation of their subject, taken on an epic quality; however, curiously, many of his biographers have been unusually reticent on the subject of the Mahatma's meeting with Narayana Guru. There is no mention of this meeting in Robert Payne's otherwise insightful and eminently readable biography.[12] The voluminous four-volume biography by the recently deceased Narayan Desai, the son of Mahadev Desai, who served faithfully by Gandhi's side for well over two decades and himself became a formidable chronicler of his mentor and the movement alike, devotes a chapter to the Vykom Satyagraha but is stunningly silent on the meeting between the two *rishis*.[13] What might that silence bespeak? Narayana Guru's biographers almost hint at something else: though he was very much an itinerant philosopher, it is Gandhi who came to the Guru's doorstep. Some element of partisanship is doubtless there; the biographers can barely resist the suggestion that Gandhi, well-intentioned though he may have been, came away with a greatly sharpened understanding of caste and its implications. Their meeting, writes K. Sreenivasan, 'had far-reaching consequences', producing 'a healthy impact on our freedom struggle and on Gandhiji's leadership of it'—healthy because, after their meeting, Gandhi was suitably enlightened and 'convinced of the irrationality of Caste. Thenceforward he vigorously worked to eradicate untouchability and caste observance'.[14] Lelyveld argues, not unjustifiably, that whatever Gandhi's reputation in the rest of India as the Mahatma, the Ezhavas had, in Narayana Guru, their own Moses.[15] He had led them out of their wilderness, wrought a social revolution not only among his own people but across all communities, and given them a slogan with which they could face the world with enhanced confidence: 'One caste, one religion, and one God for all.'

Some others, such as Ananthamurthy in this volume, have crystallized the meeting between Gandhi and Narayana Guru through certain words purported to have been exchanged between the two at the outset: Gandhi is said to have enquired of the Guru whether he was conversant in English, whereupon the Guru is reported to have retorted with the question, 'Do you know any Sanskrit?'[16] A translator or interpreter was present, but we are not merely to derive from this fact the usual conclusions about India as a multilingual country, the status of the language question in nationalist discourse, and the difficulties that India presents to those who fret about the obstacles in maintaining the country's unity. There are numerous respects in which Gandhi is incomparably more 'translatable' than Narayana Guru to the West, not the least of them being that, notwithstanding his critical role in launching a critical outlook towards colonialism and articulating a cogent critique of industrial modernity, Gandhi was very much formed in the milieu of colonialism. He was educated in London, and spent the greater part of his adult life overseas, mainly in South Africa, before returning to India for good in early 1915; though critical of the West, or rather of a certain dominant West that had colonized its own before colonizing others more remote, Gandhi was on familiar terms with the more dissident aspects of Western civilization. None of this is at all true of Narayana Guru, who was educated in village schools, interacted with other itinerant philosophers and ascetics, and remained oblivious to the intellectual mannerisms and cultural protocols of Anglophone Indian elites: we may say of him that colonialism left him untouched. The well-intentioned liberal thus at once assimilates Gandhi to the world of cosmopolitanism and earmarks Narayana Guru as a provincial, albeit influential, reformer; but this is an egregious error, since Narayana Guru had ushered in a radical transformation that broached what might be called 'the unthinkable'.

In his far-reaching study of the Haitian Revolution, the historian and political theorist Michel-Rolph Trouillot gave it an altogether novel interpretation by describing it as 'unthinkable'.[17] Many standard histories of the late eighteenth and early nineteenth centuries, overwhelmed by the canonicity of the French Revolution, that allegedly supreme moment in human history which made it possible to deliver ideas of liberty, equality, and fraternity to the elites, middle classes, and bedraggled masses alike, can scarcely be bothered with the Haitian Revolution; those which have bestowed some attention on this signal event, which established the first black republic in the world, beat a hasty retreat with the observation that the greatest rebellion of New World slaves only brought forth a country that would soon become the paradigmatic example of 'the failed state'. Trouillot, however, proposes a different reading, suggesting that the very idea of Haiti posed unusual problems, even—perhaps especially—for Europe's most 'enlightened' thinkers. 'In 1791,' he writes, 'there is no public debate on the record in France, in England, or in the United States on the right of black slaves to achieve self-determination, and the right to do so by way of armed resistance.'[18] When the revolt broke out, it was unfathomable to Europeans that 50,000 rebels in rags could defeat an armed force of 1,800 well-trained French soldiers. Yet the challenge, one to which Europe characteristically could not respond except by the imposition of draconian regimes of retribution that would persist well into the twentieth century, posed by the Haitian Revolution was still greater: it showed the emptiness at the heart of the Enlightenment, its utter incapacity to comprehend the event with the available conceptual framework.

The enterprise that underpins the present volume may well then be described as an attempt to grasp if not think the unthinkable. Some in the collective are centrally concerned with putting forward new readings of Narayana Guru, and subsequent volumes in what is projected as a series will lavish rather more attention on his thought.

Others in the collective are much better acquainted with Gandhi's life and work. But membership in the collective requires interest in neither Narayana Guru nor in Gandhi, much less anything that might be characterized as fidelity to either figure. Most of the papers in this, the first volume, provide ample testimony of the catholicity of interests among the collective's members. Some of us are interested in civilizational dialogues, since those at least seem to hold out greater promise of radical transformation in social relations than the kind of ritual exchanges that have become embedded within the structure of the nation state, while others have eschewed even these in the hope of achieving other models of inter-culturality. But I suspect that all the collective's members, both those who have formed the group's core from the outset as well as others who have been invited to share in the collective's life from time to time, can be described as morally and politically invested in a politics of knowledge that is vigorously committed to the ecological plurality of knowledges, firmly grounded in the idea that we are bound to explore and honour the sources of resistance from within the lives of ordinary peoples and their communities, and moved by the proposition that there is an imperative to continue probing the politics of metaphysics.

Notes

1. For an elaboration of this argument, see my 'Intolerance for "Hindu Tolerance": Hinduism, Religious Violence in Pre-modern India, and the Fate of a "Modern" Discourse', in *Religion und Gewalt: Konflikte, Rituale, Deutungen (1500–1800)*, edited by Kaspar von Greyerz and Kim Siebenhuner (Gottingen: Vandenhoeck & Ruprecht, 2006), 51–84.

2. Vinay Lal, *The History of History: Politics and Scholarship in Modern India* (2nd ed., Delhi: Oxford University Press, 2005), 141–85.

3. Mark Mazower, *Salonica, City of Ghosts: Christians, Muslims and Jews, 1430–1950* (New York: Alfred A. Knopf, 2005), 12.

4. Mazower, *Salonica*, 394.

5. There is some confusion, if it may be termed such, about the birth date of Narayana Guru. His disciple-successor, Nataraja Guru, does not furnish the year of his birth in *The Word of the Guru: The Life and Teachings of Guru Narayana* (3rd ed., New Delhi: D.K. Printworld, 2003 [1952]), though the 'List of Illustrations' accompanying the book mentions '1854–1928' as the years that spanned his life. The Cataloging-in-

Publication data for the same book gives '1856–1928' as the Guru's lifespan. In his translation of, and commentary on, Narayana Guru's *One Hundred Verses of Self-Instruction* (3rd ed., Varkala: Narayana Gurukula, 2006), Nataraja Guru introduces the book as a 'wisdom text of rare value written by Guru Narayana (1854–1928) in Malayalam'. The Wikipedia entry, scarcely the most authoritative source on Narayana Guru's life, but nevertheless the most likely resource for those seeking elementary information, states with some caution that he was 'most probably born in 1854' (http://en.wikipedia.org/wiki/Narayana_Guru, accessed 17 March 2015). However, one of his biographers in English displays no such uncertainty in describing the Guru's birth at Chempazhanthi, twelve kilometres north of Trivandrum, on '26 August 1856'. See K. Sreenivasan, *Sree Narayana Guru: Saint Philosopher Humanist* (Trivandrum: Jayasree Publications, 1989), 12.

All of this might justifiably be dismissed as trivial and certainly of little consequence in sketching the life of so luminous a saint-philosopher as Narayana Guru. Dates have never mattered very much in Indian history, it seems. If there is so much uncertainty surrounding the elementary details of the life of one who was so celebrated and is nearly a contemporary, one can well imagine how little can be ascertained as 'facts' in the case of those who belonged to relatively more remote times and even more so to periods of history for which we have scant, if any, evidence. The colonial writers who openly and with abandon pontificated on the 'Indian mind' would have had no hesitation in describing the uncertainty over the Guru's year of birth as indicative of the Hindu's disregard for facts, disdain for empiricism, and his inability to aim at precision. That there should be such uncertainty over Narayana Guru's birth date seems, at least on a superficial reading, all the more apposite, setting the this-worldliness of historical chronology in sharp opposition to the Advaitin's (apparent) other-worldliness.

Are, moreover, Guru Narayana and Narayana Guru one and the same? Is he the Guru that is also the Narayana, the Supreme One, or the Supreme One that is also the Guru, or the Guru that obviates the need for any other, even the Supreme One? Is the in-dwelling Narayana within him his very Guru? Let us suppose also that the Guru were travelling to another country, armed with the modern nation state's most characteristic and unyielding marker of identity, the passport. His biographers do not inform us with what papers Narayana Guru travelled to Ceylon, or even if he was armed with travel documents at all, or whether identity papers are at all required of people of his ilk. I doubt, considering that he seems to have gone under at least two names and that he is reported as having been born in two different years, that Narayana Guru would have been permitted to depart his country or enter another one in our times. But he lived in a different age, one that seems extraordinarily easy-going in comparison in relation to the behemoth that the national security state has become over the last few decades. Philosophers seldom deign to posit such questions, little realizing that the politics of the passport allows promiscuous entry into the metaphysics of identity.

6. See, for a fleeting discussion of this in a popular venue, B. R. P. Bhaskar, 'The Sree Narayana Effect', *Hindu*, 29 August 2004.

7. The phrase 'Never Never', for those conversant in Australian lore, references the more distant and demanding parts of the vast Australian Outback. The phrase first appeared in Barcroft Boake's poem, 'Where the Dead Men Lie', published posthumously in 1897: 'Out on the wastes of the Never Never—/That's where the dead men lie!/There where the heat-waves dance for ever—/That's where the dead men lie!' See the *Literature of Australia: An Anthology*, edited by Nicholas Jose (New York: W. W. Norton & Co., 2009), 260–2.

8. For a devastating indictment of the modern university's quest for 'excellence', see Bill Readings, *The University in Ruins* (Cambridge, Massachusetts: Harvard University Press, 1997).

9. Also spelled as 'Vaikom'.

10. Joseph Lelyveld, *Great Soul: Mahatma Gandhi and His Struggle with India* (New York: Alfred Knopf, 2011), 190–1.

11. For an exceedingly representative view of Narayana Guru as a social 'reformer' who challenged 'the principle of caste itself', see Ramachandra Guha, *Makers of Modern India* (New Delhi: Penguin, 2012), 14. Guha has become the voice of that segment of middle-class and upper-class India that sees itself as open-minded; he also represents India to those elements within the West who see themselves as relatively cosmopolitan and reasonably intrigued by, if not well-informed about, India. It is notable that Narayana Guru does not figure in Guha's list of the twenty Indians who were the makers of modern India; his absence is mildly lamented but justified on the grounds that Ambedkar fits better the mold of the influential reformer. When there is room for only one 'Annihilator of Caste', then enlightened opinion in India appears to be wholly in agreement that the mantle fell upon Ambedkar; see Guha, *Makers of Modern India*, 204. Narayana Guru's own disciples, it may be argued, played a critical role in disseminating the canonical view of Narayana Guru as an indefatigable reformer. 'For fifteen years he travelled incessantly', writes Nataraja Guru of Narayana Guru, 'attempting to bring more cleanliness and light to the poor people of the country. He helped them to clean

up the houses and streets. He helped them to have cleaner habits. He introduced and set an example in better diet. He gave an impetus to right moral standards. He pointed the right road to reform and more prosperity. He helped them to see clearly through maladjusted emotions.' Thus far, if that is largely what Narayana Guru sought to accomplish, in itself no mean task, there is little that would distinguish him from Gandhi. He seems to have been placed squarely within the ranks of a reformer, except that Nataraja Guru adds the following: 'But these were only preliminaries to the real teaching that was to follow. This he left behind in the form of verses and writings for his future followers to learn and interpret.' (Guru, *The Word of the Guru*, 29) The implication that Narayana Guru was much more than a reformer lurks in these passages, and it is this implication that my co-editor to this volume, Roby Rajan, seeks to bring out in his contributions to our volume.

12. Robert Payne, *The Life and Death of Mahatma Gandhi* (New York: 1969).

13. Narayan Desai, *My Life is My Message*, vol. II: *Satyagraha, 1915–1930*, translated from Gujarati by Tridip Suhrud (New Delhi: Orient Blackswan, 2009), 361–72.

14. Sreenivasan, *Sree Narayana Guru*, 5.

15. Lelyveld, *Great Soul*, 181.

16. My co-editor, Roby Rajan, has suggested to me on more than one occasion that the word 'retort' does not capture the flavour of the encounter between Gandhi and Narayana Guru; it may even, he has argued, be grievously misleading. In his words, 'These are two of India's great civilizational figures, and "retort" suggests a kind of "hurling back" of the (perceived) insult at the initial "offender"—a form of exchange that is simply inconceivable between two great souls like Gandhi and Guru' (private communication, 5 September 2015). While his suggestion has much merit to it, I have resisted the temptation to replace 'retort' with something gentler or kinder. For one thing, saintly figures are perfectly capable of retorts; saints are never just saints, whatever one's inclination and the press of received opinion about 'saints' to think otherwise. In this particular encounter, moreover, there is ample reason to suppose that Narayana Guru might just have been a bit irked by a Gujarati bania's audacity. If we are to give Gandhi the benefit of the doubt, let us suppose that he used the most matter-of-fact tone to enquire of Narayana Guru whether he was conversant in English, without insinuating, first, that English was *the* language to know, and, secondly, that whosoever commanded English was in the position of being able to command if not the world certainly much else. One can ask why Gandhi did not enquire of Narayana Guru whether he knew Hindi. It may be that Gandhi was

cognizant of anti-Hindi sentiments in south India, though the first anti-Hindi movement in Tamil Nadu dates to 1937, or that, more broadly speaking, he did not wish to appear to be a crusader on behalf of Hindi. But this would suggest that he thought of English as less imperialistic than Hindi in south India, which, considering everything we know about Gandhi, including his unapologetic critique of the colonization of English-speaking Indians at his speech at Banares Hindu University not too long after his return to India from South Africa, appears to be an untenable proposition. However charitably disposed we may be toward Gandhi, and assuming that Gandhi asked the question in innocence, looking merely for a common language—one reason why he obviously did not assume a knowledge of Gujarati on Narayana Guru's part—in which the two of them could converse, the critical consideration is how Narayana Guru received his question. He might not have thought that Gandhi was attempting to slight him, but in enquiring of Gandhi whether he knew Sanskrit, he put him on the back foot. There is writ large, in that small portion of the exchange, an entire narrative of how languages achieve hegemony, and the agonism that characterizes the relationship of two languages, one cast as the epitome of a civilizational tongue and the other as the language of triumphant modernity, rises to the surface.

17. Michel-Rolph Trouillot, *Silencing the Past: Power and the Production of History* (Boston: Beacon Press, 1995), 82.

18. Trouillot, *Silencing the Past*, 88.

ACKNOWLEDGEMENTS

It takes some kind of moxie for one of the highest-ranking corporate executives in the country to throw his weight behind an ethereal-sounding theme like 'Metaphysics and Politics', and for that we would like to extend our profound gratitude to Shri R. K. Krishna Kumar, Trustee, Tata Trust, for reposing such unflagging faith in our experimental venture. Perhaps only someone with the business farsightedness of Shri Krishna Kumar could also have mustered up the courage to place a wager on so improbable an intellectual enterprise. At a time when the academic institutions have almost wholly forfeited their responsibility to challenge prevailing dogmas, it is heartening to know that individuals like Shri Krishna Kumar who hold out the hope for a radical interrogation of contemporary ideas and institutions are still to be found in unlikely places.

This fortuitous convergence is, in no small measure, due to his continuing fidelity to a certain kind of opening that occurred in Kerala society in the early part of the twentieth century and which has come to be associated with the name of Narayana Guru. Although much ink has been spilt trying to come to grips with exactly what occurred then and how whatever did occur managed to so thoroughly transform social relations in Kerala, there persists the nagging feeling among many nearly a hundred years on that we still do not have anything close to a satisfactory account of that momentous Event. The over-hasty recourse to some ideas in common currency—'social reform' being a prominent one—has bequeathed us an understanding in which the Event has been incorporated into a 'regional' history by obscuring its most significant and enigmatic aspects so as to produce a narrative that would fit in seamlessly with prevailing social–scientific notions and with categories predominant in India's 'national' self-understanding.

However, there is now a growing realization that this unseemly haste has only served to shortchange the Kerala Event, and that nothing short of a complete jettisoning of all the understandings we have inherited of it can now enable us to return to the source so that we may start afresh, this time shorn of any anxiety to produce a readily assimilable account, and with the preparedness to accept whatever paradoxes we happen to encounter in our renewed confrontation with that Event. Only such an approach can rescue it from consignment to a dead 'history' by breathing a new universality into it so that we may continue to draw upon its resources to meet the challenges of the present.

Five conferences on the speculative theme of 'Metaphysics and Politics' have been held to date. The first of these met in Colombo, Sri Lanka in 2010 and was hosted by the Sree Narayana Guru Society of Colombo. For the flawless arrangements that were put in place there for all the conference participants, we would like to thank Shri T. S. Prakash, General Manager and Country Head of Revlon Lanka Private Limited. The prime movers for getting the Colombo conference off the ground were the dream-duo of Shri M. C. Dinakaran, General Manager, Board of Radiation and Isotope Technology, Department of Atomic Energy, Mumbai, and Shri Anish Damodaran, Director, Shree Rajlaxmi Logistics Private Limited, Mumbai, both of whom bore the brunt of the organizational burden of the Colombo meeting as well as that of the subsequent conferences. What is more, both were active participants in all the conference deliberations, and have also jointly contributed a paper to this volume. They have throughout displayed a remarkable working chemistry that ought to be an object lesson for all who might entertain the prospect of launching similar speculative enterprises in future.

All five conferences were held under the auspices of the Sree Narayana Mandira Samiti, Mumbai, and we would especially like to extend our deep gratitude to Shri M. I Damodaran and Shri N. Sashidharan, chairman and president of the Samiti respectively, for graciously putting the organizational resources of the Samiti at our disposal. For spontaneously coming to our rescue at a time when we hit an unexpected dry patch, we would like to thank Shri N. Mohandas, Chairman and Managing Director, Sterling Electromech Private Limited, Mumbai.

The Hotel Le Meridien at Maradu, Cochin, was the venue for three of our conferences, and we would like to thank Mr Sunil Nair, General Manager, for magically turning the hotel into a home away from home for the participants. We are similarly grateful to Mr P. K. Mohan Kumar, Chief Operations Officer, Gateway Hotels & Resorts, and to the Indian Hotels Company Limited for their hospitality in hosting our 2012 conference at Varkala. Sponsorship by Tata Sons and Tata Global Beverages proved indispensable to the success of our 2013 and 2014 conferences respectively.

Ashis Nandy, who remains a mentor and friend to many of us in the collective, has been characteristically generous in being with us every step of the way. Professor U. R. Ananthamurthy, an enthusiastic participant at our 2012 Varkala conference, was slated to attend our 2014 conference in Cochin but had to withdraw at the last minute due to illness. To our profound regret, he passed away shortly afterwards, leaving us (and thousands of other admirers) bereft of a kindred spirit and an exemplar of moral probity, and it is to his memory that we dedicate this volume.

Roby Rajan, Wisconsin, USA
Vinay Lal, Los Angeles, USA
1 January 2016

INTRODUCTION

Post-metaphysics and the Future of an Illusion

ROBY RAJAN

Welcome to Post-metaphysics!

The seminar circuits are abuzz today with the theme of 'religion and politics', what with everyone from the staid theologians who populate the divinity schools to functionaries of the various national intelligence services intent on deciphering the inner workings of 'the fundamentalist mind'. On the other hand, the topic of 'philosophy and politics' is as old as the hills, its place secure in undergraduate curricula, and surfacing occasionally even in the pre-election manifestos of political parties. But 'metaphysics and politics'? A more unlikely pair of bedfellows it is hard to conceive—and not because of 'politics'. If anything, recent years have witnessed an enormous inflation in the currency of 'politics' with practically every domain from the state and the university to marital relations and child-rearing now being declared 'political'. This hyper-elastic use of the word 'political' is meant to convey the idea that many areas of human life long seen as immune from questioning have now been thrown open to contestation.

It is the first half of that improbable conjuncture—'metaphysics'—which has witnessed a decline in its fortunes, a decline so precipitous that nary a respectable idea today would willingly consent to a conjunction with it. Things were not always so. Time was when the word would evoke the ultimate questions: What is the nature of reality? What is our role in the universe? What is the meaning of existence? Today however, its disrepute is such that in some circles, it has been parlayed into serving as shorthand for the sharpest possible rebuke. To be sure, a few brave souls still toil away in the musty archives of religion departments producing tenurable treatises on long-forgotten texts, but sadly these labours only serve to confirm the suspicion that metaphysics' final hour must be at hand. The over-professionalized occupant of the contemporary academy, preoccupied as he is with postcoloniality, postmodernity, post-structuralism, cultural studies, film theory, subaltern history, and other pace-setting sectors of the global knowledge industry, is only too glad to cede metaphysics as the province of cranks, god-men–charlatans, the unhinged, and a minority of the superannuated who still blissfully dwell in isolated time-warp pockets of a present that has otherwise resolutely declared itself to be 'post-metaphysical'.

A defining characteristic of this post-metaphysical era is the ever-tightening hold of expertise as it extends its reach from technocratically delineated zones such as fiscal and monetary policy or the integrated logistics of aerial bombardment and 'humanitarian' relief to the intimate crannies and crevices of filiation and sexuality. For the minutest of arenas of life may now be found a corresponding set of disciplinary paraphernalia along with a crew of accredited practitioners to whom all may turn for answers to their internal and external conundra. No problem exists today that could not be solved with the judicious application of expertise: gratuitous violence, mushrooming pathologies, debilitating anomie, all these and more are readily mendable if only the appropriate body of disciplinary knowledge were brought to bear on their seeming intractability. If something called 'metaphysics' still has a place in all this, it is either as a lapsed historical curiosity in the evolution of human thought or as a downsized technical branch of academic philosophy kept at safe remove from the 'hard realities' of social and political life.

The force that propels this post-metaphysical knowledge machine today is its drive for total 'inclusion', and the image that best captures the breathtaking scope of its ambitions is that of free iPads being distributed to children of a newly 'discovered' tribe in remotest

Amazon so that they may serve as yet another nodal point in the web of global educational connectivity. In the 'progress' ideology that powers this vision, all who happen to be currently 'excluded' by virtue of their unfavourable circumstances are in a kind of holding pattern above their designated landing strips while strenuous efforts are afoot by controllers on the ground for their eventual safe landing and full 'inclusion'. Egalitarianism, then, is the fundamental axiom of this post-metaphysics: the condition of 'underdevelopment', regrettable as it is, must therefore never be attributed to racial or genetic deficiency as was the wont of an earlier generation of civilizers. With post-metaphysics, it is only a question of *time lag* in the proper assimilation of the canons of universal rationality. But not to worry, this barrier too will be surmounted as progress takes hold universally and the promise of equality is incrementally brought to fruition for all of humankind.

Lately, however, a few discordant notes are audible beneath the smooth surface of this harmony as post-metaphysics has unexpectedly run into the problem of a rapid depletion of its pantry. Few now deny that if everyone on the planet were to reach the 'Western standard of living', the air would very likely become unbreathable, the food uneatable, the water undrinkable, and the cities unlivable for the vast majority of the planet's denizens. Indeed, for many in the Third World, this is scarcely some distant apocalyptic scenario. Savage wars are already breaking out over control of everything from water and food to oil and minerals; particulate levels in many cities today far exceed breathable levels; major rivers and lakes now harbour zero plant or animal life and are little more than sewers clogged with urban–industrial refuse; typhoons, tornadoes, cyclones grow alarmingly in frequency and ferocity, levelling towns, villages, and entirely submerging the smaller oceanic islands; mono-cropping and chemical use have turned vast tracts of farm land into 'green deserts'; rusted-out cars, obsolete computers, discarded mobile phones, and other detritus leak arsenic and mercury into the ground water; entire city neighbourhoods have turned into no-go zones where territory is carved out between rival gangs and one wrong move could invite the most violent retribution; depressive, schizophrenic, narcissistic pathologies together with their pharmacological–therapeutic correlates proliferate as jittery elites seek safety behind fortified homes and securitized buildings.

The oxymoronic expression 'gated community' best captures this phenomenon in its casual juxtaposition of the fear-stricken condition of gatedness with the warm bonhomie exuded by the word 'community'. Nearly every human habitat from the geopolitical to the familial now lends itself to being understood as a series of concentric gated communities. The First World fortifies itself against the Third to keep out the desperate multitudes crowding on to leaky boats and marching across arid deserts to escape homelands ravaged by conflict, droughts, floods, and other calamities. Against its own internal Third World of ghettoes, *banlieues, barrios,* and *favelas,* First World citizens demand intensified patrolling and monitoring even as they retreat deeper into spaces ringed by fencing systems, surveillance devices, and armoured response teams. Meanwhile within the Third World proper, mass migration into already uninhabitable cities spawns unending sprawls of improvised shacks lacking even the most basic amenities while luxury apartments, shopping malls, multiplex cinemas, and other pleasure palaces spring up within eyeshot of these shanties.

The basic unit of social life—the family—had long transmuted into a nuclear formation defending itself against sexual predators, bullying kids, demanding relatives, meddlesome neighbours, and burdensome social obligations, but now finds itself wracked from within by tele-visual addiction, drug dependence, and domestic violence. Whatever else may or may not have been universalized in this time of post-metaphysics, the Afrikaner *laager* mentality certainly has: at every level from the familial to the geopolitical, those who find themselves on the 'inside' circle their wagons ever more furiously to defend themselves against an ominous 'outside'. Meanwhile, the ballooning numbers of those 'outside' are instructed to content themselves with the promise of eventual 'equality' even as they must turn to desper-ately improvised forms of community cobbled together from the most incongruous elements (Pentecostal religion, rap music, and English Premier League football in the slums of many African cities) for sur-vival in the present.

Everyone's Favourite Whipping Boy

How then did things come to such a sorry pass? Believe it or not, some of the finest contemporary minds have laid the blame squarely at the door of metaphysics! 'Metaphysics' in this usage is held to character-ize all thought that assumes an essence that is originarily present, and from which are derived all other states as 'complication, dete-rioration, accident, etc.'[1] Thus, writes Derrida, 'all metaphysicians from Plato to Rousseau, Descartes to Husserl, have proceeded in this way, conceiving good to be before evil, the positive before the nega-tive, the pure before the impure, the simple before the complex, the essential before the accidental, the imitated before the imitation, etc.'[2] Metaphysics for Derrida is rooted in this placement of a self-present essence at the origin, from which follows the lack of full presence in the second of the aforementioned pairs: 'The history of metaphysics is the determination of Being as presence in all senses of the word. It could be shown that all the names related to fundamentals, to princi-ples, or to the center have always designated an invariable presence.'[3]

Indeed, Derrida has described the aim of his 'deconstructionist' project as one of 'making enigmatic what one thinks one understands by the words "proximity", "immediacy", "presence"'.[4] In the dual struc-ture of the linguistic sign as signified concept and signifying repre-sentation, the signified is held to be possessed of a presence that the signifier only secondarily represents: 'The formal essence of the signi-fied is presence, and the privilege of its proximity to the logos as *phone* is the privilege of presence.'[5] There is a homology, asserts Derrida, between the priority of signified over signifier and that of the spoken word (*phone*) over the 'merely' written (*gramma*): the prioritized terms in both instances are characterized by a fullness of presence. For 'deconstruction' on the contrary, every signified is always-already a signifier, every speech always-already a form of arche-writing, every privileged origin always-already shot through with *differance*. These Derridian neologisms are held to have collectively heralded our post-metaphysical age of ever-deferred, ever-displaced, ever-dislocated, ever-fluid, ever-mobile, ever-shifting, ever-ludic meanings, and to mark the end of all totalities that would establish themselves on the ground of stable identities.

From this dethroning of the signified follows the political conclu-sion that 'justice', the only ever 'undeconstructible', must also not be thought of as fully present but rather as an always-deferred *avenir* ('to come'), lest it be made to serve the ends of totalitarianism the way it did for much of the twentieth century. The deconstructionist ethical injunction is that we bind ourselves to this always-deferred future even as we realize full well that it will always remain 'spectral', never be made present. Unlike an earlier generation that believed 'History' to be on their side, the post-metaphysical universe is one of continuous deferral into an infinitely receding futurity of 'progress'. It should therefore scarcely surprise us to find Derrida unabashedly declare: 'I am for the Enlightenment, I am for progress, I am a "progressist".'[6]

Derrida borrows his use of the word 'metaphysics' from his German predecessor Martin Heidegger whose reputation as the twentieth century's pre-eminent European philosopher has been not a little tarnished by his one-time enthusiasm for the Fuehrer. If there is a politics underlying Derridian post-metaphysics, it lies in the attempt to unearth the resources necessary for resisting totalitarianism while remaining faithful to Heidegger's jettisoning of the self-present subject which continues to underpin the modern idea of democracy. Building in safeguards like *différance* and spectrality are Derrida's ways of correcting for his German mentor's political blunders while preemptively exculpating the idea of 'justice' from complicity in any future horrors.

Derrida's principal problem with Heidegger is that despite having initiated the 'overcoming of the subject', the latter remains unwittingly mired in 'metaphysics'. This is held to be especially true in the period before Heidegger's celebrated 'turn' (*Kehre*), after which he is said to have set about mending his ways by trying to expunge metaphysical remnants from his thought. From this standpoint, Heidegger's early magnum opus, *Being and Time*, is still enmeshed in metaphysical concepts such as 'man' and 'subjectivity', which are held to have spilled over into belief in the full self-presence of a collective historical subject—Nazi Germany under the leadership of the Fuehrer—that could summon up the 'resoluteness' to overthrow the nihilism of modern technological culture.[7]

In such a reading, every invocation of community invariably smacks of 'presence', opening the door to crypto-, if not full-blown, fascism. Heidegger's fatal mistake, in this view, is said to lie in the illegitimate passage from the individual freely choosing his fate-towards-death to an entire community choosing its mode of being. One philosopher's conflation of community with *Volksgemeinschaft* ('national community') is held to forever impugn the very notion of community as metaphysical, even as ever more gated communities proliferate in every direction, their full 'presence' coercively secured through a machinery of intimidation and surveillance before which post-metaphysical braggadocio stands powerless. Meanwhile, radically different traditional communities that had learned to coexist over the centuries have newly discovered ideologies like ethnonationalism, and have turned on one another as if making up for lost time, leaving in their wake dazed and uprooted men, women, and children housed in squalid 'refugee camps' and at the mercy of the global 'relief agencies'. Periodic appeals issue forth to an amorphous 'international community' for 'humanitarian relief' in what is facilely labelled as 'sectarian conflict', when it is the insatiable appetites and Machiavellian geopolitics of the very same 'international community' that are usually responsible for sowing the seeds of these conflicts in the first place.

Meanwhile Back at the Ranch

When one turns to contemporary 'postcolonial' forms of theorization, what lies in wait there is the discovery that the traditional communities that are at the receiving end of post-metaphysical machinations are in a homologously subservient position in these 'subaltern' theories as well. Here, it is inevitably 'the larger socio-historical context' through which such communities must be understood, never on the communities' own terms. Communities in this 'contextual' understanding can only have a sub-national standing, and figures who emerge at this level must necessarily be understood using categories operative at the level of the national knowledge system. As a consequence, while academic attention has been lavished on communities as objects of ethnographic enquiry, on how they have been the 'sites' of various 'insurrections', 'revolts', and 'rebellions' against some external force—colonialism, imperialism, landlordism, capitalism, the state—we know next to nothing about the dynamics of autonomous transformation from within and across communities.

The national knowledge system within which traditional communities are enfolded as objects of a 'contextual' episteme in turn subsists in a dependent relationship to the global knowledge system centred in the metropolitan knowledge capitals, for which the peripheral knowledge centres serve as field stations. In the case of India, the national political capital also doubles as the official knowledge capital hosting an assortment of development-centres, think tanks, and universities that function by processing inputs from the global knowledge system and disseminating them in the form of periodic 'policy recommendations'—pronouncements that more often than not entail deleterious consequences for the nation's far-flung populace that is entirely shut out of the capital's inner workings. Those staffing these centres are themselves products of the metropolitan knowledge system, from within which the traditional communities that command the primary affiliation of most ordinary citizens inevitably disclose themselves as infra-national entities that are to be grasped using categories through which the nation understands itself.

A significant trope in the Indian national self-understanding has been 'reform', a word first used to describe changes introduced by Brahmoism into the religious practices of the Bengali elite as a reaction-formation to the colonial encounter. The main features of this 'reform' were the excision of rituals, gods, and goddesses deemed too primitive, the adoption of a streamlined theology in line with the colonizer's Protestantism, the valorizing of selected texts to accord them a centrality hitherto unknown, and a reworking of the notion of indigenous masculinity so as to be authoritative enough to underpin these changes.[8] In the next phase of its use, the word 'reform' gradually became wedded to a galloping nationalism, and the total revamping of traditional social and religious customs now came to be seen as an integral part of the reawakening of an ancient civilization refashioning itself as a modern nation by shedding all that was obsolete and irrational in its inheritance and reviving all that was estimable and glorious.

This growth of an elite-led nationalist politics was accompanied by the first stirrings of a politics in the lower rungs of the social order, and thence also to an interrogation of the elite conception of 'nation' and what such nationhood was going to mean for the 'independent' entity that was to be brought into being after the colonizer's formal departure. The apprehension here pertained specifically to the equation of 'nation' to a 'Hindu nation' that would be indelibly stamped with upper-caste features. Whereas the elite-led anti-colonial movement was built around an inconsistent ensemble of modern and revivalist ideas such as national self-determination on the one hand and the restoration of lost glories on the other, the low-caste movements from below were directed chiefly at challenging the ritual and material inequities of the prevailing social structure while displaying a profound ambivalence towards the project of nationhood.

With the addition of this new dimension from below, an antagonism was introduced into the very heart of the idea of the 'nation'—as if in spontaneous illustration of the metaphysical proposition that the moment one defines oneself against a putative 'externality', the 'internality' which is sought to be defended suffers a simultaneous fissure from within. As the struggle against the colonizer's 'external' oppression came into sharper relief, it found itself in mounting tension with the struggle against 'internal' oppression, the latter structured around contesting traditional hierarchy and privilege rather than reclaiming territory from the colonizer. The word 'reform' was subsequently enlarged to encompass this struggle directed against the internal elites, a struggle that often allied itself with the 'external' oppressor to contain the 'internal' oppressor's ambitions of turning the nascent idea of nationhood into a plank for elite revivalism.

Separate pantheons gradually emerged for the two struggles. Gandhi, Nehru, and Tagore formed the core pantheon leading the 'external' struggle, each representing a different facet of the response to colonialism, each displaying a different emphasis of 'internal' and 'external'. Gandhi looked primarily to 'indigenous' religious sources, attempting to strike a balance between 'internal' and 'external' struggles by advocating the abolition of untouchability on the one hand while upholding the principle of caste differentiation on the other. Nehru was the quintessential worldly liberal with a secular-egalitarian outlook and unbounded faith in humanity's ability to tread the path of progress through scientific and technological advances. Finally, Tagore embodied a cultural cosmopolitanism that was rooted in native soil, eschewing any form of reactive indigenism while simultaneously embracing the best the world's cultures had to offer.

A pantheon of the 'internal' struggle would probably not command the unanimity of the 'external' pantheon—barring the exceptional figure of B. R. Ambedkar. Another name staking a strong claim for inclusion from the same Marathi-speaking region as Ambedkar is Jyotiba Phule, founder of the Satyashodhak Samaj (Society of

Seekers of Truth) in 1873 and author of a number of tracts in which Brahmins were painted as alien invaders who had subjugated the native Shudra and Ati-shudra inhabitants by force and deception. Another strong contender would be E. V. Ramaswamy Naicker (EVR for short) from the Tamil country, self-declared rationalist and founder of the 'self-respect movement' in 1925 and given to highly provocative gestures like burning copies of *Manusmriti* and *Ramayana* in public, garlanding idols of the gods and goddesses with shoes, wearing all-black attire rather than the upper-caste white—all to dramatize his protest against the ritual and symbolic privilege of the Brahmin. Although both EVR and Ambedkar began their political careers seeking to 'reform' exclusionary Hindu practices and gain equal recognition for the lower castes, they eventually arrived through their separate pathways to the common conclusion that, contrary to Gandhi's belief, caste discrimination was so integral to Hinduism that it was beyond 'reform', the only solution being to defect entirely—in EVR's case to atheistic rationalism, in Ambedkar's case by converting to Buddhism in the final year of his life.

Some of the major figures of this 'internal' pantheon have now been memorialized at the sprawling Ambedkar Park in Lucknow, a brainchild of the Dalit leader Mayawati and built intermittently over thirteen years from 1995 to 2008 during periods when she was Chief Minister of the state of Uttar Pradesh. The park hosts super-sized statues of Ambedkar, Phule, Shahu Chattrapati (a follower of Phule and erstwhile Maharaja of Kolhapur), of Mayawati's political mentor Kanshi Ram and, last but not least, of Mayawati herself. The plan to include EVR's statue had to be shelved following strenuous protestations by her erstwhile Hindu-nationalist BJP coalition partners for whom a towering memorial to one who had on numerous occasions showered abuse on their muscular warrior-hero Lord Rama proved to be one statue too many.

Stranger in the Park

Surprisingly, the park also has a statue of Narayana Guru (1854–1928), a figure of considerable importance in his native Kerala but little known outside that state. 'Surprising', because in a park dedicated to leaders for whom low-caste emancipation automatically equated to anti-Brahminism, Narayana Guru clearly does not fit the bill. Not only is there no evidence that he harboured any anti-Brahmin animus, he is commonly seen as the principal agent of the 'Sanskritization' of his own 'backward' Ezhava caste. Being an accomplished Sanskrit scholar, he authored a number of compositions in Sanskrit, the most renowned of which is the hundred-verse *Darshanamala*, a 'garland of visions' of Absolute Reality from the ten different vantage points of *adhyaropa* (superimposition), *apavada* (negation), *asatya* (non-existence), *maya* (power), *bhana* (awareness), *karma* (action), *jnana* (knowledge), *bhakti* (devotion), *yoga* (union), and *nirvana* (liberation).[9]

Furthermore, he was personally instrumental in dethroning the local gods housed in the traditional temples of the Ezhavas and installing in their place idols of Shiva, Subramania, Ganesha, Sharada, and other Brahminic gods. Not for no reason have there been some recent attempts to recruit him to the cause of Hindu revivalism, making him possibly the only figure who might one day find a place in both low-caste and Hindu-revivalist pantheons. What there is absolutely no evidence of, however, is that the idea of the Indian nation crying out for freedom from the colonizer, or of a 'civilization' mortally wounded at the hands of colonialism ever engaged him in any way. We can, therefore, rest assured that one pantheon the Guru is in no danger of being admitted to anytime soon is the national one. National pantheon-making is something of a cottage industry now,[10] but one place these pantheon-makers inevitably fall short is in supplying any kind of explanation as to why Kerala, with no pantheonal representative, is the state that underwent the most far-reaching social change of all the Indian states, emerging from it with not only its intercommunal relations radically altered but also its culture and polity thoroughly revitalized.

The central puzzle one is confronted with here is that although Narayana Guru is the figure credited with being the prime mover for these changes, unlike an Ambedkar or an EVR, he never saw 'Brahminism' as a foe of any kind nor did a political programme of 'fighting caste oppression' find any favour with him. The cosmopolitan ideal of 'world citizen', which held such sway among colonial-era Bengali elites—and of which Tagore was said to be the ultimate representative—held no appeal whatsoever for him. And if at all he could be said to have engaged in any kind of 'dialogue', it was with the *acharyas* (wisdom teachers) who preceded him, his 'praxis' (if that is even the right word) being at one with his *vidya* (knowledge), at least as far as his followers were concerned. Unlike Gandhi, he evinced no interest either in 'resisting' colonialism or in carrying on a 'civilizational dialogue' with the colonizer—or, for that matter, in even picking up rudiments of the English language.

Contemporary theorists operating in the global knowledge arena are given to a compulsive indexing of all of Indian history as 'pre-colonial', 'colonial', and 'postcolonial', as if 'colonialism' were some-how its self-evident Archimedean point. One suspects that the reason for this may well be that beneath all the high-decibel fireworks of 'postcolonial' theory, there burns bright the flame of an ineradicable fascination with the glamour of the colonizer, whether in the form of 'resisting' it as with Gandhi, or emulating it as with Ambedkar. Narayana Guru's unsettling *indifference* to it—neither 'precolonial' nor 'colonial' nor 'postcolonial' but simply dispensing with any need to reference the 'colonial'—is sought to be coarsely domesticated within this frame by casting him as a 'regional' figure preoccupied solely with the parochial goal of his caste's upward mobility. What this form of brute recuperation always betrays, however, is a confla-tion of universality with spatial geographic spread, this space being invariably construed either as 'nation' or as 'globe'.

In the more extreme versions of this doctrine, just about every-thing from the 'caste system' to the indigenous systems of phi-losophy is alleged to be a 'colonial construction'. In this conception, Vivekananda's reactive deployment of Advaita—him of 'beef, biceps, and *Bhagavad-gita*' fame—blends indistinguishably with Narayana Guru's Advaita since the prominence accorded to Advaita as a phi-losophy is, in this view, just a product of colonial philology.[11] That Narayana Guru's discovery of Advaita was through an entirely dif-ferent pathway—the millennia-old Sanskrit *pathashala* (traditional schooling) system of Kerala and not through colonial translations—matters little in this world, which, to paraphrase Hegel, is the night in which all cows (barring one) are colonial-black. The one white cow that stands out against the blackness of this night is *bhakti*, which becomes the ultimate standard-bearer of an 'authentic' people's Hinduism, when what has been indubitably established is *that it is the very distinction between 'popular' and 'philosophical' Hinduism that is colonial through and through.*[12]

Perhaps this is why Romain Rolland was moved to observe that the Guru's 'doctrine was impregnated with the monist metaphysics of Shankara, but tended to practical action showing very marked differences from Bengal mysticism, whose Bhakti effusions filled him with mistrust'.[13] Rolland goes on to say: 'He preached, if one may say so, a *jnana* (knowledge) of action, a great intellectual religion, having a very lively sense of the people and their social needs. It has greatly contributed to the uplifting of the oppressed classes of Southern India and its activities have in a measure been allied to those of Gandhi.' This observation of Rolland's, with its promiscuous intermixing of 'monist metaphysics' and 'practical action', 'a great intellectual religion' and 'a very lively sense of the people and their social needs', of 'jnana' and 'uplifting of the oppressed classes', would scarcely make sense to today's champions of bhakti for whom 'intellectual religion' and 'popular religiosity' occupy wholly different compartments—the former hopelessly tainted by its alleged colonial discovery, the latter the true religion of the people.

In his aligning of the Guru's activities with Gandhi's, Rolland's qualifier 'in a measure' betrays a degree of hesitation in advancing the comparison. Comparing the two on some putative scale of 'greatness' would surely be invidious, not least because they inhabited two entirely different conjunctures. Gandhi is of course universally acknowledged as a world-historical figure for his ethico-religious innovations and interventions in the rough and tumble world of politics, and for his unique location at the intersection of an 'external dialogue' vis-à-vis the West and an 'internal dialogue' through which ideas like ahimsa, satyagraha, and dharma received a newly mass-political articulation. The Guru, on the other hand, is to be located at an entirely different but no less significant intersection—that of the most orthodox school of Indian metaphysics and a 'gracious uprooting'[14] that saw a centuries-old social structure come gently and swiftly unravelled.

Instead of descending into chaos and bloodshed as frequently occurs with the disintegration of an old order, in Kerala this unravelling became the ground for a renegotiation of intercommunity agonisms and the heralding of a new era of constructive politics. What the Guru unwittingly demonstrated was that even in the most 'oppressive' context conceivable, the oppressor does not automatically occupy one's dialogic centre; that a deep enough 'dialogue' with one's own traditions *can* generate the resources for cultural and social renewal from within, bypassing and sidelining all the oppressor's stratagems. While Gandhi's lasting legacy is the unerring moral compass he left behind for future generations to turn to in their confrontation with new forms of oppression, what we get with the Guru is a micro-dynamics of autonomous social transformation in community-based societies, an alternative universality in which all the dominant strands of Indian metaphysics—the *vaidika*, the *baudha*, the bhakti, and the *tantrika*—converge.[15]

Some have compared the Guru with Ramana Maharshi, but this comparison between a constant peripatetic whose interventions transformed the very fabric of Kerala society, and an enlightened sage planted firmly within the confines of his ashram dispensing wisdom to his disciples can only take us so far. Even one of Kerala's foremost Marxist ideologues—a group not known for its generosity in sharing the credit for Kerala's social accomplishments, and normally given to characterizing the Guru as an 'Ezhava saint' who could only dimly perceive what later Marxist theorists like E. M. S. Namboodiripad brought to sharp clarity—has anointed Narayana Guru as the *Novodhana Rajashilpi* or 'chief architect' of Kerala's Renaissance[16] because of his foundational role in the state's social transformation. Some notion of 'politics'—insofar as politics, in however attenuated a form, is unavoidable when speaking of fundamental social change—is, therefore, indissociable from the name Narayana Guru; with Ramana Maharshi on the other hand, 'politics' is the last word that comes to mind, the Maharshi being an unambiguously 'spiritual' figure.

And yet, the Guru's was not a politics in any sense in which we might understand that word today. Where Gandhi embodied the power of religion as the source of an ethical force that could be directly deployed in politics, demonstrating this power over and over in the most intractable of situations, the Guru displayed no interest in political 'struggles' of any sort, distancing himself even from the famed Vaikom Satyagraha led by Gandhi a few kilometres away from his ashram at Aluva, much to the displeasure of his followers. The paradox to be underlined here, however, is that this distancing was *absolutely crucial* to ushering in a new era in Kerala politics and reshaping its society for all time to come. Where Gandhi was an unparalleled ethico-religious figure for whom politics was the principal domain of action, the Guru confronts us with the enigma of an 'apolitical' figure who nonetheless manages to unleash the most far-reaching autonomous social transformation witnessed anywhere in India. Add to that the oppressive presence of the colonial state in one of the most rigidly stratified regions of the country, and the enormity of the achievement begins to come into view. The central theoretical challenge posed by this paradox is precisely how we are to comprehend this 'link' between the Guru's own scrupulous self-distancing from politics, and the unprecedented political consequences of this very distancing—consequences which the connotations called forth by words such as 'religion', 'ethics', and 'politics', taken singly or in combination, fall well short in accounting for.

A Transversal Dialectic

We could call this peculiar conjuncture 'metaphysics and politics' if we wish, but only if we bracket the 'and' as not standing in for any kind of direct 'nexus' or causal relation between the two terms, neither of which can, however, be dispensed with: 'politics' because we are dealing here with a radical transformation of social relations, and 'metaphysics' because categories and methodologies derived from social and narratological sciences that in any way presuppose a notion of extant 'reality' lack the conceptual resources to account for the central feature of this transformation—*its autonomy from contextual determination*. 'Metaphysics' in this understanding is, therefore, not to be mistaken for abstract doctrine alone; what concerns us here is rather the precise modality through which abstraction becomes actuality by triggering a new politics—without in any way invoking some super-contextual agency or occult force that secretly accomplishes the work of social transformation.

An explanation that lies outside any field delineated by the twin poles of 'contextual determination' and 'inner agency' seems to be what is called for here, because no matter how sincere and talented the 'real' individuals involved in the 'actual' historical process—and the cast in the Kerala Event is stellar by any accounting—the scale of the peaceful transformation that was ushered in cannot be attributed either to the proximate categories deployed by the participants themselves or to some prior grand design that unfolded inexorably. Hopelessly inadequate for our purposes also, needless to say, is the by now ready recourse for explaining any form of social change with religious overtones in India: the staple diet of commentaries on the Puranic myths, characterologies drawn from the Ramayana and the Mahabharata, ethico-theological lessons extracted from the Bhagavad Gita, the multiple meanings of dharma, or the trendier topics of 'syncretism', 'creolization', and 'hybridization', not to mention the obligatory references to Sufism and bhakti.

One hallowed opposition the Guru definitely put paid to is that of the Sanskritic versus avarnic—the Sanskritic solely the inheritance of the *savarna*, the cruder *jatipuranas* the narrative stock inherited by the *avarna*—so that any fudging of this narratological boundary must immediately be attributed to 'Sanskritization' and the related category of 'caste mobility'. Not only is this false on empirical grounds—there was a long tradition of Sanskrit learning among the Ezhavas of Kerala for instance—*even if it were historically true*, the Guru's Sanskrit compositions, widely acclaimed as the outstanding *prakarana-granthas* of his time, coupled with his cardinal role in the overhauling of avarna–savarna relations in Kerala, should suffice once and for all to discredit this notion in its entirety. Indeed, this touches on the fundamental question raised by the Guru's pivotal place in Kerala's social transformation: both Sanskritic *and* avarnic, both 'social reformer' *and* metaphysician, both textual *and* devotional, both jnani *and* bhakta, yet neither national freedom-fighter *nor* fighter against caste oppression, neither dialoguing with the colonizer *nor* emulating or resisting him, neither gradualist reformer *nor* radical revolutionary, the Guru emerges as a paradoxical point of universal singularity that confounds every categorical opposition the national self-knowledge is structured around.

But if the national knowledge system is at a loss in trying to locate the Guru within its coordinates, 'universal history' is equally at sea. The pathway along which Kerala's social transformation unfolded undercuts the foundational premise of universal history: the decimation of traditional communities and their 'sublation' in the universality of the modern state. In this Hegelian story of universal history, the 'infinite subjectivity' of the individual is pitted against the closed particularity of traditional community, which eventually proves too brittle to withstand total incorporation by the constitutional state. Writing in the high noon of modern optimism, Hegel could probably not have imagined that the 'universality' of the modern state which he championed would soon come to host a particularism more virulent than anything the traditional communities had ever known: ethno-nationalism.

To be clear, Kerala's social transformation also witnessed a negation of traditional community, indeed a negation so thoroughgoing that the very substance of its numerically most significant community— its gods, its narratives, its rituals—stood expunged. The difference, however, was that this was a *self-negation*, not a negation foisted from without or by an overweening state seeking to bend communities to its logic of power and resource competition. It was an *autonomous negation* working its way through the constitutive inter-relationality of Kerala's communities, a negation that gave rise to the generative matrix for a revitalized form of intercommunality and the subsequent birth of a politics that saw the emergence of a cross-community Left movement that went on to win state power in 1957 and initiate far-reaching reforms in land, health, and education. Insofar as its underlying logic was also one of negation, this transformation too was dialectical at root; however, the precipitating contradiction here was not between 'infinite subjectivity' and 'closed community', *but between community and its own non-coincidence*. Unlike the Hegelian dialectic of progressive history with the modern state as its crowning sublation, in Kerala the state was subsumed as a subordinate moment in an autonomous dialectic of negation, dissolution, and reconstitution of intercommunity relations. This might also help explain why the state in Kerala remained uncharacteristically responsive to popular demands long after the most significant legislative changes had already been put into place.[17]

This Kerala dialectic runs transversal to that of universal history's subordination of traditional communities under the aegis of the nation state as meta-community. But not only that; Kerala's autonomous dialectic of intercommunality also stands opposed to a communitarianism that seeks to freeze extant communities in their present forms, freighting them for eternity with their historically inherited substance of collective narratives, memories, and prejudices. In this precise sense, Kerala's social transformation inaugurates a dialectic that lies beyond the grasp of progressive universal history as well as static communitarianism: unlike universal history, the state is thoroughly de-centred within a larger dynamic of intercommunality not beholden to any notion of 'progress'; and unlike a complacent communitarianism, it founds itself on a confrontation with the non-identity of one's communal substance, seeking to transform the inertia of this entrapped substance into a dynamic force of intercommunal regeneration. Indeed, from the perspective of the Kerala dialectic, the state's self-installation as the culminating sublation of community and the traditional community's clinging to its notion of a self-identical communal substance fully complement each other by turning such communities into reified entities that may then be seamlessly integrated into the state's logic of power and resource competition.

But the modern state's imperious subsumption of traditional communities and its seeming current invulnerability in no way implies that its supremacy is assured for all time to come. All it means, from the perspective of intercommunality, is that the state's coercive apparatus has provisionally prevailed in arresting what will nonetheless always dog it in any community-based social constellation: the insistent negativity of the intercommunal dialectic. And if that dialectic could erupt in the midst of a society crushed under the twin burdens of colonialism and untouchability, as was the case in late-nineteenth and early-twentieth century Kerala, then surely it is too early to write its obituary under contemporary conditions, no matter how dispiriting they may seem. Indeed, even in Kerala, some Dalit and Adivasi communities were left more or less untouched by the gale-force winds of social transformation, a fact sometimes used to castigate the dialectic—as if in its absence the state's machinery would have done better, a proposition quickly put to rest with even the most cursory examination of the Indian nation state's record with these communities.

Repetition of Repetition

In conclusion, it might be instructive to turn to Narayana Guru's own understanding of the task he was engaged in: 'Whatever we have to say,' he had famously remarked, 'Shankara has already said.'[18] Considering the social tremors set off by this 'mere repetition' of Shankara more than a thousand years later, the Guru's modesty seems somewhat disingenuous, yet it remains truthful in its essence. This is because 'repetition' here does not mean formulaic repetition, transmission, or exegesis, but the creative reiteration of a fundamental truth so that it can take hold under circumstances completely different from the 'original' articulation. Instead of now reposing our collective faith in the state to safeguard the welfare of marginalized communities in the name of a putative 'realism'—a folly by any measure, given what we now know about the nature of the modern state—what the inter-communal dialectic enjoins us to do is to 'repeat' the Guru afresh under contemporary circumstances. The element of contingency as to what practical form this 'repetition' would take today is unavoidable, since it is this indeterminacy that also opens up the space for creativity in social intervention.

In the domain of theory, the Guru's legacy poses no less daunting questions. What after all do we do with a figure who confounds all the standard oppositions of Sanskritic and avarnic, social-reformer and metaphysician, the textual and the practical, jnana and bhakti, national and regional, internal and external, emulation and resistance, reformer and revolutionary? What do we do with a figure who doesn't seem to have paid any heed to history of any kind, let alone universal history, yet was the bearer of a universality that unleashed a historically unprecedented transformation in his society? We could of course choose to ignore him altogether, but then how do we account for the fact that he is credited by ordinary people and intellectuals alike with initiating the most far-reaching peaceful social change witnessed anywhere, for the fact that his compositions are still recited and sung in homes large and small across Kerala, for the fact that he managed to trigger the greatest outpouring of words in Malayalam by being far and away the most written-about figure in the entire history of that language?

An analogy with what happens in the world of art when confronted with a genuinely new work might be appropriate here. Here is T. S. Eliot's description of such an encounter:

The existing order of monuments form an ideal order among themselves, which is modified by the introduction of the new (the really new) work of art among them. The existing order is complete before the new work arrives; for order to persist after the supervention of novelty, the *whole* existing order must be, if ever so slightly, altered; and so the relations, proportions, values of each work of art toward the whole are readjusted; and this is the conformity between the old and the new.[19]

Eliot is not saying that the new arrives fully formed from an alien land of utter novelty demanding to overthrow the old, nor is he suggesting that an automatism is built into the old, which makes for a spontaneous reception of the new. When confronted with 'the really new', the old may fully be counted upon to summon up all the inertia it can muster to keep the new from unsettling its established order. This is indeed what occurred in the realm of social relations with the Guru's arrival; but after displaying an initial incomprehension, the *whole* existing order had to alter itself, and the relations, proportions, values of each community toward the social whole had to be readjusted to establish conformity between the old and the new.

The striking difference from Eliot's account, of course, is that in the Guru's case, the new arrived as a 'mere repetition' of the old.

Notes

1. Jacques Derrida, *Limited Inc*, edited by Gerald Graff (Evanston: Northwestern University Press, 1988), 93.
2. Derrida, *Limited Inc*, 93.
3. Jacques Derrida, *Writing and Difference*, translated by Alan Bass (London: Routledge & Kegan Paul, 1978), 279.
4. Jacques Derrida, *Of Grammatology*, translated by Gayatri Chakravorty Spivak (Baltimore and London: Johns Hopkins University Press, 1976), 70.
5. Derrida, *Of Grammatology*, 18.
6. Quoted in Paul Patton and Terry Smith, ed., *Jacques Derrida: Deconstruction Engaged* (Sydney: Power Publications, 2001), 100.
7. Jacques Derrida, *Of Spirit: Heidegger and the Question*, translated by Geoffrey Bennington and Rachel Bowlby (Chicago: University of Chicago Press, 1989).
8. Ashis Nandy, *At the Edge of Psychology: Essays in Politics and Culture* (Delhi: Oxford University Press, 1980), 23.
9. Muni Narayana Prasad, *Garland of Visions: The Darsanamala of Narayana Guru* (New Delhi: D.K. Printworld, 2007).
10. Ramachandra Guha, *Makers of Modern India* (Delhi: Penguin Books India, 2010).

11. Ashis Nandy, *The Intimate Enemy* (New Delhi: Oxford University Press, 1983), 47.

12. P. J. Marshall, ed., *The British Discovery of Hinduism in the Eighteenth Century* (Cambridge: Cambridge University Press, 1970), 20.

13. Romain Rolland, *The Life of Ramakrishna* (Kolkata: Advaita Ashram, 2001), 110n–111n.

14. Gadjin Nagao, *The Foundational Standpoint of Madhyamika Philosophy*, translated by John P. Keenan (Albany, New York: State University of New York, 1989), 10.

15. Roby Rajan and J. Reghu, 'Backwater Universalism: An Intercommunal Tale of Being and Becoming', in *Political Hinduism: The Religious Imagination in Public Spheres*, edited by V. Lal (New Delhi: Oxford University Press, 2009), 58–95.

16. P. Govinda Pillai, 'Navodhana Rajashilpi', in *Malayala Manorama*, 30 August 1985.

17. Robin Jeffrey, *Politics, Women and Well-Being: How Kerala Became a 'Model'* (New Delhi: Oxford University Press, 2001), 227.

18. Nataraja Guru, *The Word of the Guru: The Life and Teachings of Guru Narayana* (New Delhi: D.K. Printworld, 2008), 62.

19. T. S. Eliot, 'Tradition and the Individual Talent', in *The Sacred Wood: Essays on Poetry and Criticism* (London: Methuen, 1920), 43–5.

I

IS METAPHYSICS POLITICAL?

SUNDAR SARUKKAI

Rather than ask what metaphysics is in the context of politics, I would like to begin with the question: what are the stakes in a metaphysics of politics? Before listing the problems of metaphysics in the context of politics, consider a simple question of origin. The origin of metaphysics lies in the attempt to describe that which lies beyond 'physics'. But why this shift to metaphysics in the first place? It is because the philosopher realizes that the descriptions of the physical need a substratum. Metaphysics arises as a condition of the possibility of the physical and as something that orders the physical as physical. Metaphysics is that which supplies an idea of what the physical is about. But since the fundamental characteristic of the physical was seen to be the 'real', metaphysics has been understood as the foundation of fundamental structures of reality.

There is a historical lesson in this, which is relevant to any discussion on politics and metaphysics. It is that the metaphysics of politics should not be concerned with questions of the real and categories of the real that underlie physical reality. The essence of a metaphysics of the political should be to supply an idea of what the political is—and more importantly, to show how the political is ordered *as* the political.

Perhaps we can consider the possibility that the alienation of the metaphysical with respect to the political has arisen primarily because metaphysics in the traditional sense is not an attempt to explicate the foundations of the political but only of the physical— that is, the 'real' for the physical world is different from the 'real' for politics. If we get stuck with the metaphysics that originates in response to the physical, we can expect to inherit many of the same problems we encounter with 'the physical'. Moreover, to use the traditional elements of metaphysics blindly in the context of politics is itself a political move, and hence in any such use, metaphysics itself becomes political. Thus, the questions I address in this paper are: (a) what are the fundamental philosophical structures of politics and (b) what is the metaphysics of politics that can describe how the political is ordered as the political?

This is where Indian metaphysical approaches might be helpful. Unlike the metaphysical categories of the Greeks (and later modern European philosophy), Indian philosophical systems did not draw clear distinctions between metaphysics and epistemology or between metaphysics and ethics.[1] This is why the metaphysical categories of many Indian schools differ in the number as well as in the types of categories. If metaphysics is not completely separated from epistemology (a move which, among other things, makes many European philosophers believe that Indians had no idea of 'philosophy'), what is the consequence of this world view for constructing philosophical ideas of the political?

Suspicion towards Metaphysics

First, I will begin with some comments about an enduring suspicion about metaphysics. For instance, understanding a figure like Narayana Guru, for many of his disciples, means an immersion in his texts, words, messages, and practice. According to some of them, thinking, reflecting, and enquiring into the larger theme of Guru's works negates his essential spirit. This stance is not unique to the followers of Narayana Guru nor even to followers of spiritual movements generally. Nor is it surprising that the first target of such ire is metaphysics, for somehow, the very word seems to connote a distance from the 'real' purpose behind their practice. As far as these critics go, metaphysics might as well be the last refuge of the academic scoundrel.

However, this very suspicion of metaphysics betrays a politics, an agenda, and an ideology. One, there is this real fear that reflecting on the foundations of practice might somehow paralyse the person who is involved in that practice. In other words, one can only 'be' spiritual; the moment she engages with understanding the nature of spirituality (which automatically would draw her into the world of metaphysics), she would negate her search for the spiritual. It is surprising how prevalent this view is, and what is ironic is that this position is completely contrary to the deep insights of the very spiritual leaders they claim to follow. For example, reading Narayana Guru's writings, it is obvious that a profound philosophical insight is integral to his 'prescriptions' and practices. Why then this continued suspicion of metaphysical reflection?

There are many different trajectories along which this reaction to metaphysics has taken place. We could even trace this back to Buddha's and Mahavira's reaction to Brahminical texts, traditions, and metaphysics. In the Western tradition, an example would be the influential critique of metaphysics by Mach, followed by the call to remove metaphysics from the practice of science. This is a movement that has had a deep influence in the evolution of the sciences, which includes their movement away from engaging with philosophical issues related to science. Or, in the context of political action, Marx's critique of philosophy based on his popular slogan that the task at hand is to change the world and not understand it (presumably the task of abstract philosophy). These views have led to the well-established schism between practice and theory that has especially been useful for those who are involved in various religious, political, and spiritual movements.

However, those who are agents of action do themselves a disservice when they create this artificial boundary between practice and metaphysics. After all, metaphysics is an exploration of the foundations upon which practice rests. Those who act are already doing so based on certain beliefs and judgements. They might want to ignore them since 'questioning' or 'understanding' these might hinder their actions. But this is to claim that one prefers to act in ignorance of the motivations and the presuppositions behind their act. In other words, the person who is acting is already immersed in a metaphysics of her own, whether she is aware of it or not. Reacting against explicit reflection on these metaphysical moorings is, therefore, a way to protect oneself from having to enquire into the deeper desires and motivations that underlie one's actions.

The Stake of Metaphysics

I will first make some preliminary remarks on the nature of metaphysics. While noting that the definition of metaphysics is a matter of continuing dispute, I will nevertheless identify some elements of it that are useful for this paper. Basically, metaphysics is about describing fundamental structures of reality. It is a description of the fundamental categories that characterize any 'thing'. These categories are best understood as elements that are common to all things which are existent. Existence as physical object is just one mode of existence. But even in this mode there are categories that are common to all physical objects. What are they? The first and most important category is substance. One can understand the spirit of metaphysical enquiry by following the argument for substance as a category. Suppose there is an object that has properties such as shape, size, and colour. Now, what happens to the object if we keep stripping away each of these properties? Eventually will we be forced to acknowledge that there is a fundamental substance upon which all these properties 'rest'? Or, to express this in the language of metaphysics, is there finally a substance in which properties inhere? In this attempt we can see the continued preoccupation of philosophy with defining notions of sameness and difference. What is similar to all things that exist? What is different between individual things?

Aristotle's influence on metaphysics is well known. I will only briefly discuss two points of his metaphysics. One is the set of metaphysical categories that he describes. Standard accounts of this give a list of ten categories: substance, quality, quantity, relation, place, and so forth. The second important point is that following this tradition, metaphysics becomes the foundation of all philosophical enquiry and, as a consequence, is clearly distinguished from other themes such as epistemology, logic, aesthetics, and ethics. The implication of this is that metaphysical categories cannot be epistemological or ethical categories. In this sense, metaphysics is not grounded in empirical observations—that is, we do not discover metaphysical categories by experience. It is this idea of transcendence that is so important to Western metaphysics—at least to that tradition that builds on the Aristotelian one.

Now, when we look at Indian philosophical traditions, there are some fundamental differences in the meaning and applicability of the idea of metaphysics. These differences, interestingly, are to be found in those elements that are the 'same'. First, there are the categories that characterize Indian metaphysics. These are grouped under *padārtha*, which is usually translated as categories. Padārtha is nothing more than the meaning of words, or that which a word stands for. The Greek category has nothing to do with words or language. In fact, they cannot be related to words or language since that would make metaphysics empirical. Why would we then consider padārtha as metaphysical categories? One good reason is that the list of categories has much in common with the Aristotelian categories. For example, the list of categories in the Vaiśeṣika system (one that is used by Nyāya also) consists of substance, quality, inherence, action, individuation, universal, and absence (which is added later). Padārtha seems to do a parallel job of describing the fundamental structures of the real. In this system, there is a substance upon which qualities inhere. (We should note here that *guna* is translated as quality, although there are some subtle differences between them.) Already there are fundamental differences even in the meaning of terms that are translated into the same idea such as quality and universal. Moreover, if one considers other systems of Indian philosophy, the problem gets doubly compounded. For example, the padārthas that are given in these traditions include power (*śakti*), number (*sankhyā*), time, space (*desha*), sorrow (*dukkha*), and so forth.[2] It is very clear from this list that a cardinal rule of categories à la the Greeks is violated by the Indians—these categories do not make a rigid distinction between epistemology, ethics, and so on. Thus, Indian 'metaphysical' categories are not disjunctive in the way the Aristotelian ones are. Similar points about fundamental metaphysical ideas like mental, physical, self, causality, relations, and so forth need to be understood when we talk of Indian metaphysical systems.

There is an added implication which relates to the second point about the categories discussed above. If Indian metaphysical categories do not, in principle, make a distinction between epistemology and metaphysics, then can metaphysics be seen as meta-physics, a level beyond the empirical? This question is very important since the answer to it will define the task of metaphysics. If metaphysics is in a sense the 'beyond', then for Western thought, a metaphysics of politics will be the fundamental structure of politics but one beyond the practice of politics. However, in the framework of Indian categories, if metaphysics is not about the 'beyond', then these categories and the philosophical reflection using these categories perform a completely different task.

General Reflections on the Metaphysics of Politics

Let me begin with some standard analysis of metaphysics from contemporary philosophy. The use of metaphysical categories often signals the metaphysical commitment inherent in that use. The terms that are of central importance to metaphysics are the following: substance, quality, inherence, individuation, persistence, causality, identity, and so on. So whenever we use these or related notions, we are already in the domain of metaphysics. Given the centrality of these terms, one can see why we are never far away from metaphysics in any intellectual activity.

I want to focus on a few defining characteristics of politics that illustrate its metaphysical underpinnings. First is the question of identity: what really constitutes the political? Nowadays it is often said that everything is political: knowledge, science, religion, sports, tradition, and anything else you might care to name are all political. What exactly is meant by this statement? If everything is political, then what exactly is the mark of the political?

Second, I am interested in engaging with the metaphysics of two very important concepts in politics: public and the notion of necessity. The notion of the public hides within it the idea of 'all', and this simple word has proved to be philosophically most truant! The notion of necessity in politics has deep implications for ideas of justice for example. Both 'necessity' and 'all' are metaphysical terms.

I also use these terms not just to illustrate one strand of thinking about metaphysics in politics but also to point out how these terms have been looked at very differently by Indian philosophers. So these terms actually serve as a useful comparative device for how one could draw meaningfully from the Indian traditions to understand the metaphysics of politics.

How Is Politics Possible?

Metaphysics is really about the possibility of physics (although the notion of possibility itself gets taken into metaphysics later). It delineates the foundational structure of the world that is necessary for something like physics to be possible. We can begin our reflections on metaphysics and politics by asking a similar question: how is politics possible?

One way to approach this question—a way that is relevant in any comparative enterprise—is by responding to claims that the idea of politics is a European one; for instance, the well-known political philosopher Oakeshott has claimed that 'politics is an European invention'.[3] Such a statement is an assertion of a certain politics of metaphysics. The politics of this metaphysics is best understood when we place this claim alongside similar claims about Indian logic, science, ethics, aesthetics, and philosophy. There is a long tradition of European scholars ranging from Locke, Hume, and Hegel to more contemporary figures like Husserl, Heidegger, and Gadamer who seem committed to the belief that the Indian intellectual world did not possess sound ideas of logic, science, reason, philosophy, and so on. Without imputing a Eurocentric bias to all these thinkers (although one cannot wish that away either), we can understand why they claimed this in the face of considerable evidence to the contrary. Western logicians familiar with Nyāya logic argued that it was not really logic since those formulations did not seem to distinguish the empirical and the logical. Parallel assertions were made about Indian mathematics: that it did not have any notion of proof. Similarly, Indian philosophy was held to be only about the other-worldly. Part of the problem was the lack of material available to these philosophers, but the other significant part of the problem was the desire to hierarchize cultures based on certain intellectual virtues. For our purposes, what is of interest here is the way these claims are legitimized, because in examining this process, we can also detect the metaphysics inherent in their presuppositions.

What is the basis for this problematical claim that politics itself is a European idea? Oakeshott begins by arguing that there are some fundamental conditions required for politics to appear. One, there should be a plurality of beings who are associated as a community that has to exemplify diversity—as he suggests, politics may be said to be the activity in which a society deals with its diversities. Two, there should be a presence of an authority figure in this association of beings such as a government, which, as a consequence, leads to the appearance of the ideas of public and private in the society. Three, the government and instruments and policies of governing must be determined by human choice and action. In explaining these rules, Oakeshott makes these additional observations: politics is not about just ruling; politics is about the possibility of change brought about through deliberate thought; politics is thinking about what should be done and persuading or inducing those who have the authority to act to make certain choices and not others; one cannot do politics with god (unless they are like human beings) nor politics with animals. From these observations, he deduces that politics is a European invention, although even within Europe it arises in bits and parts over time.

As Oakeshott notes, these conditions for the appearance of politics are particularly important for the appearance of political thought, which is manifested by the use of new terms such as freedom, power, democracy, and so forth. He then discusses four examples of political cultures which illustrate these conditions of being political and which are located in ancient Greece, ancient Rome, medieval Europe, and modern Europe. While his analysis is primarily historical, we can already note the metaphysical assumptions in this definition of politics. Part of it is signalled explicitly in the use of putatively 'political' terms such as state, freedom, power, and so forth. Much of it is hidden in the presuppositions of the notions of community, diversity, choice, action, and so on. And finally, the politics is very clearly staked out by understanding these terms in an exclusive manner, in a manner in which other cultures, *by definition*, cannot possess them. By not making this metaphysics clear, Oakeshott's analysis exemplifies a particular politics of metaphysics.

This politics of metaphysics rests to a large extent on a particular 'metaphysics' of concepts, one that is not only used by Oakeshott but also by many other writers in the past and in the present. A simple illustration of this is the argument that certain political/scientific/ philosophical concepts are not found in the vocabulary of a society and, therefore, that society did not possess these ideas. This naïve argument has been used so much in the case of Indian society that it has had deleterious consequences for the growth of contemporary Indian thought. This argument misses the meaning of how concepts accrue meaning; it also negates the processes of negotiation integral to the conceptual imagination. Concepts cannot be matched like things, so the argument that there is no 'exact' word for some of these terms is based on a mistaken idea of concepts and meaning.[4]

An extension of Oakeshott's argument has been provided by Candea where he discusses the possibility of discovering the non-political in a world in which everything is politics.[5] Today, knowledge, science, religion, and all these traditionally non-political worlds are seen to be political in some fundamental sense. While this has liberated the historical and philosophical understanding of these terms, it has also led to a complete universalization of politics: politics is everywhere and in everything. In an interesting twist to this debate, Rancière points out that politics is a 'way of repartitioning the political from the non-political', that is, politics arises in the very attempt to discover the non-political as distinct from the political.[6] Candea attempts to discover spaces of the non-political through anthropology and concludes that the 'political is itself a result and condition of non-political action'.[7] One can see how such a view of politics negates Oakeshott's conclusion that politics is a European invention, and also makes possible a comparative metaphysics of politics from an Indian perspective.

It is worth placing this question of identity within the larger problem of metaphysics and politics. There are two important metaphysical issues here: one of identity and the other of 'belongingness'. More on this later, but first I want to briefly consider this debate between metaphysics and politics within the German philosophical tradition.

Thornhill makes an important point in this context. He points out that post-Kant, political philosophy in Germany was primarily about themes related to humanism and specifically 'attempts to outline the anthropological specificity of the human' in contrast to theological or metaphysical views on humanity. Interestingly, he argues that the notions of 'legality' and 'law' are central to modern political German thought. For Kant, political legitimacy arises only from law and this, as Thornhill observes, makes the legitimacy of politics metaphysical. If, for Kant, law was the 'objective medium of human self-realization', after Kant, it was 'politics' that 'replaces law as the medium of possible human freedom and fulfilment'. Without entering into the complexities of this development in German thought, I use this example to point to the importance of the idea of necessity in politics. If there is a paradigmatic metaphysical term, it is that of necessity. I am also interested in this term since it allows us to engage with another problematic argument about the notion of necessity in Indian metaphysics, namely its purported absence from the Indian philosophical imagination. But by looking at this a little more carefully, we can see how to begin to unpack the larger set of ideas surrounding necessity and the problems Indian philosophy had with this concept.[8]

Indian Metaphysics and Politics

Let me motivate this problem by describing some peculiarities of Indian philosophy. First of all, philosophical descriptions are primarily cognitive descriptions in all Indian systems. That is, processes are defined in terms of cognitive states. Second, the way they understood some common concepts were quite different from the Western systems. For example, the idea of a property that an object possesses has a rather different meaning in Indian philosophy as compared to Western philosophical systems. What is common though to the many Indian systems are these specific ways of describing cognition by using concepts such as locatee, location, pervasion, property of possessing, *vyāpti* (invariable concomitance), and so on. There are fundamental differences in how the world is described. For example, the correct expression in Sanskrit of a sentence like 'there is a pot on the ground' will be 'the ground (is) pot-possessing', thus converting the 'subject-predicate sentences into their locus-locatee model'.[9] These modes of describing the world as well as our cognition of it mark a fundamental difference in the ways of talking about 'similar' things.

Let me illustrate this with a simple example. Consider the inference of the presence of fire from seeing smoke. There is a cognitive process which infers that the mountain has fire when one sees smoke

on the mountain. If asked to give an account of this process of inference, many would invoke memory and the fact that it has happened
before. Indian philosophers of almost all hues discuss this problem
of inference in great detail. In Greek and modern thought, we would
call the study of inference as 'logic'. In this sense, one of the pillars
of Indian thought was logic and an associated world of 'rationality'.
But in this activity, there were not only some fundamental conceptual differences but also a difference in the aims of this enterprise.
Unlike many observations that suggest that liberation was the goal
of all Indian philosophy (which is true but not significant), I would
suggest that one particular concept in Indian philosophy becomes
the master concept, one that resonates across the popular understanding of the world as well as in philosophical and soteriological
descriptions. It also arises in medical discourses and sometimes in
literary canons.

This concept is vyāpti. It would not be an exaggeration to say that
this single concept and the task of defining it took the Indian logical
traditions away from what happens in Greek and European philosophy. It has within it a very different vocabulary of pervasion and the
pervaded to describe countless scenarios. We need to begin with this
pervasiveness of pervasion in Indian thought in order to understand
its characteristics. To give an example: when we say we infer fire from
seeing smoke, we give an account of this by saying 'fire causes smoke'.
But the jump to causality is too quick and unclear since it could only
be a matter of smoke always being seen with fire.

The Indian description of this process is that smoke is pervaded by
fire. In other words, this means that wherever smoke is present there
is fire. Smoke and fire are in a pervaded–pervasion relationship. It is
remarkable how much this language of pervaded–pervasion is used
in so many different contexts. One idea can be pervaded by another;
two concepts can also be in a pervaded–pervasion relationship. While
this may seem like an idiosyncratic way of talking about properties or
of something being present somewhere, it is much more than that.
For Indian logic, the task of logic (anumāna) reduces to the analysis of
the invariant in this relationship—vyāpti. It is to give an account of
why two things always occur together even as it is a method that gives
us a set of rules to detect whether two things indeed occur together.

It is important to note that all these traditions, which otherwise strongly criticize each other, nevertheless accept the primacy of vyāpti, although they have different formulations of this idea. The Buddhists following Dharmakīrti accept three modes of inference: analyticity, causality, and inference from non-perception. Consider this simple example of analyticity: seeing an oak tree, we infer that it is a tree. This is not a trivial inference since it is an inference of the class the object belongs to. And the Indian logicians understand this by noting the pervaded–pervasion relationship between 'oak tree' and 'tree'. Tree pervades all oak trees—this means that whenever we see an oak tree we are also seeing/inferring a tree. Thus class-inclusion becomes an inference, one that has its special relation of vyāpti. Similarly, for these Buddhists, smoke-fire is described through causality but they are nevertheless in a pervaded–pervasion relationship.

What exactly is pervasion? I would suggest that pervasion is an alternative way of looking at set or group membership. A group consists of individuals and a set is a collection of these individual members. A relation of pervasion is spatial and not discrete like set membership. A group or a community in the vocabulary of pervasion is not reduced to a collection of individuals but is a distribution. The metaphysics of distribution is far more complex and interesting than individual, discrete membership. Suppose we accept that a chair has the property of chairhood, a universal that characterizes the chair. Then we can say that chairhood pervades the chair; it is present in all the locations where the chair is present. Pervasion is so important for the Indian philosophers as they give great importance to the idea of location and locatedness. We can distinguish the Indian and the Western metaphysical enterprise in terms of this discrete and continuous nature. There are important consequences of this distinction. The abstract concepts arising from a discrete view of the universe include points, sets, geometrical entities, Platonic ideal forms, and so on. Such abstractions do not arise in the Indian case—note, for example, how Platonism is largely absent in Indian thought even in the case of mathematics! This locatedness of concepts and properties in Indian metaphysics constitutes its strength as far as modern political and scientific thought is concerned, since these disciplines are increasingly distancing themselves from a Western metaphysics that was ungrounded, transcendent, and unverifiable.

Before we lose track of why we are talking about pervasion, let me give an example from politics. When we talk of citizenship or belongingness to a country, how exactly do we characterize this? We can do it in terms of numerical enumeration or we can think of a spatial distributive description. Consider also terms such as justice or equality. What does it mean to say that all people are equal? Is it the same as saying that every individual is pervaded by 'equality'? And how much of our ideas of equality are based on the structure of sets with individual members rather than a distributive relationship?

The idea of pervasion is not just a different rendering of other concepts but a fundamentally different world view with its own unique consequences. Indian logicians spend an inordinate amount of time trying to define vyāpti. How do we detect that two terms are indeed in a relation of pervasion? First, we expect the two terms to occur together all the time. But this definition is circular because we are using all to characterize all. Dignāga, the great Buddhist logician, came up with a process of ascertaining with certainty whether two terms always occur together. The first step in this process of checking whether two things occur together all the time is to first have an instance of it happening, and second to have some positive examples of their occurrence together. So one would look at the kitchen as an example of smoke and fire occurring together. However, we cannot conclude that two things are in a pervasion relation even if there are many examples where they are together. What we need are negative examples where one term occurs and the other does not occur. So to show that smoke and fire are not essentially related, all we have to do is to find locations of smoke where there is no fire. But the Buddhist formulation is more complex than merely finding counter examples. The third condition of Dignāga's description of vyāpti is that smoke should not be found where fire is necessarily not to be found—such as in a lake.[10] In other words, this condition of counter example is not merely an empirical one but one that is grounded metaphysically.

I will not enter into the long debate on how to define vyāpti here. But we can look at the Navya–Nyāya formulations of vyāpti to get a glimpse of the theoretical complexity of pervasion. Already from the Buddhist formulation we can see the possibility of absence as an important category to define pervasion because pervasion is grounded in absence. The third condition says that two things occur together if and only if one of them is not found in a location where the other is absent. It is not an accident that absence as a category plays such an important role in the Nyāya system as opposed to the Buddhist one. In fact, the Vaiseṣika consider absence as a metaphysical category. The latter Navya–Nyāya developments are primarily centred on refining the definition of pervasion so that it almost seems to be the defining concept for this tradition.

Without discussing the details of this definition, let me just point to the importance of the idea of pervasion, the associated world of metaphysical terms that are needed for it, and how this offers another metaphysical approach to central themes in politics.

Like so many other similar claims, there has also been the assertion that there is no idea of necessity in Indian logic. However, one needs to ferret out ideas of necessity that are strewn around other conceptual terms such as vyāpti, absence, delimiters, and so on.[11] The idea of vyāpti is primarily about a formulation of necessity, particularly necessity as it occurs in scientific laws.[12] There is a long debate between the Buddhists and the Naiyāyikas on necessity and universality. There are elements of this debate that are also found in Kant and in some contemporary discussions on whether universality is enough, or whether there should also be a commitment to necessity. Given the importance of necessity for political philosophy, we can ask how this alternative metaphysics can be useful for contemporary discussions on political philosophy.

I will give a very brief outline of the potential and possibilities of such an exercise. Consider the ideas of public, democracy, and justice. What is a public? While there are many defining characteristics of the public, let me isolate one 'ordinary' idea about it that has to do with access to all. A public space is open to all unlike a private space. So we could ask, what is the relationship between public and 'all'? How do we come to know that a particular space is a public space? We come to know of it only when somebody is denied entry into that space. That is, a public space does not attain the characteristic of a public space just because many people may have entered it. It only attains the idea of public space when somebody is denied entry into it—the third condition of Dignāga! The metaphysics of this is again based on absence or negation. Thus, the essential definition of public will then be about non-entry and not really about entry to all. This example also illustrates well the conflict between universality and necessity: Is it enough to know that everyone is allowed entry into a public space or should we expect that a public space is one that necessarily allows anyone to enter? The consequences of these two positions are metaphysically very divergent.

Consider the following question: what is it that pervades ideas of public, equality, and justice? This is nothing more than asking: what characteristic will you find in these terms wherever they happen to occur? Note that my expression of this question follows the way Indian philosophers might have asked this question—in terms of 'locus'.

We can also look at the example of equality and the problems surrounding theories of equality. First, we can begin with the formulation that all human beings are equal. However, this statement is blatantly false unless we define what is meant by a 'human being' and what is meant by 'equality'. Each one of our bodies is different from the other. So if we want to establish equality as an important concept, we have to redefine humanity and not equality. Given our evident bodily inequality, perhaps we can look at the claim that all human beings are equal in terms of their 'minds' (whatever this actually means!). But this claim is also obviously not true. Then we try out different ideas of what is to be human, not in terms of actualities but in terms of potentialities and capacities. Furthermore, we might think of entitlements and rights as defining humans. Or like Kant did, draw on respect and duty for example, to define the human. Or like Agamben, who drawing on Aristotle, argues that politics is metaphysics and that the 'metaphysical task par excellence' is the 'politicization of bare life'.[13] This is a task which is primarily about defining and redefining the human. But we can see how these definitions of 'human' seem to always be subservient to some other term. Let us say that we accept the Kantian idea of respect as a fundamental attribute of human beings. What would this mean? It would be that every human being should be respected or is an object of respect. We could perhaps express this equivalently in terms of the language of pervasion: respect pervades human beings. What does this re-expression give us? First of all, note that when we say that all human beings are deserving of respect, we need to have a metaphysics which will describe this relationship between 'respect' and 'human being'. How does respect inhere in humans? Is it a particular property? How then is it instantiated? And so on.

But when we talk of pervasion, we understand that the human and the notion of respect are co-located all the time and in all places. It does not commit us to a metaphysics where we have to accept the reality of propositions or other similar categories. There is also another way to view this relationship. Some philosophers, including Kant, might express this in a different way: respect is necessary for one to be considered human. The use of necessity always signals a deep metaphysical problem. In Western philosophy there has been a long debate on the nature of necessity. What does it mean to say that some truths are necessarily true? The philosophical interest in this topic also arises because of the close relationship between necessity and possibility, the terms referred to as modal terms. For Kant, these modal terms are so important that they figure in his fundamental categories.

But it is as difficult to give an account of necessity as it is of pervasion. One can see how this difficulty is exemplified in the definitions of vyāpti by Gangesa Upadhyaya. He discusses nearly twenty definitions of vyāpti before offering his own. And the definition is so complex and based on notions of absence and limiters that it seems as if a lot of 'metaphysical obfuscation' has taken place. However, if we look at any contemporary theory of necessity, we find very similar problems in developing a consistent definition of necessity.

I offer this example because this illustrates a ready-made approach of Indian philosophy to a similar problem in Western philosophy. Thus, there are grounds for a meaningful comparison to examine the strengths and weaknesses of the two approaches. We could do a similar exercise for the idea of justice, which is also primarily to do with the idea of equality. For example, many important theories of justice are based on the idea of equality, liberty, and autonomy. Equality is often equality of rights to attain liberty and/or equality of opportunity. The difficulty in finding consistent definitions of these terms drives some to invoke the idea of natural law. But all these terms are fundamentally about necessity, which is fundamentally about pervasion.

This is only a preliminary sketch of a larger project of an Indian metaphysics of politics. The main point I wish to underline here is that different imaginations of metaphysics illuminate the world differently. While one might think that metaphysics has been banished (in science post-Mach, or in German political thought post-Kant), the reverse is in fact the case. Deeper involvement in non-metaphysical traditions (implying, for the Western tradition, a kind of empirical grounding such as anthropological humanities) has paradoxically driven these theories deeper into metaphysical issues. The reasons for the contemporary disavowal of metaphysics are many, but as we saw in Thornhill's analysis, it is not clear whether such a disavowal has really 'displaced' metaphysics or merely ignores it. As he points out, legality becomes the central core of political philosophy, but its association with the idea of law makes the entire project metaphysical.

But that in no way implies that it is metaphysics which is at fault. If these thinkers had looked at how the Indian philosophers formulated their metaphysics, it may have pointed them to a different way of looking at metaphysics, one which is empirical but which can simultaneously accommodate the ethical. However, I would also add that the world views are so fundamentally different that I am not sure such a metaphysics would have found a sympathetic reception with these political philosophers. And I am not talking about soteriology or liberation theology. I am referring to a more fundamental problem that distinguishes the Indian metaphysical system from the modern European one, and this has to do with the autonomy and primacy of the individual. As I mentioned above, there is much in political philosophy, including concepts such as justice, equality, liberty, and so forth, which revolves centrally around this specific idea of the individual. But the metaphysics of the individual is quite different in Indian reflective traditions. The potential for a radical rewriting of politics lies buried in the metaphysics of the individual as drawn and developed from Indian traditions. To give a flavour of this potential and the related issues that would need addressing, here are some questions: Is the individual really an autonomous agent? Should an individual be an autonomous agent? What is the metaphysics of the relationship between the individual and the larger group to which she belongs, whether it be the family or the community? Should notions of freedom, equality, and justice be tied to an ideology of the free-floating individual? Do the radically different theories of the self in Indian and Western reflective traditions allow us to reformulate the metaphysics of the individual? Is intervening in the hegemonic

Western discourses on these topics by drawing on the metaphysics of non-Western traditions not also another manifestation of the politics of metaphysics?

Notes

1. K. Bhattacharya, 'Classical Philosophies of India and the West', *Philosophy East & West* 8 (1958): 17–36.

2. J. N. Mohanty, *Classical Indian Philosophy* (Lanham: Rowman & Littlefield, 2000).

3. Michael Oakeshott, *Lectures in the History of Political Thought*, edited by T. Nardin and L. O'Sullivan (Exeter, UK: Imprint Academic, 2006), 36.

4. Sundar Sarukkai, 'Translating as Method: Implications for the History of Science', in *The Circulation of Knowledge between Britain, India and China*, edited by Bernard Lightman, Gordon McOuat, and Larry Stewart (Leiden: Brill Press, 2013), 311–30.

5. Matei Candea, 'Our Division of the Universe', *Current Anthropology* 52, no. 3 (2011), 309–34.

6. Quoted in Candea, 'Our Division of the Universe', 321.

7. Candea, 'Our Division of the Universe', 321.

8. C. Thornhill, 'Politics and Metaphysics: A Problem in German Philosophy', *Studies in Social and Political Thought* 5 (2001): 3–24.

9. Biman K. Matilal, *The Character of Logic in India*, edited by J. Ganeri and H. Tiwari (Albany: State University of New York, 1998), 29.

10. Sundar Sarukkai, *Indian Philosophy and Philosophy of Science* (Delhi: Motilal Banarsidass/CSC, 2005).

11. Sundar Sarukkai, 'Possible Ideas of Necessity in Indian Logic', *Journal of Philosophical Logic* 40, no. 5 (2001): 563–82.

12. Sarukkai, 'Possible Ideas of Necessity in Indian Logic'.

13. Andrew Norris, 'Giorgio Agamben and the Politics of the Living Dead', *Diacritics* 30, no. 4 (2000): 38–58, 41.

2

A DISOWNED FATHER
OF THE NATION IN INDIA
Vinayak Damodar Savarkar and the Demonic
and the Seductive in Indian Nationalism[1]

ASHIS NANDY

The ideology and political legacy of Vinayak Damodar Savarkar (1883–1966) trigger anxieties that centre around the ethical demands of a national state on individuals and societies in those parts of the world where communities have not obligingly died out and where the violence involved in creating a modern nation state does not enjoy any intrinsic legitimacy. Many sense the presence within them of the same ruthlessness and calculative cruelty that Savarkar sought to bring to the process as inescapable parts of nation-building and state-formation; they are doubly hostile to a person who has come to personify the psychopathic tendencies that the processes of state-formation and nation-building tend to unleash and legitimize.

This essay traces the trajectory of Savarkar's life through its many vicissitudes and the internal contradictions, to examine the deeper consistencies in his political beliefs and the deeper sources of his absolute, uncritical faith in the modern state system and its secular imperatives. Probably more than any other Indian leader of his time, he was in awe of Europe's achievements in the area of nation-building and state-formation. And such was the wide acceptance of these achievements in urban, middle-class India that few noticed that the basic categories of Savarkar's political ideology—nation, national state, nationality, and nationalism—always remained aggressively European. It was his misfortune that, in his lifetime, this middle class was not a sizeable part of the country and he never emerged as a popular leader with a large mass base, not even as a leader of the Hindus. That position was occupied by Mohandas Karamchand Gandhi (1869–1948), much younger than Savarkar in Indian politics even if older in age, much less erudite, and full of strange, hare-brained ideas of politics that, Savarkar felt, could only hobble the future of the Indian state.

I

However, before entering the world of Savarkar, a few comments on the context of this essay on his life. First, Savarkar is often seen as a Hindu extremist. Like everything else in this part of the world, this also has its own distinctive features. Those concerned not with academic puzzle-solving, but with live problems of religion and violence in South Asia know the anomalies that mark the public career of 'religious extremism', caught between the culture of the global nation-state system, the remnants of nineteenth-century colonial culture, and the everyday practices, values, and categories of popular religion in the region. Thus, under the umbrella of fundamentalism, there are clear differences between those who insist on total, literal allegiance to a sacred text and those who carefully avoid the issue and bypass the substantive contents of faith, to pursue the secular interests of a religious community, invoking faith as only a strategy of mobilization.

This is not a matter of personal whimsy. Political communities and movements often oscillate between the two poles. Thus, the content of Islam for many decades was not a serious concern of Muslim nationalism in South Asia, though it has increasingly become so. Both strands are still visible in Pakistan, but it has become more difficult to admit publicly that the founder of the state, Mohammad Ali Jinnah (1876–1948), was an anti-clerical, secular, Westernized liberal in personal life, routinely breaking some of the injunctions of Islam in matters of food and drink. Among Sikhs, too, there has been a similar oscillation between Sikh nationalism and fundamentalism.

For a while during the 1980s and 1990s the latter was more visible; now it is less so.

The Hindu nationalism that has become an important player in Indian politics has mostly thrown up leaders to whom contents of faith hardly matter, even though their politics and rhetoric have changed the contours of Hinduism among some sections of Indians. It took the Rashtriya Swayamsevak Sangh or RSS, deemed the steel frame of Hindu nationalism, something like fifteen years to find a serious, believing Hindu interested in theology and religious rituals to head it. And only during the Ramjanmabhumi movement in 1989–92 did the RSS flout its conventions to allow religious icons to enter its precincts.

Such anomalies are clues to the inner world of those who participate in or shape ethno-religious movements and an invitation to empathetically, yes empathetically, plumb the complexities of persons involved. Yet, this has become increasingly difficult because it is now seen either as an attempt to whitewash the violence and hatred such leaders and their acolytes spew or as an insult to the religious or cultural sentiments of a community. As a result, serious cultural psychological explorations of militant nationalism as well as millennialism are becoming rarer in South Asia. Now, in the wake of 11 September 2001, such cultivated blindness and tacit censorship are also being indirectly endorsed by the global cultures of politics and knowledge.

Second, the early post–World War II scholars of religious and ethnic prejudice and violence—particularly those that were a response to the European genocide of the 1940s—worked in an environment in which there was inchoate, vague tiredness with cruelty, hatred, and gratuitous violence. By studying the authoritarian personality as a clinical syndrome, some of them sought to universalize their work, but they remained captive to the dominant culture of European modernity and heritage of the Enlightenment, both self-consciously oblivious of the way massive genocidal projects had been mounted and successfully executed with impunity outside Europe over the previous 150 years.[2] Indeed, such violence was often seen as an ugly but unavoidable part of statecraft and justified in social evolutionary terms or as parts of a new medical regime of social hygiene and eugenics. Joan Robinson, the radical economist and manifestly an opponent of colonialism, used to famously claim that the only thing worse than being colonized was not being colonized.

This is not unique to our times or to the culture that produced Savarkar. Everyone has his or her own ideas of the sanctity and meaning that must attach to some instances of mega-deaths and the reasons why those responsible for it should not be allowed to 'over-contextualize' their genocidal acts as products of a sick society or mind. Even the psychoanalytic tradition, which has significantly deepened our insight into contemporary Satanism, was not free of such debates. The psychoanalyst Bruno Bettelheim was convinced that fellow psychoanalyst Robert J. Lifton's book, *Nazi Doctors*, based on intensive interviews with homicidal doctors, humanized the Nazis and, hence, was politically and ethically culpable.[3] The fear of de-demonizing an enemy with a proven record of Satanism persists. Hatred has become more respectable when directed against the hate-ful and the 'hatable', whether the target is Osama bin Laden or George Bush. The global culture of common sense now leaves one lesser scope to empathize with one's subjects, even for purposes of research. As a result, what Philip Rieff used to call the 'analytic attitude', has often been sacrificed at the altar of political and academic correctness, masquerading as commitment to secular humanism and radicalism.[4] On the one hand, ethno-religious and ultra-nationalist extremism demands a one-dimensional, heroic picture of sacrifice and martyr-dom; on the other, those fighting it fear that any humane treatment of the subjectivities associated with such extremism will only acknowl-edge the humanity of the enemy and legitimize its politics. There is the unacknowledged fear in both that the enemy may not turn out to be an alien, infra-human species, but a dangerous human potentiality within everyone, that serious psychological explorations might reveal continuities rather than unbridgeable gaps. It is not easy to say these days what Lifton once did: 'Yes, that was the Germans, that has been the Jews, but it's anyone. It's a universal potential which different groups may embrace or feel victimized by.'[5]

Thus, in South Asia in recent years, the growth of religion-based violence has spawned an array of demonologies and a rich vocabulary that eschews shades of grey. Terms such as fundamentalist, fascist, fanatic, terrorist, and religious right are routinely bandied, to set up what Erik Erikson used to call a new 'pseudo-species', which has to be annihilated the way the enemy would like to annihilate its targets and opponents. The vocabulary establishes a regime of indignation, disgust, and revulsion, and of censorship imposed on enquiries into human motivations and technologies of self.[6]

This essay makes this point in a more roundabout way by entering the world of one such ideologue, to show that what appears at first to be an unforgivable depravity could be an ideological solution that an era and a globally dominant culture of public life promoted as part of sanity and rationality. Indeed, in many Afro-Asian societies, such solutions constituted a psychological trap in colonial times; some escaped it but most did not. Savarkar, the freedom fighter turned Muslim-baiter turned the man behind the assassination of Mohandas Karamchand Gandhi, arrived at an ethnonationalism that could only be called an illegitimate child of modern Europe, at the time routinely dumping its intellectual wares in the colonies as culture-free, universal components of secular salvation. Savarkar is an extreme case of the way an entire generation of South Asian political activists and ideologues thought.

Here I shall disobey Clifford Geertz's maxim and supply only a thin description of the person and his times. Data on Savarkar's personal life is scarce, though some of the ongoing works on him promise to do better. His best known, full-length, serious biography is also, as its title suggests, a hagiography; it mostly shuns his private life and interpersonal relations. Even the names of his wife and children, though mentioned cursorily in the text, find no place in the index. Following the conventions of life stories in many South Asian cultures, the biographer reads Savarkar's childhood and family life strictly through the prism of the adult Savarkar's political career and ideology.[7] Savarkar's own autobiographical writings are not much better; they too are, apart from being self-righteous, fearful of all human subjectivities, in an attempt to be rational, logical, secular, scientific, and modern.

II

Sections of urban, middle-class, modernizing Hindus of British India were reborn as fragments of a pan-Indian Hindu nation only in the 1940s, roughly a hundred years after the idea itself was born. This process of nation-building is not yet complete and it may never be complete. However, it has gone far in urban, educated, middle- and upper-middle class India, where individualism and social and occupational mobility have steadily grown since the nineteenth century. (The process has gone farthest among diasporic Hindus in the First World, some of whom have begun to think of themselves as part of a Hindu ummah, but that is not our concern at the moment.) Both the individuation and the mobility have taken place in a relatively impersonal, contractual, anonymous, urban–industrial context, where mainstream Hinduism in all its diversity—its innumerable castes (some figures go as high as 70,000), tens of thousands of village gods and goddesses, hundreds of sects, thousands of vernacular religious epics and jatipuranas,[8] family priests and personal and family deities, rituals and practices specific to castes, sects, and regions— cannot be sustained. The demand for Hinduism as a religion that an ordinary, socially and geographically mobile householder—as opposed to a world-renouncer—could carry within him or her as a portable device was a direct product of colonial political economy and the growth of presidency towns. At the moment of its birth, this new Hinduism—also sometimes called reformed Hinduism, proudly by some, wryly by others—did not look like Hinduism at all to a vast majority of Indians, Hindus, and non-Hindus. To them, such an 'essentialized', desiccated Hinduism, seeking to cover so many incompatible religious practices, lifestyles, and theologies, seemed absurd.[9] This majority was to be surprised; it had not reckoned with the new psychological demands crystallizing in colonial India.

It was a slow and painful process of birth. Among Hindus, the first well-known group to talk of the Hindus as an incipient national community was probably the Young Bengal Group in the 1840s at Calcutta, then the capital of British India. The group saw itself as a collection of reformers and talked of the Hindus and Hinduism critically, sometimes with contempt. The process was underwritten by the colonial tendency, reflected in the ruling culture of the Raj and in missionary tracts, to see Hindus as a community defined—and doomed—by their religion and the gradual institutionalization of this tendency in colonial law, education, administration, and census. Partly as a reaction, within a decade or two, the idea of the Hindus as a nation found a different status and intellectual respectability in the writings of Bhudev Mukhopadhyay (1827–94), a social and political

thinker, and Bankimchandra Chattopadhyay (1838–94), India's first
important novelist. They, too, were critical of many things Hindu
but were even more critical of the anglicized Indians who thought
Hinduism could not be retooled for modern times.[10] In another two
decades had emerged Brahmabandhab Upadhyay (1861–1907), a
Catholic theologian and Vedantic scholar, who ran into trouble with
the church in his lifetime but was to be rediscovered towards the end
of the twentieth century as a pioneer in indigenous Christian theology. In his other incarnation, Upadhyay was a Hindu nationalist,
scholar-activist, and theorist of violence—so at least it seemed to his
friend Rabindranath Tagore (1861–1940). As is well known, Tagore's
novel *Chār Adhyāya* is built around Upadhyay and Upadhyay's guilty
awareness of nationalism as a sanction for ruthless, machine violence
that involved viewing human life and human emotions instrumen-
tally.[11] One could argue that it was the desacralized, secular part of
Upadhyay's political Hinduism that finally ended up as Savarkar's
theories of state and nationality.[12]

The idea that the Hindus were the carriers of an overly diverse
religion called Hinduism by default—and, to that extent, were an ill-
formed, sleep-walking crypto-nation that had not actualized its
possibilities—was to later become a central assumption of Hindu
nationalism. Naturally, a certain admiration for Christianity and Islam,
as religions in better touch with the processes of state-formation
and nation-building, was the obverse of such nationalism. All Hindu
reform movements borrowed from these two faiths to correct the
'inadequacies' of Hinduism. Such a stance was then popular among
the modernizing middle class, which endorsed the contempt and
hostility that often tinged Hindu nationalist attitudes towards the
Hindus. The overdone emphases on Hindu pride and masculiniza-
tion of the Hindus was built on such self-hatred.

Vinayak Damodar Savarkar in 1923 reinvented a term previously
used by the likes of Brahmabandhab Upadhyay to describe this ideology—Hindutva.[13] Hindutva, Savarkar made clear, was not the same as
Hinduism, despite what an unthinking Indian Supreme Court was to
declare eighty years later.[14] Hindutva was a form of political Hinduism
that sought to organize and militarize the Hindus as a nationality.
Without such nationality, the argument went, there could be no basis
for nationalism in a highly diverse society, and without nationalism

there could be no nation state. From the beginning, Hindutva had a strong masculine content. Savarkar was probably the first and the last to call India a fatherland (*pitrubhu*) and not a motherland (*matrubhumi*). To introduce this Continental usage, he had to dredge Sanskrit grammar to shed the common term *bhumi* (land), which was feminine, and use the rarer *bhu*. To this pitrubhu you could not even sing one of the unofficial national anthems of the freedom fighters, *Bande Mataram*, a paean to Mother India.

To this fatherland, by virtue of the sacred geography associated with it, the Hindus had an exclusive right, Savarkar believed. Amnon Raz-Krakotzkin defines the secular Zionist as the one who believes that there is no God but insists that He has given the land of Israel to the Jews nonetheless.[15] Savarkar, a hardboiled atheist who did not believe in sacred geographies, was even less embarrassed to claim the whole of India for the Hindus on the ground of sacred geography.

When Savarkar propounded his two-nation theory—the first to explicitly do so in South Asia—it was a clear sixteen years before the Muslim League embraced the idea of the Hindus and the Muslims as two distinctive nations and demanded the division of India. His pioneering efforts in this respect were recognized. Historian R.C. Majumdar, who called Savarkar a 'great revolutionary leader', was clear about where the League got its inspiration from: it 'took serious notice of the frank speeches of Savarkar'.[16] But the idea of nationhood as the marker of a people was not Savarkar's either; he borrowed it from European thinkers like Giuseppe Mazzini (1805–72). Mazzini was not unknown in India, thanks to the early Bengali Hindu nationalists such as Upadhyay. Only, the likes of Upadhyay did not include in their repertoire an ideology of political and cultural exclusion, leavened with hatred, as Savarkar openly did. In a public speech in 1925, Savarkar said that Indians had to learn to eschew soft values like 'humility, self-surrender and forgiveness' and cultivate 'sturdy habits of hatred, retaliation, vindictiveness'.[17] Occasionally, he went further. At one place in his writings, he seems miserable that his heroes, Shivaji and Chinaji Appu, did not rape Muslim women, 'because of then prevalent suicidal ideas about chivalry to women, which ultimately proved highly detrimental to the Hindu community'.[18] To spite admirers who might think this to be an aberration, in 1965 at the age of 82, Savarkar wrote in the wake of the

India-Pakistan war that took place that year: 'Pakistan's barbaric acts such as kidnapping and raping Indian women would not be stopped unless Pakistan was given tit for tat.' One suspects that violence to Savarkar was not merely a revolutionary tool, but an end in itself, as if he was seeking legitimate targets to express the free-floating anger within him.[19]

Savarkar may not have been honest about many things but he had a Brahminic respect for ideas. When in the 1940s Mohammad Ali Jinnah began to go places with his two-nation theory, Savarkar was honest enough to say: 'I have no quarrel with Mr. Jinnah's two-nation theory. We Hindus are a nation by ourselves and it is a historical fact that Hindus and Muslims are two nations.'[20]

III

At this point let me quickly outline Savarkar's life. Vinayak Damodar Savarkar was born in a Chitpavan Brahmin family in a village near Nasik in 1883.[21] It was a landed family but his father Damodarpant was known more for his poetry and his knowledge of Sanskrit and Western classics than for his land holdings. Vinayak was the second son of his parents. His two brothers were also to become freedom fighters and one of them was to be sentenced to life imprisonment at Andamans. He also had a younger sister. Biographies suggest a Hindu nationalist atmosphere in his house, but that was not rare then in educated Chitpavan households. One of the few Brahmin communities to have tasted real political power in the declining years of the Mughal empire, Chitpavans were highly successful in the professions under the Raj but seemed to resent their loss of power. Perhaps more significant were the vague indications of an amoral, violent streak in young Vinayak. Keer tells how Vinayak, as a child, proudly vandalized a local mosque and then had a brawl with angry Muslim boys.[22]

From his early years Vinayak was a voracious reader and had a superb memory. His poetry was first published when he was ten. This might have been a response to the sudden death of his mother from cholera the same year. Young Vinayak was particularly fond of his mother and she had been his refuge from a stern, disciplinarian father, not averse to occasionally meting out heavy doses of physical punishment.[23] Her death must have been traumatizing.

Vinayak also turned out to be a good public speaker; at the age of fourteen, he won a prize for elocution. At around the same time, deeply moved by the hanging of the Chapekar brothers by the British regime, he took a vow at the altar of his family goddess, Durga, to fight for India's freedom. He even started in 1899, as a sixteen-year-old student, an anti-imperialist Friend's Circle, *Mitra Mela*. The same year his father and uncle died of plague. His two brothers also contracted the disease but recovered. Vinayak's elder brother Babarao had to now bear the burden of maintaining the family. Life for the three brothers had suddenly become unpredictable and cruel; there were reasons for them to be bitter with fate and its treacherous ways.

After matriculating from the city of Nasik in 1901, Vinayak joined Fergusson College at Poona in 1902, where he completed his studies and passed his examination. His degree, however, was withheld because of his political activities. Fortunately, he won a scholarship to go to England in 1906. There, at the age of twenty-three, he established another anti-imperialist group called Free India Society. They produced a manual on bomb-making and sent copies of it to India and Savarkar himself produced a Marathi translation of Mazzini's writings, which was published from India.

In 1908, to commemorate the fiftieth anniversary of the rebellion of 1857 against British rule, the Sepoy Mutiny, Savarkar published his well-known tract, *The First Indian War of Independence—1857*, which many consider to be his best work. A. G. Noorani, no admirer of Savarkar, calls it a 'veritable classic'.[24] The government duly proscribed it but it was republished from Holland. He also led the Indian students in celebrating martyr's day on the fiftieth anniversary of the 1857 uprising. He was then not even twenty-five. In 1909, he heard in England that his brother had been sentenced to transportation for life at Andaman for his revolutionary activities. Soon afterwards, Madanlal Dhingra, Savarkar's one-time colleague and protégé, was caught after he killed a colonial bureaucrat in London at his instigation.[25]

Savarkar met Mohandas Karamchand Gandhi (1869–1948) for the first time at London. Much of Savarkar's life was to be later defined by his differences with and antipathy towards Gandhi. He had contempt for Gandhi's 'unscientific' and 'unscholarly' mind and he despised Gandhi's critique of the urban–industrial vision and modern technology, and preoccupation with things like truth force, fasting, and concern for the cow.[26] Above all, as an obedient student of Europe's political history, he hated Gandhi's non-violence, which Savarkar thought irreconcilable with modern—and, of course, European—politics and statecraft. 'Absolute non-violence', he would later declare, was 'absolutely sinful'. Later, he came to develop as strong a dislike for the *charkha* or spinning wheel and Gandhi's pacifist interpretation of the Gita. They all seemed to Savarkar forms of primitivism, gloriously ignorant of what modern science and political theory had to offer India. What remained unmentioned at the time was Savarkar's strong belief that the Hindus had been de-masculinized over the centuries and his own desperate search for masculinity in a political environment where Gandhi's androgynous presence, he was to find out to his utter chagrin, had a natural space and legitimacy. It is said that when Gandhi once came to meet him in London at India House, Savarkar was cooking prawns, his favourite. When Gandhi broached some issue, Savarkar cut him short, 'We can discuss it later ... first come and have your food with us.' When Gandhi said he was a vegetarian, Savarkar reportedly retorted, 'If you cannot eat with us, how on earth are you going to work with us?' Savarkar's contempt for the effeminate, retrogressive, vegetarian, Gujarati Bania never subsided.[27]

This story is symptomatic of a basic personality difference between the two persons and their rival ideologies of freedom. The four years of his exposure to the West at the prime of his youth, as his doting biographer Harindra Srivastava recognizes, had remade Savarkar as a secular, modern, Western-educated Indian who had studied mainstream British life, literature, culture, and the British mind.[28] Mazzini was already his God and he suffered from what some biographers have called a 'Mazzinimania';[29] his stay in England now equipped him with European concepts and methods of statecraft and protest. Gandhi, on the other hand, had cussedly chosen to decide which West would influence him and how much; he searched for and discovered another West that could be an ally of not only his political but also his cultural self. He refused to be retooled as a standardized, progressive nationalist or as a conventional revolutionary.[30]

In due course, Savarkar qualified as a barrister from Grey's Inn, but he refused to give an undertaking that he would not participate in seditious activities and was not called to the bar. (As we shall see, that might have been the last time Savarkar refused to give an undertaking under pressure from authorities.) Such incidences of dissidence and his earlier secret revolutionary activities had a cumulative effect. In 1910, he was arrested and deported to India. On the way to India, he tried to escape at Marseilles but was recaptured and turned over to British authorities, even though it was French territory. Presumably, even post-revolutionary, republican France, when it came to anti-colonial violence, knew where and when to draw a line so far as its ideas of freedom and sovereignty went.

Savarkar was tried in India and was sentenced to transportation for life twice over, which meant jail for fifty years. His property, too, was confiscated.[31] The university cancelled his B.A. degree. At the age of twenty-seven, Savarkar was sent to the notorious Cellular Jail at Port Blair in the Andaman Islands. The journey to Port Blair was itself traumatic. He was to later write:

> Climbing into the steamer to be transported for life was like putting a live man in his own coffin. Hundreds and thousands must have gone to the Andamans ... and not ten in a thousand had returned alive to India! Young men of 18, as soon as they put their step on the steamer, became old and the shadow of death was visible on their faces.[32]

The Cellular Jail, Savarkar soon found out, took its notoriety seriously and tried to live up to its image the hard way. The jail's walls were adorned with manacles and other items of torture and sadism was a part of everyday life.[33] He was allowed one letter a year and had to wear a plaque which said that he was sentenced in 1911 and would be released in 1960. His punishments included solitary confinement for six months, seven days of standing handcuffs and ten days of cross bar fetters, which did not allow him to bend his knees for ten days. He was also yoked to an oil mill like a bullock—along with two other revolutionaries, Indu Bhushan Roy and Ullaskar Dutt—to produce 30 lbs of mustard oil. (Roy committed suicide, unable to bear the torture and the humiliation, and Dutt went mad and was put in an asylum in the Andamans for 14 years.) However, what the finicky Brahmin hated the most were the filthy, primitive, grossly inadequate toilet facilities. As prisoners were locked up and not allowed to use the jail toilets for about twelve hours at night, many eased themselves in their cells and had to learn to sleep next to their faeces and puddles of urine.

All this, but particularly the solitary confinement, began to induce subtle but decisive changes in the personality and world view of Savarkar, still a young man who could hope to return home only as an old man. 'He often felt that his mind had been on a rack all the time, his nerves completely shattered.'[34] And the hardened revolutionary began to show signs of physical fright and psychological collapse. The culture of violence, cruelty, and totalism in the jail was a constant invitation to suicide and madness. One could survive that extreme situation only by radically retooling oneself to ensure survival and the costs of that retooling could be distasteful, both for the victim and the onlookers.[35]

Savarkar's ideological self always had two axes: along one he worshipped modern scientific rationality and Machiavellianism, along the other he used European romanticism to empower his ideas of nationalism and revolution. His ethics probably came from the latter. The Cellular Jail crippled the romanticism, so that it now survived mainly as a rhetoric that allowed him to give fuller play to his amoral, reason-driven, Machiavellian self as a technology of survival. Contrary to the impression he gives in his autobiographical writings, within a year of his arrival at Andamans he began to write abject appeals to the authorities, seeking clemency and promising loyalty, obedience, and good behaviour. There had been a manipulative streak even in his revolutionary career and he now began to take even greater care not to antagonize the jail authorities. There is at least one other respected revolutionary, Trailokya Nath Maharaj, a fellow-prisoner of Savarkar in Andamans, who complained to historian R.C. Majumdar that the Savarkar brothers egged on the political prisoners to call a strike and then did not join it.[36] Rumours say that Savarkar's experiences in jail sharpened his antipathy towards the Muslims, for the torturers included Muslim warders, two of whom allegedly sodomized him. Savarkar does mention that the warders for political prisoners in Cellular Jail were all Muslims and they were nasty.[37]

However, Savarkar's own account forces one to ask if his sufferings at the hands of his Muslim warders were not at least partly a result of his self-fulfilling, anti-Muslim prejudices. For instance, once an infamous, low-level functionary of the jail, a Pathan called Mirza Khan, came to Savarkar and complimented him for the loyalty, courage, and determination of Nani Gopal, a political prisoner who had gone on

hunger strike and was nearing death. Khan called Gopal a 'true disciple' of Savarkar and 'verily a Pathan lad'. Savarkar's response to this
attempt to establish a relationship was:

> Bada Jamadar, you are wrong. Your father was a Pathan and you are
> a Pathan. If he [Nani Gopal] were a Pathan, he would not have rotted
> in this jail for the sake of his country; he would have, like you, licked
> the shoes of Mr. Barrie and would not have defied him.... It is because
> Nani Gopal is a born Hindu that he is so brave.[38]

That Savarkar shared the widespread stereotype of the Pathans and
considered the Pathan warders to be 'ignorant blockheads'—apart
from being, like the Sindhi and Baluchi Muslims, 'cruel', 'unscrupu-
lous', 'bigoted', and 'fanatics'—did not help matters.[39] At one place in
his jail memoirs, he mentions that there were exceptions among the
Muslims, but his narrative has no place for any of these exceptions
and his ideology does not allow him to talk of them.[40]

Savarkar's admirers claim that the mercy petitions and the undertakings he signed so readily were strategic; he wanted to be released
to participate in the freedom movement. It is true that the British
never fully trusted his petitions and his relationship with the colonial
regime did not automatically become cosy immediately afterwards, as
some of his detractors insinuate. It is also true that some degree of
manipulative cunning was part of Savarkar's repertoire. Filing of such
petitions by political prisoners, too, was not rare. But it is also true
that the authorities trusted him enough to appoint him a foreman in
the jail, and Savarkar never again played any significant or insignifi-
cant part in the anti-imperialist struggle. On the contrary, he openly
began to look upon the British empire as a boon and an opportunity to
cleanse India of the Muslims, his version of the 'yellow peril'.[41] There
was in his new politics identifiable strains of what some clinicians
will diagnose as authoritarian submission and identification with his
tormentors.

Savarkar's petitions paid dividends nonetheless; the colonial authorities probably had a more rounded understanding of his personality
than his Indian admirers and detractors. He was considered harmless and released in 1921 at the age of 38. But the authorities did not
take any chance either. After his return from the Andamans in 1921,
he was kept in Ratnagiri Jail for three years. The ghosts of Andaman

still haunted him and this new sentence was probably the last straw. At least at one point he was depressed enough to think of suicide: 'High up in that cell was a barred window as in the jail in the Andamans. I thought out in my mind how to reach my hand to the window and how to put an end to my life by hanging myself by a rope to its bars ... my mind was overcast with complete darkness.'[42]

In 1924, Savarkar was finally released on the condition that he would not participate in politics and not go outside Ratnagiri district. Indeed, 'seeing his spirit broken and willpower completely shattered', the government also suggested that he should state that his trial was fair and the sentence awarded was just. At the same time, it told him this was 'in no way ... a condition of his release'. Yet, he went ahead and made the statement.[43] The colonial system was more efficient than it itself thought; Savarkar had returned from Andaman a shadow of his old self and the three additional years in jail, too, had done their job. When released in 1924, it has been said of him, 'At forty one he looked sixty and resembled a lean and hungry hawk, with bitter mouth and eyes that looked hooded.'[44]

It was in Ratnagiri Jail that Savarkar wrote the tract, *Hindutva* (1923), which still serves as the Bible of Hindu nationalists.[45] Savarkar had started public life as a secular, reasonably non-sectarian, anti-imperialist activist. He might have already been a bit of a Hindu chauvinist but that did not distort much his political ideas. One indicator is his book on the 1857 uprising. Even his favourite argument that the holy land, *punyabhu*, for Muslims and Christians was outside India—and hence they could not be equal partners in a common nationality—does not find a place in the book.[46] *Hindutva* was the milestone in a journey that was to devour him. There are hints in the book of a totalism that induced him to marry even his classical scholarship to concerns that had little to do with classicism and everything to with imperial Europe and what had already become an imperial knowledge system—nationality and national culture, nation-building and state-formation, secular rationality and a social–evolutionary concept of history. Each of these imported ideas were absolutized, seen as sacrosanct and all traditions, however sacred, were made subservient to them.

In politics, if you wear a mask long enough, it becomes your face. The peculiar mix of collaboration and xenophobia gradually

overwhelmed Savarkar and helped to hold together his post-Andaman
self. Politics had always given him the scope to publicly express
his more psychopathic and violent traits and he was learned enough
to know that modern nation-building and state-formation had been a
violent, criminal enterprise in all societies. At the same time, being
a typical product of the late nineteenth-century colonial knowledge
system, he could think of India only as a potential, European-style
nation state. Once he had thought through this issue, his authoritarian traits did not permit him any ambiguity in this matter. The 'prince
of revolutionaries' now openly redefined British colonial rule as an
apprenticeship, which taught the Indians the principles of 'normal'
nationhood. He was too deeply seeped in history, the new obsession
of India's modern elite,[47] not to notice that the basis of nation- and
state-building in each and every European country had been, to start
with, religion and ethnicity. He was one of those who had not only
taken to heart the 'lessons' of Europe's political history, but also
wanted all Indians to live by that history.[48]

Whether Savarkar himself fully shared the passions and symbols
on which the Hindu nation was to be built is, however, another issue.
Realpolitik, too, was a part of his ideological kitbag and under his
leadership, his party, the Hindu Mahasabha, often collaborated and
formed governments in alliance with parties that others did not
expect him to touch (with the Muslim League, for instance, when the
League was demanding the division of India). This manipulative use
of religion and culture could not but boomerang; in Savarkar's later
years it looked as if he himself had turned into the soulless instrument that he wanted the Hindus to be.

In 1937, Savarkar became the president of the Hindu Mahasabha.
This was not surprising; the party was his in any case. More important
was the publication of his novel *Kalapani* in the same year. Savarkar
was already the author of a novel, *Mopla* (1924), and a play, *Ushap*
(1927). Both mirrored his ideology. *Kalapani* was something more—
it reflected his and perhaps Hindutva's only attempt to envision an
ideal or desirable India. He had written in 1907 *The First Indian War
of Independence–1857*, which projected the idea of a unified, Indian
resistance to colonialism, cutting across all socio-religious barriers.
At the centre of the new work, shaped by his days in the Andamans,
was an imaginary, futuristic, post-penal colony as the epitome of a

postcolonial society. It was the vision of a secular, egalitarian, homogeneous, Hindu community where people married across linguistic and caste boundaries and shared the same culture, language, and ideology—a terribly insipid, deadly version of a fully modern nation state with all its unmanageable angularities ironed out. *The First Indian War* was evidently a distant memory now.

Magnanimously, *Kalapani* confined its thought experiment to the Hindus. They were the ones who were to be thus homogenized for the sake of a viable national state and cured of the Hinduism that a chaotic, amorphous Indian society had thoughtlessly inculcated in the 'slumbering' Hindus over the centuries.[49] Unfortunately, though Savarkar exiles Muslims and Christians from his utopia, they are there in his novel in full strength. They haunt Savarkar's utopia as monolithic ghost communities, as fully formed nations running full-fledged states. They are there in the novel as the unacknowledged future of the Hindus.[50] *Kalapani* represents the hope of the author that, despite rebuffing him and his party, the Hindus would someday be rational enough to gulp the heavy dose of uniformity he was prescribing, for the sake of *his* idea of India.

The Hindus proved to be more headstrong; Savarkar's ideology and politics only further distanced him from the freedom movement. Once World War II started in 1939, the gap widened because he began helping the colonial regime to recruit Indians as soldiers. He argued that this was his way of militarizing the Hindus. By the end of the war, he was even more of a lonely figure, excluded from virtually all serious negotiations on transfer of power and the division of British India into two nation states. Savarkar must have been hurt that though Gandhi had helped a recruitment drive in South Africa many years ago, it was never held against Gandhi, while his recruitment drive for the British-Indian army, in a war that enjoyed much more legitimacy among the liberals and the Left, further isolated him.

Though it was Savarkar's two-nation theory that triumphed at the end and justified the partitioning of India, he was deeply distressed by the division and held Gandhi primarily responsible for it. Savarkar was never terribly self-exploratory and anti-intraception was almost an article of faith with him; like many revolutionaries he feared looking within, perhaps because he thought it would soften his resolve. In 1947, the ageing rebel got involved in a plot to kill Gandhi who

was threatening to become a long-term liability for the young Indian
nation state. This time Savarkar found his willing instruments in
Nathuram Vinayak Godse and Narayan Apte, two of his young admirers. They were members of the Hindu Mahasabha and former members of the RSS. Godse was the one to pull the trigger on an unarmed,
unprotected Gandhi on 30 January 1948.

The police and the government could have easily prevented the
killing, for one of the plotters, Madanlal Pahwa, who had thrown
a bomb at one of Gandhi's prayer meetings a few days earlier, was
caught, and within a few hours revealed all the relevant details and
names of the persons involved in the plot. However, many in the
ruling circles were fed up with Gandhi's 'eccentric', 'effeminate',
'irrational' defiance of the canons of modern statecraft, his non-
violence, and what some Indian intellectuals had already begun to
call 'pulpit politics'.[51] Payne directly accuses the Bombay police of
being involved in the conspiracy to kill Gandhi. Embarrassment and
perhaps a touch of guilt pushed them to act more decisively after
the assassination. The conspiracy was unearthed soon enough and
Savarkar was arrested within eight hours of the assassination. He
was tried, along with seven others, for murder. In February 1948,
before the trial began, he had predictably offered to give another
undertaking abjuring politics if let off. The offer was rejected and the
trial finally ended the political and intellectual career of this gifted
but troubled vendor of hate and violence. However, he 'escaped conviction by the skin of his teeth', for this time too he had taken his
usual care to hide his links with the assassins.[52] Also, some of the
most powerful political leaders too wanted Savarkar to be acquitted.
Deputy Prime Minister and Minister of Home Affairs Vallabhbhai
Patel, for instance, admitted that the government had annoyed the
Muslims and 'could not afford to anger the Hindus too'.[53]

Godse—the naïve, ideologically driven killer of Gandhi, pushed
by forces that he neither controlled nor fully understood—faced
the other Savarkar, the one whom he had not met during his long
acquaintance with the guru, only during his trial in 1948. Though he
had directly inspired Godse to kill Gandhi, Savarkar during the trial
was not merely aloof and distant, he was careful to avoid any show
of concern or fraternal feelings towards his protégé, lest it weak-
ened his plea of innocence. Advocate P. L. Inamdar, an admirer of

Savarkar who unsuccessfully defended Nathuram's brother Gopal in the same trial, found Savarkar very nervous and agitated during the trial. Savarkar, himself a barrister, repeatedly sought reassurance from Inamdar and asked the lawyer if he would be acquitted; he did not ask a single question about the fate of the others.[54] He was still phobic about jails.

Godse, we learn from those close to him, was deeply hurt. He worshipped Savarkar as a selfless, heroic, father-figure and was not prepared to discover in the former freedom fighter a self-centred, manipulative politician desperately trying to save his skin. Inamdar says:

> During the various talks I had with Nathuram, he told me that he was deeply hurt by Tatyarao's [Savarkar's] calculated, demonstrative non-association with him either in court or in the Red Fort Jail.... How Nathuram yearned for a touch of Tatyarao's hand, a word of sympathy, or at least a look of compassion ... Nathuram referred to his hurt feelings in this regard even during my last visit with him.[55]

Savarkar had reasons to be careful. Though the trial court acquitted him, a judicial enquiry later established his complicity. The Supreme Court judge J. L. Kapur, who headed the enquiry, was clear in his finding: Savarkar *did* lead the conspiracy that killed Gandhi.[56]

The assassination was the last political act of Savarkar. Though he lived another eighteen years, he withdrew into a cell and took care not to offend the government even indirectly. He had already mastered the art of buying peace with authorities. Once in 1950, when he tested waters in the wake of the Nehru–Liaqat Ali Pact and the government frowned upon his political activities, he once again offered to abjure politics to avoid prosecution. When the authorities asked for a formal undertaking, he promptly gave it.[57]

Savarkar died in 1966, a bitter, defeated man. He had fought for the Hindus for nearly sixty years, but the Hindus had failed to appreciate it and had not given him or his party a respectable voice in any election in independent India.[58] The man he had loathed for more than fifty years, Gandhi, was triumphant even in death. Not only was he already being called a saint but, horror of horrors, the father of the nation by the same Hindus whom Savarkar had tried so hard to organize as a nation and wean away from the bewitching guiles of the retrogressive counter-modernist and crypto-anarchist. Savarkar, a

nineteenth-century European rationalist caught in the hinges of time,
could only 'retaliate' by showing his contempt towards his ungrateful
compatriots and their fake hero one last time. He declared that he did
not want any Hindu rituals after his death and insisted that he should
be carried to an electric crematorium, not on human shoulders, as
conventions demanded, but on mechanical transport.[59]

IV

It is a peculiar sensation, this double consciousness ... this sense of
always looking at one's self through the eyes of another, measuring
one's soul by the type of a world that looks on in amused contempt
and pity ... two souls, two thoughts, two unreconciled strivings, two
warring ideals in one dark body, whose dogged strength alone keeps it
from being torn asunder.

—W. E. B. Dubois, quoted in Charles Long[60]

Savarkar's life became controversial only after independence, more
so after his death. As details of his role in Gandhi's murder and his
obsequious letters to British authorities, seeking forgiveness and
promising loyalty, began to get better known, they led to all-round
embarrassment. However, that does not fully explain the attempts to
undervalue his anti-imperialist record in recent years, why even the
fifty-year sentence passed on him is not considered a proof of his cre-
dentials as a freedom fighter. Nor does it explain why there has been
so little acceptance that, after being sentenced to jail for fifty years
in one's mid-twenties, one may have failure of nerve and collapse of
self-esteem. True, the criticisms often come from those who have no
direct or indirect link with the freedom struggle against the world's
then-reigning superpower and have the luxury of demanding total
constancy and persistent self-sacrifice. But it is also true that there has
been no in-depth enquiry into the inner drives that pushed Savarkar
to his particularly petty version of xenophobia. Was his violence an
unrealistic, adolescent search for a heroic stature, which collapsed the
moment he confronted its 'natural', inevitable consequences under a
colonial dispensation? Did the Muslims become for him a safer target,
once he sensed the might of the British empire? Did he represent or
tap a political–psychological potentiality in urban, middle-class, educated India during the last hundred years? Is that potentiality a price

India has paid for its modernization? Are the attempts to demonize Savarkar ultimately a form of exorcism?

The last two questions are especially important. The hostility Savarkar arouses is the hostility towards one who dares to remind us that the post-seventeenth-century idea of nation state and secularism have both been complicit with ethno-religious violence during the last two centuries. For Savarkar's hatred for Muslims came not from ideas of ritual purity and impurity or caste hierarchy but from his prognosis of communities that could or could not be integrated—assimilated or dissolved—within the framework of a modern Indian state. The standard conventions of a nation state within the Westphalian model constituted his religion and he brought to it the fervour of a fundamentalist. He was not willing to wait for the decline of communities, the spread of literacy, and urban–industrial values—individuation, secularization, and instrumental rationality—to ensure nation-formation in a society organized around a different set of principles. Actually, he was searching for something more substantial than territoriality to give Indian nationalism a stable base. The search was not unknown to modern Indians; many had mounted it before Savarkar and many others were to do so after him. But most of them avoided facing the full implications of it. Savarkar was more open and honest about his goals. Hence the periodic, obsessive concern in India with the life of a person who throughout life remained at the margin of Indian politics and whom mainstream India and Hinduism never knew well enough to forget.

The second part of the story is the record of secularism in genocide, particularly ethno-nationalist genocide, in the last hundred years. Data on mass violence show that secular states, backed by secular ideologies, account for at least two-thirds of all the deaths in organized mass violence during the twentieth century.[61] Savarkar typifies the attitudes and the motivational structure—the genocidal mentality—that underlies politically engineered mass violence.[62] The conservative folk theory of secularism in many parts of the globe, particularly its South Asian variants, cannot cope with this reality. G. P. Deshpande acknowledges this when he calls Savarkar a 'secular communalist' vending a 'supra-religious ideology', but does not sense how absurd these expressions sound in South Asian intellectual circles where secularism is seen as a magical cure of all communal passions.[63] Nor is Deshpande willing to take the next step and to read Savarkar as a pathological by-product of the modern idea of a secular nation state rather than that of Hinduism.

This love–hate relationship with Savarkar in sections of India's urban middle class and the political identity he offered can be read, more aptly, as a lesson on the limits of nineteenth-century modernity, scientific rationality, and political realism rather than as pathological ethnophobia. He was one person who had grasped the scope modern rationality offered to act out the hate within him, and his attitudes to Hindutva and the Hindus were as instrumental as his attitude towards the Muslims. His rationalist, amoral, anti-religious self had paradoxically arrived at the conclusion that only religion could be an efficacious building block for nation- and state-formation in South Asia and he did not know where to stop. In his impersonal, reified, Brahminic ideas of statecraft and politics, there was not much place for emotions, certainly not for compassion. The aloof ruthlessness came packaged in an arrogant trust in his own cleverness and strategizing skills.

Even Savarkar's atheism was not the philosophical atheism associated with Buddhism and Vedanta, but the anti-clerical, hard atheism of fin-de-siècle scientism, increasingly popular among sections of the European middle class and, through cultural osmosis, in parts of modern India.[64] His politics paralleled the way European racism in the 1940s drew upon modern science, particularly nineteenth-century biology and eugenics, and saw itself responsible for doing the dirty work of scientized history.[65] The sceptics might like to look up Savarkar's comments on the cow, worshipped as sacred by most Hindus, and compare it with the position of the organizations and parties that constitute the Hindu nationalist formation today. While the latter try to pander to the sentiments of the Hindus, Savarkar publicly supported cow slaughter when necessary and declared the cow to be a useless animal with no sacredness about it.[66] He also advised Hindus to give up vegetarianism and eat fish and eggs.[67] When Gandhi's assassin and Savarkar's protégé Godse complained in his last testament in court about Gandhi's 'superstitious' use of ideas like soul force and fasting in modern politics, it was not the accusation of a Hindu fundamentalist. It mirrored Savarkar's statism.

Over the last eighty years, most ideologues of Hindu nationalism have neither come from orthodox Hinduism nor have they flaunted their orthodoxy the way Gandhi did, by proclaiming himself a Sanatani Hindu. They have proudly affirmed their links with the nineteenth-century Hindu reform movements, which they see as analogues of a masculine Protestantism, cleaning up a degraded, distorted faith to make it fit the needs of a national state.

These ideologues borrowed from ideas that were in the air during their formative years. Not only among European fascists but also among the European intelligentsia in general and among westernized Indians trying desperately to cope with their feelings of inferiority and attain global respectability through tough-minded, secular rationality wedded to ideas of national interest, social evolutionism, political realism, and progressivism. Savarkar's contempt for the likes of Gandhi came partly from that. Savarkar was not alone. The first head of the RSS, Keshav Baliram Hedgewar (1889–1940), too, could hardly be called a run-of-the-mill, believing Hindu. An urban, well-educated, modern doctor, with poor links with rural India and mainstream Hinduism, he like many pioneers of Hindu nationalism was an aggressive critic of Hinduism and was exposed to religious and social reform movements, especially the Ramakrishna Mission founded in 1897 by Swami Vivekananda (1863–1902). Hindu nationalism, on this plane, was popular European political theory and political history telescoped into South Asia as a form of toady Hinduism. In retrospect, one realizes why Gandhi insisted that the nineteenth-century religious reform movements had done more harm than good to Hinduism in the long run.

The entire process has remarkable parallels with the experiences of Sri Lankan Buddhism and Indian Islam under colonialism and the dual impact of urbanization and industrialization. There is in them the same efforts to rationalize one's faith and to set up demonic others who seemed better equipped to handle the demands of the modern world and its amoral ways; they too, consequently, initiated the same kind of self-engineering to be able to flirt with the Dionysian in human personality.[68] As if they were all caught in a larger, inescapable, evolutionary process that enjoyed intrinsic legitimacy even among those hostile to religious nationalism.[69] That partly explains why most conservative Muslim clerics in India opposed the idea of a separate country for South Asian Muslims as un-Islamic, whereas the leadership of the Pakistan movement sought a modern Muslim state, the way many secular, liberal Jews sought a Jewish state. Is the dream of a liberal, ethno-nationalist, modern state sustainable in the long run? Or is it an oxymoron? No final answer has yet been given.

The founder of Pakistan, Mohammed Ali Jinnah—Westernized, loyal to constitutionalism, staunchly secular in personal life—had as his avowed role model the classical liberal Gopal Krishna Gokhale (1866–1915). Jinnah kept the ulema at a distance throughout his life, but was perfectly willing to use them to advance the cause of a separate homeland for South Asian Muslims. Exactly as Savarkar, who despite all his anti-Muslim rhetoric and passion for united India, not only established coalitions in Sindh and Bengal with the Muslim League, fighting for Pakistan, but was proud of these alliances. He argued that the alliances were more nationalistic than the ministries formed by the 'pseudo-nationalist' Indian National Congress, led by Gandhi and Nehru.[70] There *are* parallels between the trajectories Savarkar and Jinnah traversed and the reason they chose religion as a vehicle of nation-building despite being non-believers or casual believers. Both had internalized contemporary European political categories and saw nationality as a crucial module of sovereign, modern republics. Both sought to replicate in South Asia existing wisdom in the global citadels of knowledge. Both represented the triumph in the South not so much of history as of European history. If they were fundamentalists, their fundamentals came from conventional European wisdom about nation-building and state-formation. Defying the warning of Rabindranath Tagore, they owned up the 'motive force' of Western nationalism as their own.[71] Not surprisingly, the personal relationship between Savarkar and Jinnah never soured. Nor did Savarkar ever entirely lose the respect of the likes of Subhas Chandra Bose, M. N. Roy, and B. R. Ambedkar.

V

I have used some scrappy biographical details on Savarkar to pose a series of questions: Has it become more or less inevitable for a social group—be it a religion, caste, denomination, sect, or ethnic entity—to gradually acquire the features of a nationality because that seems the only way community grievances can be aggregated and effectively articulated in a culture of state based on a concept of citizenship enmeshed with the idea of nationality? Do claims made in the name of a nationality have more political impact than the same claims made in the name of other aggregates and, as a result, has there grown, in the last hundred years, a tendency in religion-based or ethnic political formations to act as nationalities to empower themselves? Does that allow more effective mobilization in modernizing societies, particularly among the newly modern, uprooted by social changes and seeking new communities, real or imaginary? Does it also mean that such nationalism has natural limits in a society that is not fully modern? Does Savarkar's marginalization in Hindu society have something to tell us?[72]

Everyone knows that the Western history of state-formation and nation-building is simultaneously a story of how religions, denominations, and ethnicities were bludgeoned into nationalities. For those entering the realm of history for the first time in Asia and Africa—and facing the hierarchies and exclusions of the global state-nation system for the first time—the temptation is not only to construct their own history, but also to read into Europe's history their own past, present, and future. Even when they construct their own history, the categories and concerns that frame it are 'universal' or, it comes to the same thing, European. When that reading is deployed as an evolutionary grid in an Asian or African society, there is a natural fear that unless one builds a nation, whatever its cost in human suffering, one will not get justice locally or globally.

Vinayak Damodar Savarkar and Mohammed Ali Jinnah were not personally as culpable as many like to believe. The evil that many locate in them resided, at least partly, in the political ideas that dominated the world. Savarkar and Jinnah were, like most first-generation builders of South Asian states, faithful and obedient pupils of the Bismarckian state and post-medieval European republicanism, both vital parts of the dominant culture of common sense in their times. Once they accepted that culture, they could not but try to duplicate Europe's history in South Asia, whatever the cost. Not surprisingly, neither of the two is known to have ever mourned the unnecessary death of more than a million people in the bloodbath that came with the division of British India.[73] For both, human beings were means of implementing important historical designs, and in their versions of nationalism, the sufferings of the nations they represented were probably only instances of collateral damage. The rationality they worshipped overlay deep emotional voids, created by personal losses that came almost like betrayals by fate. Both coped with the betrayal through uncompromising, dispassionate, ruthless pursuit of a form of political rationality that allowed and even glorified withdrawal from or avoidance of personal emotional involvements.[74] Both lived with fragile, perhaps anchorless self-definitions that pushed them to embrace aggressive, ideological postures that tallied with their deeper psychological needs. As I have said, in politics if you wear a mask long enough, it becomes your face.

Jinnah's case was more tragic. In his famous speech of 11 August 1947, three days before the birth of Pakistan, he declared inclusive nationalism based on territoriality as his project and sought to distinguish between inclusive and sectoral nationalism exactly the way Jawaharlal Nehru did.[75] He wanted Pakistan not to exclude non-Muslims in principle and in practice. Himself a Shia, Jinnah included in Pakistan's first cabinet an Ahmadiya as the foreign minister and a Hindu Dalit as the minister of law.[76] Pakistan's first national anthem was written by a Hindu and, it is said, Jinnah had a hand in that choice. These did not help; it was too late or, perhaps, too early. Nor could Indian nationalism, despite the presence of leaders such as Jawaharlal Nehru, avoid full-scale militarization, nuclearism, and intermittent religious and ethno-nationalist violence. Nationalism, once let out of the bag, tends to become self-sustaining and to plot its own political–psychological agenda.

Many Southern scholars, blinded by nationalism's anti-imperialist role in the South, believe it can be tamed and used creatively. The experiences of South Asia in the last two centuries suggest that usually religions and cultures change to accommodate nationalism, not the other way round. Savarkar, whom many see as a minor pawn of South Asian history, did change not only South Asian Hinduism but also South Asian Islam and Buddhism. All three had to accommodate strains that have more in common with house-broken versions of Christianity in Europe and North America than with home-grown, South Asian Hinduism, Islam, and Buddhism.[77]

Ultimately, Vinayak Damodar Savarkar is the name of a blown-up, grotesque temptation inherent in the Southern world's encounter with the global nation-state system and with religious traditions that facilitate the internalization of the motive force of Western nationalism. That temptation is a part of everyone dreaming of working with tamed versions of nationalism and nation states armed with ideas of rationality, secularism, progress, and the so-called lessons of history, careful not to be ensnared by empathy, compassion, and other such subjectivist traps.

Notes

1. This paper has grown out of a small paper that was presented, under a different title, at the Panel on History of Religions as Hermeneutics of Contact Situations: Colonialism, Imperialism and Popular Religions, organized by Michio Araki for the 19th World Congress of the International Association for the History of Religions, Tokyo, 23–30 March 2005. A revised and expanded version was delivered as the Sankari Prasad Bannerjee Memorial Lecture at the Department of Philosophy, Calcutta University on 29 August 2006. The present version was written for a public lecture at the Ruprecht-Karls-Universit, Heidelberg, on 23 October 2008 and a section of it published in the website of the Karl Jasper Centre of the University. This, the final version, was prepared for the 2012 Shanghai Summit of the Asian Circle of Thought, held in connection with Shanghai Biennale. I am grateful to Mohan M. Trivedi, who, thirty years ago, helped me read some of the Marathi writings of Vinayak Savarkar and Nathuram Godse. Others who have contributed to my insights into Savarkar's personality are Gopal Godse, whom I interviewed some thirty years ago, and Siegfried O. Wolf, who drew my attention to some materials on Savarkar's sojourn at London.

2. Theodor W. Adorno, Else Frenkel-Brunswick, Daniel Levinson, R. Nevitt Sanford, *The Authoritarian Personality* (New York: Harper, 1960); see also Milton Rokeach, *The Open and Closed Mind* (New York: Basic, 1960).

3. Robert J. Lifton, *Nazi Doctors: Medical Killings and the Psychology of Genocide* (New York: Basic Books, 1986); Bruno Bettelheim, 'Their Specialty Was Murder', review of Robert J. Lifton's *Nazi Doctors, New York Times,* 5 October 1986.

4. Philip Rieff, *Freud: The Mind of the Moralist* (New York: Viking, 1959).

5. Robert J. Lifton, 'Wellfleet Conference on Historical Memory', *The Psychohistory Review* 14, no. 3 (1986): 5–66; see p. 20.

6. Arindam Chakrabarti, 'The Uses of Revulsion: Ethics and Aesthetics of Disgust', plenary lecture at the 9th East-West Philosophers' Conference, East-West Centre, Honolulu, June 2005. See also Martha Nussbaum, 'Danger to Human Dignity: the Revival of Disgust and Shame in the Law', *The Chronicle of Higher Education*, 6 August 2004, available at http://chronicle.com/free/v50/i48/48b00601. html. I am grateful to Chakrabarti for drawing my attention to this work.

7. Dhananjay Keer, *Veer Savarkar* (Bombay: Popular Prakashan, 1950). Nevertheless, the present essay has gained much from Keer's work and the correctives to it in A. G. Noorani, *Savarkar and Hindutva: The Godse Connection* (New Delhi: LeftWord, 2002); and Suresh Sharma, 'Savarkar's Quest for a Modern Hindu Consolidation', *Studies in Humanities and Social Sciences* 2, no. 2 (1996): 189–215. For an insightful, nuanced discussion of the cultural status of the autobiography in India and the bifurcation of the genre into *jīvanvrittānta* and *ātmakathā* by Gandhi, see Bhikhu Parekh, 'Indianization of Autobiography', in *Colonialism, Tradition and Reform: An Analysis of Gandhi's Political Discourse* (New Delhi: Sage, 1989), 247–66.

8. Jatipuranas may be understood as often-changing, sometimes-mythic, caste-specific accounts of the origins and the past of communities.

9. Years ago, I plotted the process of this reform along two axes— Semiticization and revaluation of Kshatriya virtues—mainly to supplement the socially more critical process of Sanskritization that M. N. Srinivas has studied. Ashis Nandy, *The Intimate Enemy: Loss and Recovery of Self under Colonialism* (New Delhi: Oxford University Press, 1983). The third axis was missing—the emergence of a generic, 'portable', tamed Hinduism that would make sense not only to scholars and theologians but also to a socially and geographically mobile householder, cut off from his or her local, vernacular roots. To survive in the contemporary world, that new Hinduism had to be more open to Hindu nationalism and more compatible with a modern nation state.

10. Sudipta Kaviraj, *The Unhappy Consciousness: Bankimchandra Chattopadhyay and the Formation of Nationalist Discourse in India* (New Delhi: Oxford University Press, 1995).

11. Upadhyay in many respects served as Tagore's double. All three explicitly political novels of Tagore—*Gorā* (1909), *Ghare Bāire* (1916), and *Chār Adhyāya* (1934)—negotiate the personality and ideology of Upadhyay. For a while in his youth, Tagore himself was close to Hindu nationalism and, when he was moving out of that phase, he found Upadhyay moving towards his abandoned ideology. Ashis Nandy, *The Illegitimacy of Nationalism: Rabindranath Tagore and the Politics of Self* (New Delhi: Oxford University Press, 1989).

12. Nandy, *Illegitimacy of Nationalism*. For a detailed and insightful look at Upadhyay, see Julius Lipner, *Life and Thought of a Revolutionary* (New Delhi: Oxford University Press, 1999). Others elsewhere in India were moving towards Upadhyay's position, indicating that it was something more than an idiosyncratic, personal choice. Only a few years later, Har Dayal (1888–1939) in North India began articulating a similar idea of political Hinduism, though without an explicit theory of violence.

13. Vinayak Damodar Savarkar, *Hindutva: Who is a Hindu?* (Bombay: Veer Savarkar Prakashan, 1969 [1923]).

14. Justice J. S. Verma, who delivered the judgement, was to, however, later claim that politicians had misused his judgement, without admitting that the judgement gave a suspect political ideology the status of a religion, which even Savarkar and the RSS had not claimed or done. On Justice Verma's self-justification, see 'My Verdict was Misinterpreted', *Hindustan Times*, 7 February 2003.

15. Amnon Raz-Krakotzkin, presentation in the session on 'Contemporary Debates in the West: Secular Norms, Multiculturalism, and Immigrant Incorporation', Conference on The Secular, Secularizations, and Secularisms at the Wissenschaftskolleg, Berlin, 7–10 June 2006.

16. R. C. Majumdar quoted in Noorani, *Savarkar and Hindutva*, p. 25.

17. M. R. Jayakar, *Story of My Life*, vol. 2, p. 541, quoted in Noorani, *Savarkar and Hindutva*, 25–6.

18. V. D. Savarkar, *The Six Golden Epochs of Indian History* (New Delhi: Rajdhani Granthanagar, 1970), 71, quoted by Kavita Krishnan, 'Unveiling Savarkar: Picture Imperfect', available at www. Cpiml.org/liberation/ year-2003/April. For a detailed, well-researched discussion of Savarkar on rape and his belief that a woman's body can be a political instrument and weapon and that the Hindus must learn to use this weapon, see Purushottam Agarwal, 'Savarkar, Surat and Draupadi: Legitimising Rape as a Political Weapon', in *A Review of Women and the Hindu Right*, edited by Tanika Sarkar and Urvashi Butalia (New Delhi: Kali for Women, 1996), 29–57.

19. Even this may not be the whole story. Lloyd deMause has argued that the origins of war lie partly in the fantasy of war as righteous rape. Savarkar might have reversed the process, imagining rape as a form of war that allegedly makes nations. Lloyd deMause, *The Emotional Life of Nations* (New York: Karnac Books, 2002), Chapter 6. Suresh Sharma argues that Savarkar reneged on the inclusive nationalism of his earlier years 'not because Hindu rashtra represented a higher ideal' but because he came to the conclusion that his earlier project was not a feasible one, whereas a Hindu nation was a realizable goal. Sharma, 'Savarkar's Quest', 202.

Sharma is not wrong but his interpretation does not fully explain the low rhetoric and passions of an otherwise Machiavellian politician who was proudly dispassionate and impersonal. For that one must take into account the inner demons that populated Savarkar's world.

20. *Indian Annual Register*, vol. 2 (1943): 10, quoted in Anil Nauriya, 'The Savarkarist Syntax', *Hindu*, 18 September 2004.
21. On the political–cultural context from within which Savarkar emerged and within which he made sense, see Enrico Fasana, 'Deshabhakta: The Leaders of the Indian Independence Movement in the Eyes of Marathi Nationalists', *Asian and African Studies* 3, no. 2 (1994): 152–75; and *From Hindutva to Hindu Rashtra: The Social and the Political Thought of Vinayak Damodar Savarkar (1883–1966)*, presented at the 13th European Conference on Modern South Asian Studies, Toulouse, 31 August–3 September, 1996, manuscript.
22. Keer, *Veer Savarkar*, 4–5.
23. Keer, *Veer Savarkar*, Chapter 1.
24. It is a remarkable coincidence that Savarkar's book was published more or less at the same time as Gandhi's *Hind Swaraj*, which projected an entirely different view of India's self-definition and political future, and Rabindranath Tagore's novel *Gorā*, a sophisticated rebuttal of Savarkar's ideology from a prescient, proto-Gandhian point of view.
25. S. S. Savarkar and G. M. Joshi, eds, *Historical Statements by V.D. Savarkar* (Bombay: Popular Prakashan, 1967), 114.
26. Keer, *Veer Savarkar*, 530.
27. Harindra Srivastava, *Five Stormy Years: Savarkar in London* (New Delhi: Allied, 1983), 28–9. One result was that when Gandhi next visited India House in 1909 to preside over Dusserah celebrations, he made it a condition that only vegetarian food will be served. On the basic philosophical clash between Savarkar's modernism, including his total commitment to modern science and technology, and Gandhi's radical, futuristic critique of modernity, the urban–industrial vision, and Baconian science and technology, see Sharma, 'Savarkar's Quest'; A. Raghuramaraju, *Debates in Indian Philosophy: Classical, Colonial, and Contemporary* (New Delhi: Oxford University Press, 2006), 66–91; and Ashis Nandy, 'From Outside the Imperium: Gandhi's Cultural Critique of the West', in *Traditions, Tyranny and Utopias: Essays in the Politics of Awareness* (New Delhi: Oxford University Press, 1987), 127–63.
28. Srivastava, *Five Stormy Years*, 4.
29. Srivastava, *Five Stormy Years*, 33; also see S. L. Karandikar, *Savarkar Charitra* (Pune: Modern Book Depot, 1947), 33.

30. For Savarkar's version of his days in England, see *Inside the Enemy Camp*, available at www.Savarkar.org.

31. .The property was not returned to him in independent India either. When the last request in Savarkar's lifetime was made to Morarji Desai, then chief minister of Bombay, Desai was unambiguous. He said that the harm Savarkar had done to the country in his later life outweighed the good he did to it earlier. Keer, *Veer Savarkar*, 406.

32. V. D. Savarkar, quoted in M. V. Kamath, 'Savarkar: The Limits of Human Endurance', in Verinder Grover, *V.D. Savarkar* (New Delhi: Deep and Deep, 1993), 444–51; see 445.

33. To get a flavour of the sadomasochistic environment of cellular jail as it was experienced by Savarkar, see Damodar Vinayak Savarkar, *My Transportation for Life*, translated by V. N. Naik (Bombay: Veer Savarkar Prakashan, 1984). The original, *Mazi Janmathep*, was serialized in two Marathi journals in 1925–7 and later published as a book by Savarkar. For those who might be tempted to read the account as exaggerated and self-serving, there is also the more recent invocation of the concentration camp–like ambience of the jail by two British journalists in Cathy Scott-Clark and Adrian Levy, 'Survivors of Our Hell', *Guardian Unlimited*, 23 June 2001, available at http://www.guardian.co.uk/Archive/Article/0,4273,4207876,00.html. Scott-Clark and Levy depend not only on survivors' testimony but also on official records. See also S. N. Aggarwal, *Heroes of Cellular Jail* (New Delhi: Rupa, 2006).

34. Kamath, 'Savarkar', 445.

35. Some amount of doublespeak, ingratiation, and manipulative behaviour was common in the sick environment of Andamans, both among the prison staff and the prisoners, including some of the most respected freedom fighters. These had become inevitable tools of survival, even resistance. See Savarkar, *My Transportation for Life*, Chapter 16. However, Savarkar's attempts to cast himself in a heroic mould and judge others by impossible standards, standards by which he himself could not live, did not make him particularly popular among other freedom fighters in the jail. Ideologically, he could not accept in freedom fighters the normal 'weaknesses' of human beings. He was not sensitive to the inner life of persons and his ideology had little space for human subjectivities, which he tended to see as emasculating. One revealing instance was his inability to see through the weak, fearful, insecure, scheming Barrie, the Irish jailor who at one level was a tyrant and a sadist, and at another, a self-hating, colonial subject trying to ingratiate him by talking to Savarkar about his early hatred of the English and the unpleasant duties his job imposed on him. Savarkar's attempts to score debating points whenever

Barrie opened a conversation with him quickened Barrie's feelings of inferiority and his lurking awareness of his moral degradation and made him doubly dangerous.

36. R. C. Majumdar cited in Noorani, *Savarkar and Hindutva*, 58–9.
37. These rumours probably induced two popular writers to suspect that there was homosexual bonding between V. D. Savarkar and Nathuram Godse. Larry Collins and Dominique Lapiere, *Freedom at Midnight* (1975) (New York: Harper Collins, 1997). Could it be that in the masculinized world view of Hindu nationalism, these rumours, even if untrue, were a metaphoric means of recognizing the emasculation of Savarkar?
38. Savarkar, *My Transportation for Life*, 91–2, 254.
39. Savarkar, *My Transportation for Life*, 252–3.
40. Things were seemingly different before Savarkar went to the Andamans. On the way to the Andamans, when he was staying in a jail at Bombay, he was helped by one of his Muslim warders and, he openly acknowledged that.
41. See G. N. S. Raghavan, 'In Search of the Real Savarkar', *Indian Express*, 8 July 2003. Raghavan tries hard to sell the colonial regime's natural suspicion of Savarkar's motives behind his mercy petitions as a proof of Savarkar's persistent faith in his political tactics. Actually, such proof is not necessary. His participation in Gandhi's murder is a more than adequate proof that his tactics did not change over a period of four decades. The question is: Was he willing to or psychologically capable of taking on the colonial state or, for that matter, any state after his experiences in the Andamans? Savarkar was an incurable statist, but the Cellular Jail taught him a thing or two about the power and ruthlessness of states. The tone of his mercy petition to the government sent from the Cellular Jail says it all. Not only did he promise to 'serve the government in any capacity' it wanted, he also added, '... the mighty alone can afford to be merciful and therefore where else can the prodigal son return but to the parental doors of the government'. Noorani, *Savarkar and Hindutva*, 18.
42. V. D. Savarkar quoted in Kamath, 'Savarkar', 445. Ideologically Savarkar was against suicide, but the idea did come fleetingly to him even at the Andamans. When Indu Bhushan Roy committed suicide unable to bear the life at the Andamans, Savarkar said to himself, according to his own admission, 'Who knows, one day your fate will be the same as his.' Savarkar, *My Transportation for Life*, 216.
43. Savarkar wrote: 'I hereby acknowledge that I had a fair trial and just sentence. I heartily abhor methods of violence resorted to in days gone by, and I feel myself duty bound to uphold Law and the constitution to the best of my powers and am willing to make the Reform [Montagu-Chelmsford

proposals of 1919, rejected by virtually every Indian political party] a success insofar as I may be allowed to do so in future.' Krishnan Dubey and Venkitesh Ramakrishnan, 'Far from Heroism—The Tale of 'Veer Savarkar' and a Response', *Frontline*, 7 April 1996, available at www.hvk. org/ articles/ 1196/0047.html.

44. Robert Payne, *The Life and Death of Mahatma Gandhi* (London: Bodley Head, 1968), 208.

45. When Madhavrao Sadashiv Golwalkar (1906–73), the head of the RSS during 1940–73, attempted an updated handbook on Hindu nationalism, he ended up crudely parroting Savarkar, even though he had been the butt of Savarkar's biting sarcasm for his softness towards Hindu rituals and beliefs. See M. S. Golwalkar, *We or Our Nationhood Defined* (Nagpur: Bharat Prakashan, 1939). Golwalkar reportedly showed the manuscript of the book to one of Savarkar's brothers for comments, criticisms, and suggestions. It did not help, for Savarkar's aim was to produce nothing less than a house-broken, defanged version of Hinduism that would be subservient to a modern nation state.

46. It is surprising that to a person as obsequiously and uncritically European in his political thought as Savarkar, it never occurred that every European nationality had its holy land not only outside their country but outside Europe as well. Probably he thought that Europe was advanced and modern enough to have outgrown its ethno-religious past and denominational differences, and could sustain its nationalities on rational and secular grounds alone.

47. Kaviraj, *Unhappy Consciousness*, 109. By Indians, Kaviraj of course means the small, modernizing, urban, middle-class India that dominated public discourse at the time.

48. As he put it in a speech unearthed by historian Prabha Dixit (Hindu Mahasabha Records, File 13, quoted in Noorani, *Savarkar and Hindutva*, 34), 'in Hindustan it is the Hindus professing Hindu religion and being in overwhelming majority that constitute the national community and create and formulate the nationalism of the nation. It is so in every country of the world's.

49. As he once said in a maudlin homage to the martyrs of 1857: 'And then, oh Martyrs, tell us the little as well as the great defects which you found out in our people in that experiment of yours. But above all, point out that ruinous, nay, the only material draw-back in the body of the nation which rendered all your efforts futile—the mean selfish blindness which refuses to see its way to join the nation's cause. Say that the only cause of the defeat of Hindusthan was Hindusthan herself.' V. D. Savarkar, *Echoes from Andamans* (Bombay: Veer Savarkar Prakashan, 1984), 53–6; see 55–6.

50. Though he never directly wrote on the subject, Savarkar had swallowed hook, line, and sinker European social evolutionism. He did not approve of the Indians writing on Vedanta. He would have them write rather on political history, science, economy, and such other subjects, because, he said, 'The Americans need Vedanta and so does England; for they have developed their life to that fullness, richness and manliness—to Kshatriyahood and so stand on the threshold of that Brahminhood. But ... we are ... at present all Shudras and cannot claim access to the Veda and Vedanta.' Savarkar, *Echoes from Andamans*, 5.

51. For more details see Ashis Nandy, 'Final Encounter: The Politics of the Assassination of Gandhi', in *At the Edge of Psychology: Essays on Politics and Culture* by Ashis Nandy (New Delhi: Oxford University Press, 1980), 70–98; and 'Coming Home: Religion, Mass Violence and the Exiled and Secret Selves of a Citizen-Killer, *Public Culture* 22, no. 1 (2010): 127–47. Payne in his *Life and Death of Mahatma Gandhi* neatly describes the political ambience in which the assassination took place. He talks of the '... shadowy presences lurking in the background.... Their names are unknown to history, or can be guessed at. The attentive reader of the voluminous trial reports soon finds himself haunted by the certainty that many others who never stood trial were involved in the conspiracy'. Payne, *Life and Death of Mahatma Gandhi*, 646.

52. Noorani, *Savarkar and Hindutva*, 4.

53. Tushar A. Gandhi, *Let's Kill Gandhi: A Chronicle of His Last Days, the Conspiracy, Murder, Investigation and Trial* (New Delhi: Rupa, 2007), 732–3. Tushar Gandhi also suggests that Patel made peace with his conscience by choosing to believe that Gandhi was killed for going on fast to force the Government of India to give Pakistan the Rs 550 million due to it. Actually, the same group of conspirators had made at least two earlier attempts to kill Gandhi years before the issue of money came up.

54. P. L. Inamdar, *The Story of the Red Fort Trial 1948–49* (Bombay: Popular Prakashan, 1979), 23.

55. Inamdar, *Story of the Red Fort Trial 1948–49*, 14. These details do not support Tushar Gandhi's belief that Savarkar wrote or edited Nathuram Godse's powerful testimony in court. Gandhi, *Let's Kill Gandhi*, 606–7. However, the testimony does show how deeply the assassin had internalized Savarkar and wanted to act as an extension of Savarkar's self.

56. Justice J. L. Kapur, *Report of Commission of Enquiry into Conspiracy to Murder Mahatma Gandhi*, vol. 2 (New Delhi: Government of India Press, 1970), 303.

57. By this time, giving obsequious undertakings to authorities had become a way of life with Savarkar. The last undertaking was also his most abject. In independent India, despite his total opposition to

the pact, he promised, in writing, to 'exhort the people to observe the Nehru-Liaqat Ali Pact'. Even his fawning biographer Keer is forced to admit that 'for a moment, the physical agonies [of preventive detention] must have overpowered his stubborn will'. Keer, *Veer Savarkar*, 432. This undertaking, too, was given under Morarji Desai, then the home minister of Bombay. Understandably Desai, who was in excellent spirits when jailed during the freedom struggle and was to improve in his health when jailed by the Indira Gandhi regime at about the age of eighty during the Emergency and suspension of civil rights in 1975–7, had utter contempt for Savarkar.

58. Payne puts it succinctly when he says, 'Long before he died, he knew that he had been like a man waiting in the wings for the call to occupy the centre of the stage, but the call never came.' Payne, *Life and Death of Mahatma Gandhi*, 209.

59. Keer, *Veer Savarkar*, 544.

60. Charles Long, *Significations: Signs, Symbols, and Images in the Interpretation of Religion* (Aurora, Colorado: The Davies Group, 1995), 178.

61. See for example R. J. Rummel, *Death by Government: Genocide and Mass Murder Since 1900* (West Hanover, Massachusetts: Christopher Publishing, 1994).

62. See for example Robert Jay Lifton and Eric Markusen, *The Genocidal Mentality: Nazi Holocaust and the Nuclear Threat* (New York: Basic Books, 1990).

63. G. P. Deshpande, 'An Occasion for the RSS', *Economic and Political Weekly*, 25 March 2006. Deshpande also points out that Savarkar conceptualized Hindutva as some kind of Hegelian Geist. It is not clear from his brief but insightful comment whether Savarkar borrowed as directly from Hegel as he did from Mazzini.

64. Nothing expressed Savarkar's tough-minded atheism better than his refusal to allow any Hindu religious ritual or rite when his wife died, notwithstanding public protests and *Satyagraha* by some of his followers. He did not want even her body to be brought home, saying that it was 'no use lamenting over the dead body'. Keer, *Veer Savarkar*, 529–30.

65. Aditya Nigam in a comment has differentiated between two styles of Hindu nationalism, one typified by Savarkar and the other by Golwalkar, the believing Hindu who came to head the RSS in the 1940s. He suggests that Golwalkar's is the more dangerous version. See Aditya Nigam, 'Reading between the Chinks in Pariwar Armour', *Tehelka*, 25 June 2005, 20. Nigam may be right, because the likes of Golwalkar can take Hindu nationalism *into* Hinduism and reshape the culture of Indian politics and, at the end, Hinduism in a way that Savarkar could never do. On the

other hand, Savarkar seems to conform more faithfully to the profile of the fascist personality as portrayed in post–World War II psychoanalysis and social and political psychology. Could it be that, despite the rhetoric of public debate in India, the 'classical' European fascism in India can be the ideology of only a conspiratorial political fringe and the more danger-ous sources of political authoritarianism lie elsewhere?

66. Dayanand Saraswati, the founder of Arya Samaj, also approved of eat-ing beef in the first edition of *Satyārthaprakāsh* (1874) but the remark was dropped from the second edition in 1882. P. C. Ghosh, *The Development of Indian National Congress (1892–1909)* (Calcutta: Firma K.L. Mukhopadhyay, 1960); quoted in Sharma, 'Savarkar's Quest', 69. As is well known, similar comments are attributed to Vivekananda, too.

67. Keer, *Veer Savarkar*, 443–4.

68. See for instance, Stanley J. Tambiah, *Buddhism Betrayed? Religion, Politics and Violence in Sri Lanka* (Chicago: University of Chicago, 1992); and T. N. Madan, *Modern Myths, Locked Minds: Secularism and Fundamentalism in India* (New Delhi: Oxford University Press, 1998). The overall cultural-psychological framework within which Savarkar worked has been discussed in Ashis Nandy, Shikha Trivedi, Achyut Yagnik, and Shail Mayaram, *Creating a Nationality: The Ramjanmabhumi Movement and Fear of the Self* (New Delhi: Oxford University Press, 1995).

69. For instance, the early Hindu nationalists were role models for Sri Lankan Buddhist nationalists. Anagarika Dhammapala (1864–1933) lived in Calcutta, the capital of British India till 1911, and was an admirer of Vivekananda. The Mahabodhi Society that Dhammapala established was directly inspired by the Ramakrishna Mission and less directly by the theosophical society.

70. Savarkar and Joshi, *Historical Statements by V.D. Savarkar*, 96–105; see particularly 99–101.

71. Rabindranath Tagore, *Nationalism* (London: Macmillan, 1917), 77–8.

72. I should clarify at this point that I view nationalism as an ideology that is radically different from the sentiment called patriotism, though the first kind of territoriality may build upon or mobilize for its purposes the second kind. For a more extended discussion of the issue, see Ashis Nandy, 'Nationalism, Genuine and Spurious: A Very Late Obituary of Two Early Post-Nationalist Strains in India', Third Usha Mehta Memorial Lecture, delivered at the Nehru Centre, Mumbai, on 9 September 2005. Also published in *Economic and Political Weekly*, 12 August 2006, 3500–4.

73. I have already drawn attention to Savarkar's fascination with gratuitous violence in political matters. That fascination, though it came pack-aged in the rhetoric of revolution, preceded his ideological convictions.

Many have found more disorienting the openness to violence of Jinnah, whom Eqbal Ahmad has called a liberal constitutionalist. Eqbal Ahmad, *Confronting Empire: Interviews with David Barsamian* (London: Pluto Press, 2000), 10. Kuldip Nayar, for instance, says that when asked in 1946, after the call for Direct Action given by the Muslim League, whether Direct Action would be violent or non-violent, Jinnah said, 'I am not going to discuss ethics.' Kuldip Nayar, *Scoop: Inside Stories from the Partition to the Present* (New Delhi: HarperCollins, 2006), 25.

74. See Salman Akhtar and Manasi Kumar, 'Destiny and Nationalism: Mohammad Ali Jinnah', in *The Crescent and the Couch: Cross-Currents Between Islam and Psychoanalysis*, edited by Salman Akhtar (Lanham, Maryland: Jason Aronson, 2008), 79–102.

75. Mr Jinnah's first presidential address to the Constituent Assembly of Pakistan, 11 August 1947, available at http://www.stanford.edu/group/pakistan/pakistan/legislation/constituent_address_11aug1947.html.

76. It is remarkable that the passage of modern, secular constitutions of both India and Pakistan were officially piloted by two Dalits, Babasaheb Ambedkar and Jogen Mandal. The former, who of course played a more significant role in shaping the constitution of his country, is virtually deified in India; the latter is forgotten in both countries.

77. For instance, E. Valentine Daniel, 'The Arrogation of Being by the Blind-Spot of Religion', *Hitotsubashi Journal of Social Studies* 33, no. 1 (July 2001), 83–102. True, surveys done in India suggest that only about 10 per cent of those who vote for Hindu nationalist parties do so on ideological grounds, but in absolute numbers that is a substantial presence. Data Unit of the Centre for the Study of Developing Societies, 1998 Survey of General Elections in India.

3

BACKWATER DISCLOSURE
Ontological Politics and the Dialectics of Intercommunality

ROBY RAJAN

His Master's Blunder

One name seems hard to avoid in any contemporary juxtaposition of the words 'metaphysics' and 'politics': that of Martin Heidegger and his 'uncircumventable meditation'.[1] Here is a man widely considered the greatest European philosopher of the twentieth century—one who called into question the entire tradition of Western philosophical reflection from Plato down to the present, one to whom we owe our current understanding of the very word 'metaphysics' and its pitfalls[2]—making the most egregious political blunder it was possible for anyone to make: finding common cause with the Nazis.

How this most fundamental of thinkers could go so spectacularly wrong is a question that can scarcely be sidestepped today by anyone choosing to locate himself or herself in the lineage of Western philosophy. One can deny the very validity of the Heideggarian problematic as Habermas has chosen to do,[3] one can disentangle the thought from the political (mis)judgement as Derrida has tried to do, what one cannot do is ignore this gaping wound at the very heart of Western philosophical reflection. The case of Derrida is doubly pathos-filled: he had barely put the finishing touches on a highly contorted defense of a kindred spirit,[4] when the full extent of the Master's own Nazi involvement was revealed. With two major shocks close on each other's heels, the new 'deconstructive' philosophy was truly in a bad way.

Now, this particular cross need not of course be every metaphysical tradition's to bear, nor need every contemporary use of the word 'metaphysics' necessarily refer back to the troubled Teutonic philosophy. Besides, given the volume of commentarial accretion around the question of how the West's greatest contemporary philosopher could have gone so disastrously awry, one is surely well advised to consider carefully the consequences of wading into that particular bog. Nonetheless, a number of reasons argue for what Derrida has termed its 'uncircumventability', not least of which is the newfound use that contemporary 'postcolonial theory' has found for it.

Had the great philosopher's entanglement with National Socialism been a case of opportunism pure and simple, things would have been more straightforward. To be sure, the matter would still stand in need of explanation, but at least a line of demarcation could be drawn between the thought and the politics—as for instance in the case of the notorious anti-Semite logician Gottlob Frege. The philosopher's case is more troubling precisely because of the possibility that the thought may have had some bearing on the politics, that something integral to the thought may have led the philosopher down the blind alley of his politics. And if this was the fate of the loftiest philosophy of our time, what then of lesser ideas? Where was one supposed to turn for any kind of guide to action? Could fundamental ontology ever furnish sufficient grounds for an ethics or a politics? Are these questions every tradition ought to pose to itself in light of the philosopher's gargantuan blunder?

Provincializing Postcolonialism

Curiously, however, it is not as a cautionary tale that Heidegger makes his entry into contemporary 'postcolonial theory'. In *Provincializing Europe*,[5] the best known work of Dipesh Chakrabarty, one of the theory's leading lights, Heidegger furnishes the philosophical categories necessary to offset 'the figure of the universal human',[6] a figure Chakrabarty deems 'both indispensable and inadequate in helping us think through the various life practices'.[7] This universal figure is defined not by any sense of rootedness or belonging but by categories such as 'rights, citizenship, fraternity, civil society, politics, nationalism, and so on',[8] which afford us 'glimpses of the Enlightenment promise of an abstract, universal but never-to-be-realized humanity'[9] that is indispensable in the 'pursuit of social justice'.[10] Chakrabarty brings in Heidegger to supplement the 'inadequacy' of the 'indispensable' universal abstraction with the requisite quantum of concreteness that enables particular communities caught up in the throes of 'a non-European modernity' (exemplified for the author by 'literate upper-caste Hindu Bengalis'[11]) to make 'a world out of this earth'.[12]

The central idea that Chakrabarty borrows from Heidegger to underpin these communal life-worlds,[13] even as they are caught up in universal history, is the contrast between the ready-to-hand stance that designates a pre-analytical everyday relationship to one's surroundings, and the present-at-hand stance for which these surroundings turn into an object of analysis and manipulation. Marxist and liberal histories are constructed on the model of the analytical present-at-hand, which must, for Chakrabarty, be held in a state of permanent tension with the ready-to-hand of communal life-world histories accessible only to lived pre-analytical relationships through an exercise of translation. Totalities constructed entirely on the analytical model are far too abstract to actually exist anywhere because any concrete historical formation is inevitably a compromise between universal abstraction and concrete particularity.

Chakrabarty also credits Heidegger for furnishing him with the philosophical ground for his claim that the two cannot but coexist, each communal life-world 'modifying'[14] the universal in its own specific way; this ground is 'the "constantly fragmentary" and irreducibly plural nature of the "now"'.[15] The inherent fragmentariness and plurality of 'the now' 'makes it impossible to sum up a present through any totalizing principle' while opening up a plurality of futures that similarly 'do not lend themselves to being represented by a totalizing principle'. Through specific examples of such 'translation' work, Chakrabarty seeks to demonstrate how particular life-worlds may be 'released into'[16] into the abstract totalities of universal histories so that these worlds are not condemned to become excrescences excised by history's scalpel in the course of its surgical forward thrust. Towards this end, he mobilizes not only the abstract universal logic of the European Enlightenment which he calls History 1 but also a History 2, which contaminates the pure universality of History 1 by forcing it to make accommodations for local particularities. In the case of the universality of the logic of capital for instance, Chakrabarty asserts, 'No global (or even local, for that matter) capital can ever represent the universal logic of capital, for any historically available form of capital is a provisional compromise made up of History 1 modified by some-body's History 2.'[17]

Although his book's main claim to fame has been the proposi-tion that these two histories must be held 'in tension', Chakrabarty gives away much of the store at the very outset by ceding the entire terrain of universality to the Marxist and liberal accounts—with concrete life-worlds being brought in to lend to these histories the local colouration that would suitably 'modify' and 'unsettle' the totalities. As for universal history itself, Chakrabarty avers: 'We, whether decisionist or historicist, cannot but have a shared com-mitment to it (in spite of all the disagreements between Marxism and liberalism).'[18]

In making this pronouncement on our collective behalf, Chakrabarty is implicitly relying on Ferdinand Tonnies' (ready-to-hand, one is tempted to add) late nineteenth-century distinction between *Gemeinschaft* (community) and *Gesselschaft* (society) as the universal transformation that frames both Marxist and liberal histories. For Tonnies,[19] 'community' is characterized by the organic unity of ties of blood, place, and customary law forged through family, village, and worship. Modernity brings about the shift to 'society' with its artificial associations regulated by state and contract, and governed by utilitarian logic, disinterested knowledge, public opinion, and anonymity. Once this mode of universality is granted its totalizing privilege in the Marxist and liberal versions, 'concrete life-worlds' are the slim pickings communities must content themselves with in any work of 'translation' *a la* Chakrabarty. Even in conceptualizing this shift to the abstract universal, Chakrabarty wants to ground its emergent institutions—state, bureaucracy, and capitalist enterprise—in 'categories and concepts, the genealogies of which go deep into the intellectual and even theological traditions of Europe';[20] for Chakrabarty, whatever be the case elsewhere, in Europe at least the abstract universality manages to retain a 'deep' continuity with the prior concreteness.

Chakrabarty also asserts in multiple places in the book that one should bear no 'ressentiment towards European thought',[21] that 'provincializing Europe cannot ever be a project of shunning European thought',[22] that 'at the end of European imperialism, European thought is a gift to us' and so on, but in his cosmopolitan eagerness to have it both ways, universality inevitably appears on the horizon of a community as a vast flotilla sailing in from the Occident. Upon landing on its shores, however, it is the concrete life-world of the community that sets about 'modifying' and 'unsettling' the universal's abstraction. *That universality could emerge from within communal life-worlds themselves* is one figure too far for this provincializer of Europe to contemplate, lest these life-worlds be led astray and start 'shunning' universal history entirely.

However, the prospect of universality emerging from within communality is not only allowed for by Heidegger, it forms the very centrepiece of his thinking on community. The core of Chakrabarty's book is a critique of what he calls 'historicism', which posits a unilinear development from traditional societies to secular modernity, but he appears quite unaware that such a use of 'historicism' as well as his conception of community as bereft of any universalizing potential of its own is diametrically opposed to Heidegger's. As James Phillips has recently argued, communality for Heidegger cannot be understood as an 'insurrection of the particular against the universal';[23] indeed, a community's self-positing as a distinct particular is the surest way to its thorough assimilation by the very universal it opposes itself to: 'A *Volk* that insists on its singularity, on its condition as "this" *Volk*, is in the end ... always betrayed to the universal by its very "thisness".'[24] A 'reprise of the nominalist cult of the particular'[25] is, therefore, not at all what Heidegger's critique of the universal aims at; rather, it 'pursues a different course from ... avowals of the particular's independence'.[26]

Historicizing the Volk

What then is this 'different course'?[27] Here is Phillips's answer: 'The questionability of Being as presence, and not the independence of the particular, is what Heidegger brings up against the traditional logic.'[28] 'Questionability' for Heidegger is not a form of interrogation in search of an answer; rather, it designates a disclosedness of the community's constitution vis-à-vis the question of being *contra* beings as entities. Or, as George Steiner has put it, 'To inquire into Being is not to ask: What is this or that? It is to ask: What is "is"?'[29] Insofar as a community 'is', 'questionability' means that in its being, it is its very being that is at issue. This 'reaching beyond the presence in which a people could recognize itself in its oneness'[30] through its questionability, a reaching beyond 'the isolation of individual subjects, as well as the isolation of an individual ethnic group', but which can also 'just as little become the humanity that is the oneness of the peoples' is what Heidegger calls *historicizing*. 'Historicizing' then is an ontological category that is to be clearly distinguished from the ordinary understanding of history as 'the past'.[31] As Miguel de Beistegui points out, 'the existential-ontological interpretation of History must be grasped in spite of and almost against the way Dasein's historical happening is ordinarily interpreted' because 'Dasein's ordinary historical self-understanding serve[s] to cover up its fundamental historicity' and is, as a consequence, 'Dasein's fallen interpretation of its own historicity'.[32]

'Dasein'—literally 'there-being'—is the word Heidegger uses to distance his conception of human being from the object-cognizing 'subject' of epistemology so as to redirect attention towards the question of being, which, according to him, had fallen into forgetfulness for close to two and a half millennia. Such a distancing is crucial for Heidegger because the centrepiece of his notion of Dasein is the claim that ontologically prior to the explicit act of cognizing, there always-already exists a pre-understanding of Dasein's there-being in the world as a fore-structure of meanings and existentially rooted dispositions that are constituent features of being-in-the-world. Among the most significant of these features are practical involvements with the ready-to-hand and the social relations of being-with-others. This 'being-with' is in no way an external addendum to some more fundamental 'being self'—it is co-originary with the self.

Heidegger's point is that the notion that the subject first encoun-
ters present-at-hand objects and other selves, which it then grasps
with its cognizing faculty falsifies the proper order of things. It
is our engaged immersion with the ready-to-hand and with others
that is primordial; all other modes of presence are derivative. For
Heidegger then, the true problem of philosophy is not how to pass
from mental representations of objects to the objects themselves,
but that this was seen as a problem at all. Our being-in-the-world—
our dealing with objects as ready-to-hand, our irreducible embed-
dedness in a concrete life-world of a network of meanings—is
consubstantial with our always-already being-with-others, so that
Dasein's historicizing is also inextricably interwoven with the community's. Steiner puts the matter succinctly: 'Being-in-the-world,
says Heidegger, is a being-with.'[33]

As for 'Volk', it stands neither for an agglomeration of individual
subjects nor for a specific ethnic group nor for 'humanity' in general,
but designates a community's collective historicizing by raising the
question of Being in confrontation with its (non-)presence: 'The *Volk*
thinks the difference of Being from that which is present-at-hand ...
and it thinks this difference as the truth of its own historicality'[34] just
as Dasein's distinguishing feature and privilege is that 'in its very
Being, Being is an issue for it'[35]. The Volk in this sense is not an
entity present-at-hand in the world like other beings; it is constituted
only through its questionability.

This alternative to 'universal history' on the one hand, and the
immediacy of pre-reflexive belonging to a substantial life-world on the
other, is laid out in the famous Section 74 of Heidegger's magnum
opus *Being and Time*:

> But if fateful Dasein, as Being-in-the-world, exists essentially in Being-
> with-Others, its historicizing is a co-historicizing and is determinative
> for it as *destiny*. This is how we designate the historicizing of the com-
> munity, of a people. Destiny is not something that puts itself together
> out of individual fates, any more than Being-with-one-another can
> be conceived as the occurring together of several Subjects. Our fates
> have already been guided in advance, in our Being with one another in
> the same world and in our resoluteness for definite possibilities.[36]

The first thing to note about this controversial passage is that the line
between the present-at-hand of universal Reason and the ready-to-hand

of communal substantiality is not as clear-cut as Chakrabarty appears to believe. The distracted busy-ness of *das Man* that is aligned with universal abstraction has its own version of ready-to-handness in his non-reflective immersion in 'everydayness'. On the other hand, communal belonging for Heidegger is in no sense confined to the limited role of 'modifying' and 'adapting to' universal history as it is for Chakrabarty, but fully capable of 'wrest[ing] a destiny from ... *within itself*'.[37]

Fate and Destiny

For Heidegger, such a 'wresting' occurs on the model of the individual's being-toward-death as the full assumption of one's fate through an advance confrontation with death. And it is at this precise place that the majority of Heidegger commentators have located the source of his fascist temptation—in the allegedly illegitimate analogical leap from individual 'fate' to communal 'destiny'. de Beistegui,[38] for instance, asks how being-toward-death as the resolute assumption of one's innermost possibility could be transposed to the level of the collective without invoking some form of sacrificial death—since authentic death is uniquely one's own, not sharable with anyone else. How is a community to collectively take up an 'authentic' stance towards its 'death'? What could terms such as 'death' and 'resoluteness' possibly mean in the context of an entire community?

In the passage immediately following the one quoted above from *Being and Time*, some have read a kind of 'bridge' between individual fate and collective destiny. In being thrown-into-the-world, Dasein can assume its fate by choosing a past 'hero' and 'repeating' his acts: 'The authentic repetition of a possibility of existence that has been—the possibility that Dasein may choose its hero—is grounded existentially in anticipatory resoluteness.'[39] Since 'anticipatory resoluteness' is a purely formal category whose content cannot be auto-generated at the level of the individual, the reference to communal tradition becomes unavoidable here. It is the 'heritage' in which Dasein's existence is caught up that must supply the content for this resoluteness; communality insinuates itself into Dasein's fate as the source from which resoluteness must draw.

However, 'heritage' in no way grounds communal destiny in the resoluteness of individual Dasein; rather, community for Heidegger is possessed of an autonomous capacity, which it is its 'destiny' to disclose. But if Dasein can repeat a past possibility with its choice of 'hero', how is this repetition to occur at the level of the community? Not, as de Beistigui asserts, through 'common resolve for a common history, the origin of which is the phenomenon of death as the constitutive horizon of the people'[40] but by a repetition of the 'heroism' of its own contingent having-come-to-be. *What is repeated is not some ancient content of the collective heritage but the primordial emergence of the communal form itself.* Heidegger puts it this way: 'Anticipation of one's uttermost and ownmost possibility is coming back understandingly to one's ownmost "been".'[41] The past that is repeated is, therefore, not a chapter from its history, but the past 'loss' that was constitutive of community. It is in this collective 'asking-again' that Dasein's being-with-one-another (what Heidegger calls *Mitsein*) assumes its proper destiny—a repetition that also 'confronts Dasein with its essence in Being-with-one-another'.[42]

'Death' here is not to be understood as a terminal event that befalls the individual, nor should it be read as a form of heroic–tragic self-extermination in the service of community. As with Dasein's 'there-being', so with Mitsein's 'being-with-others', in its being-towards-death is raised the question of the being of that being for which its very being is at issue. And it is here that Heidegger finds the modern conception of the political lacking: 'For modern consciousness', writes Heidegger, 'the "political" is the necessary and unconditional lack of questioning.'[43] The 'political' of universal history becomes, for Heidegger, a contrivance for the extreme forgetfulness of being.

The 'parallel' between the levels of individual and community is, therefore, to be sought not as a one-to-one mapping of Heidegger's categories of 'thrownness', 'resoluteness', 'projection', and so on across the two levels, but in what Heidegger calls 'ecstatic temporality'. By fully assuming their respective finitudes and 'running ahead of themselves' (*Vorlaufen*), Dasein and Mitsein are autonomously capable of opening out to the dimension of ecstatic temporality that slumbers within the un-ecstatic time of linear succession. Furthermore, such an opening-out is as far removed as it is possible to be from Tonnies' sterile opposition of *Gemeinschaft* (traditional community) and *Gesselschaft* (modern civil society) that de Beistigui mobilizes to circumscribe communal destiny as a category of organicism.[44]

de Beistigui also raises a number of other objections to Heidegger's conception of communal destiny: 'How can we move from this solipsistic encounter with one's self to a shared temporality, a co-history?'; 'How can a community face its own death as its ownmost possibility without imposing a peculiar kind of closure upon its singularities?'; 'Do such words [as 'community' and 'people'] imply a shared resoluteness, in which a given community would exist *qua* community or people?'; 'Does this mean that a people comes to be constituted as such only in the anticipation of death as its ownmost possibility?'; 'Who is/are "we"?'; 'Where does the unity of the "we" lie?'; 'Can we say "we" in the same way Dasein speaks its own singularity through the "I"?'; 'Can "we" be at once singular and plural?'; 'What does resoluteness mean for the "we"?'; 'Must a community consist in the sharing of such a horizon [of death]?'; 'Must it perpetuate the model of communion around a founding sacrifice?'[45]

All such objections are premised on the belief that any assertion of a community assuming its collective destiny must come at the expense of Dasein's singularity. However, the problem here is not one of finding a 'bridge' between Dasein and Mitsein; to be sure, Dasein *is* only in 'being-with-others' nor can there be Mitsein without Dasein, but this in no way implies forsaking either's autonomy. de Beistigui's question, 'Can we say "we" in the same way in which Dasein speaks its own singularity through the "I"?'[46] is answerable in the affirmative if by 'the same way' we understand both communality and singularity as autonomously capable of opening out to the dimension of ecstatic temporality.

The problem with the concept of 'communal destiny', therefore, lies elsewhere than in the analogical parallel with individual fate. On the one hand, Heidegger's philosophical stance was one of overturning the conception of 'subject' as a distanced observer of objects—his entire effort consisting in a search for categories that would ground Dasein in concrete existence. When it comes to the notion of 'communal destiny', however, Heidegger resorts to the idea of a free-standing unitary community devoid of any appropriate grounding. To provide such a grounding, however, Heidegger would have had to turn to a different conception of community—and to a mode of becoming that discloses itself otherwise than as 'resoluteness'.

Backwater Disclosure

One such disclosure, associated with a charismatic figure who came to be called Narayana Guru, unfolded in late nineteenth-/early twentieth-century Kerala in southern India and has now gained entry into the history books as a regional footnote to the putatively more momentous transformations ushered in by various national-level movements launched as a reaction to the colonial encounter. 'Reform' was the operative word used to describe these movements—of which the Brahmo Samaj and the Arya Samaj were the most prominent—directed at divesting Hinduism of its unruly undergrowth of 'redundant' beliefs and practices so that it could be pared down to a rational core that bore more than a passing resemblance to the Protestant Christianity of the colonizer. The word 'reform' subsequently secured for itself a permanent place in the national–religious lexicon, being slapped onto any and every form of socio-religious change, no matter how different in origin and spirit they may have been from the pan-Hindu 'reform movements'. In the particular case of the 'movement' associated with the name of Narayana Guru, the indiscriminate use of words like 'reform', 'Hinduism', and 'religion' has served to thoroughly obfuscate the distinctive dialectics of continuity, discontinuity, and temporality of this 'movement'.

This effort to normalize it within the larger narrative of 'reform' at the level of Hinduism as a 'religion' was, from the outset, at odds with Narayana Guru's own unequivocal rejection of 'Hinduism' as a religion:

> There is no religion that may be called Hinduism. Outsiders styled the people of Hindustan as Hindus. Therefore, if by 'Hinduism' one denotes the religion of 'Hindus', then the Christianity and Islam professed by thousands of inhabitants here should also be called Hinduism.... Today 'Hinduism' covers the agglomeration of an immense variety of beliefs belonging to an entire scale of values that span customs, manners, rites, and philosophy among different groups and believers. *Veda*, *Mimamsa*, *Samkhya*, *Dvaita*, *Advaita*, *Vishistadvaita*, *Saiva*, *Sakteya*, *Vaishnava*—all these are forms of 'Hinduism', not excluding the innumerable modes of belief that differ

from place to place and caste to caste.... If this entire gamut of beliefs can be called 'Hinduism', then all religions—Islam, Christianity, Buddhism, Jainism, etc. can also collectively be known as 'one religion'.... If a religion preached by its founder, and subsequently elaborated into different branches by its followers can be called a 'religion' and given the name of the founder, the spiritual tenets preached by the different *acharyas* can also, by an extension of this principle, be termed 'religions'.[47]

In this brief paragraph is to be found as thoroughgoing a 'deconstruction' as one is likely to find of the idea that the word 'religion' is a genus containing the multiple distinct 'isms' of Islam, Christianity, Hinduism, and so forth, as its species.

A major obstacle that stands in the way of a proper understanding of the 'movement's' distinctiveness is fear of the loss of narrative coherence and the consequent hasty resort to a conception of temporality and allied notions of cause-and-effect that combine to produce a well-ordered chronological sequence. Udaya Kumar's capsule account of Narayana Guru's life and social role is typical:

Sree Narayana Guru was born of Ezhava parents in 1855 in Chempazhanti near Tiruvananthapuram. He received education in Tamil and later in Sanskrit. He worked as a teacher in his village for some time, and married under familial pressure. He left home soon after this, and wandered as an *avadhuta*, undertaking *tapas* in remote forested areas.... In 1888, Sree Narayana consecrated a Shiva temple at Aruvippuram, the first in a series of places of worship that he established for the use of lower castes. In 1898 he founded a society to look after the affairs of the Aruvippuram temple, and in 1903, with the help of Dr. Palpu, transformed it into Sree Narayana Dharma Paripalana [SNDP] Yogam.... [He] promulgated the message 'One caste, one religion, one god for all mankind' in 1920. He convened a congress of all religions in 1924. In 1928 he entered Samadhi.[48]

Virtually every such account locates the consecration of the Shiva Temple at Aruvippuram mentioned by Udaya Kumar as the moment Kerala's social transformation was launched—an event that has come to be collectively memorialized as the *Aruvippuram Pratishta*. This consecration is said to have been performed on the banks of the river Neyyar when Narayana Guru was still a wandering mendicant and had made a nearby mountain cave his temporary home. The local villagers had by then begun to venerate him as a *siddha*, and he undertook the consecration in response to a request from them for a temple they could worship at. The story goes that on a moonless Shivaratri night, the villagers had erected a platform on a large rock by the river bank and decorated it with flowers, mango leaves, and palm-leaf buntings. The prescribed hour for the consecration was fast approaching, but no one had prepared the idol that was to be installed.

The 'actual moment' of the *pratishta* has been etched deep into the collective memory, thanks to this powerful rendering by Kumaran Asan, one of Kerala's pre-eminent modern poets:

> At the midnight hour, the Guru waded into the river and disappeared. For what seemed like an eternity to the villagers who had thronged the river bank, he remained under water. When his shape finally reappeared, he began walking slowly toward the shore, and in his hands was held aloft a *shivalingam*. He strode to the decorated platform and stood there, his eyes closed in meditation, his hands holding the lingam close to his chest, tears running down his cheeks, lost to the world. For a full three hours, he stood motionless while the crowd around him rent the midnight air with cries of *Om Namah Shivayah, Om Namah Shivayah.*[49]

When subsequently queried by a Brahmin as to the sacerdotal validity of a consecration performed by a lowly Ezhava, the Guru is said to have responded spontaneously with a line that has now gone down as the most famous riposte in modern Kerala: 'I have only consecrated an Ezhava Shiva', he reminded the Brahmin.

This act of consecration and the accompanying rejoinder are conferred an unparalleled inaugural significance both in historical accounts such as Udaya Kumar's as well as in popular memory—but for entirely divergent reasons. In the historical accounts, the pratishta derives its unique significance from its status as a first act of 'subaltern resistance': the consecration of idols had always been the Brahmin's prerogative, and the Aruvippuram Pratishta was the first-ever instance of a non-Brahmin performing such a symbolically important ritual. The incident is usually cast in 'subaltern' narratives as a calculated act of defiance meant to undermine the Brahmin-dominated social order, and from which there subsequently ensued a rapid-fire series of similar defiant acts of idol-consecrations and temple-building.

Typical of such accounts is that furnished by V. K. Krishna Iyer, former judge of the Supreme Court of India and prominent public personality who was also a law minister in Kerala's first communist government:

> The Guru adopted an extraordinary strategy of installing idols, a function traditionally the exclusive preserve of Brahmins. This masterstroke of Narayana Guru was a radical challenge to the status quo ante. The entire edifice of Brahminism and the caste structure suffered a collapse when, by installing Siva in a temple built by him, Narayana Guru worked a miracle of spiritual transformation and social reformation. What was at stake was not an Ezhava Shiva installed by an Ezhava Sadhu with access to all regardless of caste, creed, or religion or sect but an irreverent subversion of an obscurantist order which dominated and blinded the masses of Hindus.[50]

Here we have all the ingredients of a 'progressive history' within which Narayana Guru is sought to be subsumed by historians of the Left in Kerala: an oppressive pre-modern order; a crafty representative of the subaltern classes bent on subverting it; a carefully worked out plan to accomplish this goal; a strategy of 'irreverent subversion' finally rewarded with success; the era of obscurantism finally left behind in the march towards a full-blown scientific temper; the goal of social justice unshackled from the fetters of faith and superstition.

The contrast with the popular memoration of this act could not be starker; especially noteworthy is the absence of any trace of 'defiance' in the popular recounting of the event. Here, the act's unparalleled significance is attributed solely to its luminosity as a *dharmic* act, and it is for this reason *and this reason alone* that the aura attaching to the Aruvippuram Pratishta is held to be indestructible. As to the Guru's rejoinder to the Brahmin, there are all manner of disputes among historians as to exactly when and where it was made, and even about who made it. Some claim it occurred immediately after the pratishta; others place it a full twenty years later some five hundred miles north of the original site of the pratishta. According to K. V. Subramanyam,[51] the incident took place in Tellicherry when, in the course of a conversation in Sanskrit between Kumaran Asan

and a group of Brahmins in the presence of Narayana Guru and
some local people, Narayana Guru abruptly intervened in Malayalam
to enquire of the Brahmins whether there was any injunction in
the *dharmashastra* texts prohibiting the pratishta of an Ezhava
Shiva. Others claim that it was Kumaran Asan himself who made
the rejoinder.[52] None of these disputes centring on the veracity of
the riposte, however, appear to matter to the ordinary Malayali; as the
American writer Bill McKibben observed in the course of his travels
through the state, the rejoinder's irresistible mix of self-deprecation
and sending up of the Brahmin 'still makes Keralites laugh'.[53] In
Narayana Guru's own writings—a corpus of some sixty compositions
in three languages (Sanskrit, Malayalam, and Tamil)—neither the
consecration nor the rejoinder find any mention, nor is there anything in these writings to suggest that he would view such an act as
anything resembling 'resistance'.

The curious paradox about the two contrasting accounts is that
while the inconsistencies surrounding the event's narration in no
way diminish its force in popular memory, it is the brute facticity of
the historical accounts that seems highly improbable. Aruvippuram
has now become a place of pilgrimage because of its association
with Narayana Guru, but this hamlet in the foothills of the Western
Ghats still takes some effort to get to. Back in 1888, when the
pratishta purportedly occurred, there was not even a road leading to
the village nor any media that could have rapidly disseminated this
news. Add to this some key additional features of the account—that
the only people present were the local villagers, that Narayana Guru
was then just a young unknown mendicant, that he had not even
earned the appellation 'Guru'—and it begins to look highly unlikely
that this consecration in a remote village in the dead of a Shivaratri
night was the shot heard throughout Kerala triggering a collapse
of its traditional order. Judged by its own criteria of verisimilitude,
the historical placement of the pratishta as the initial impetus in a
linear chronological flow of events cannot stand. Indeed, to arrive
at a more plausible account by the very criterion of 'realism' the
historical accounts are wedded to, it becomes necessary to suspend
the nexus between the pratishta as prior cause and 'social reform'
as posterior effect, and to admit the possibility of other modes of
determination.

Farewell to Old Gods

It is upon turning to the community where the memory of Narayana Guru is strongest—the Ezhavas—that we obtain our first clue to unravelling this puzzle. Narayana Guru is revered in the community for initiating a number of innovative practices such as the simplifying of wedding and funeral rites, devising of new worship rituals at temples, abolition of puberty celebrations and child marriages, assurance of inheritance rights for women, and so on. What is often collectively glossed over in the eagerness to cast everything he did as stemming from his superior spiritual cognition that helped the community evolve from primitive to civilized forms of worship is that he was also the bearer of a radical negativity. The term 'Sanskritization'[54] has often been used to describe this phenomenon, but in subsuming Narayana Guru under this sociological label, there has been a rather too-quick sleight of hand. Is it really credible that in the space of a couple of years, an entire community managed to pull off a seamless transition from the gods they had been worshipping for centuries to a new set of gods with wholly different characteristics?

From afar, the experience of the community may well lend itself to such a reading. In the older temples of the Ezhavas where village gods and nature spirits had been worshipped since time immemorial, liquor was the standard offering to the deity and animal sacrifice was widely prevalent. Some of these deities were explicitly characterized by Narayana Guru as 'malignant' (*durdevata*) and at these temples, he proceeded to '*unseat the gods*, replacing them with idols of Shiva, Subramania, and Ganesha' as Murkot Kunhappa has put it.[55] Of the many local gods who were 'unseated', the writer K. Sreenivasan mentions Marutha, Madan, Muthappan, Yakshi, Poothathan, Vankaramadan, Chudalamadan, Isaki, Mallankankali, Karuppan, and Irulan. 'The Guru', according to Sreenivasan, 'gave the lead in demolishing all of them.'[56] On one such occasion, when he happened to walk into the middle of a drunken temple celebration and asked the revellers how exactly the slaughter of a poor fowl would appease the god, the worshippers were reportedly so overwhelmed that they turned on the very deity they had been worshipping, admonishing the god for his bloodthirstiness, and banishing him from the temple for good.[57] Sreenivasan also recounts a different occasion when not only was a prominent deity unseated, her very abode was obliterated: 'At Kulathoor, a suburb of Trivandrum, he sponsored a drastic step. He asked the existing Bhadrakali temple to be demolished. Many a devotee of the goddess was scared by this advice. They feared the wrath of the vengeful deity. Many deemed it sacrilegious. But the Guru's advice prevailed. The substitute was Lord Shiva.'[58]

When Murkot Kunhappa uses the word 'unseat' to describe the fate of the old gods at the hands of the Guru, he does so advisedly: after these 'malignant deities' had been dethroned, there was an actual historical period during which the Ezhavas still held together as a community despite their gods having fled—a community that was still a community, but divested of its very substance. The true extremity of this condition can only be gauged retrospectively in the anguished debates about which gods the community ought to adopt and which religion it should convert to. The writer C. Krishnan used the columns of the journal *Mithavadi* to argue for a mass conversion to Buddhism. Other prominent community leaders such as Sahodaran Ayyappan and C. V. Kunjuraman, who were self-declared rationalists, had also thrown their weight behind Buddhism. A group of Ezhavas in the southern district of Neyyatinkara embraced Christianity to become a new community of 'Ezhava-Christians'. Around the same time, some in Alleppey district converted to Sikhism; there were also multiple instances of individual and family conversion to Islam. However, for the community as a whole, these possibilities quickly receded when it became amply clear that 'mass conversion' of any kind was nowhere on the Guru's horizon.

In the traditional sacred landscape of Kerala dominated by high Brahminic temples such as the Krishna temple at Guruvayur and the Shiva temple at Trichur, the new temples consecrated by the Guru stand out for their diminutive size, surrounding garden, and attached buildings housing primary schools, high schools, technical institutes, working women's hostels, and libraries. When doubters wondered if these new temples would continue to attract devotees for long—considering the great antiquity and symbolic standing of the traditional Brahminic temples—he expressed his readiness to convert the temples into schools, libraries, assembly halls, or weaving sheds, should the day arrive when they cease to draw worshippers.[59]

And it was Narayana Guru himself who decided which gods to admit into the inner sanctums of these new temples; there were even

occasions when he changed his mind midway. A Shiva idol was originally to be installed at the Shivagiri temple, but halfway through the
construction he decided in favour of the goddess Saraswati (Sharada).[60]
He literally cherry-picked the gods to be assigned to other well-known
temples: Subramania at Kunnumpaara; Shivalingam at Vakkom;
Sreekanteswaram at Kozhikode; Jagannath at Tellicherry; Gokarnath
at Mangalore, and so on. In an unheard-of reversal, the very gods that
had for centuries refused him entry into their sacred precincts would
now come knocking on his door seeking admission. These gods live
on today in temples large and small, ancient and recent, throughout
Kerala—*but only as mediated by the Narayana Guru event.*

'The [new] Sree Narayana temples', observes Murkot Kunhappa,
'were like and yet unlike the old temples in the land.'[61] What Kunhappa
is adverting to is that although in the vast majority of these new temples, the presiding deities were drawn from the Brahminic pantheon,
some were utterly unlike them. His temple at Karamukku houses only
a lighted lamp in its inner sanctum. At the Murukumpuzha temple,
there is only a slab of stone with the words '*Satyam, Dharmam, Daya,
Sneham*' etched on it. At the centre of the temple at Kalavamcodam, the
Guru placed a mirror with the sacred letter 'Om' formed by scratch-
ing away its rear mercury coating. The *Advaita Ashram* founded by
him in Aluva on the banks of the river Periyar has neither temple nor
idol; instead, there is a prayer hall for people of all faiths, a library
housing the scriptures of the world's religions, a high school, and
a hostel for students drawn from all castes and religions. The construction of these new 'Sree Narayana temples' caused considerable
alarm among established guardians of the faith; in some quarters,
it aroused fears that they would eventually lead to, in the words
of one Brahmin High Court judge, 'a parallel belief system within
Hinduism'.[62]

The void that had opened up in the life of the community between
the departure of the old gods and the arrival of these new gods is
usually sought to be quickly passed over in all the existing narratives,
whether of Left-liberal persuasion, *Advaitic* inspiration, or social science's realist aspiration—as if this voiding were of no great consequence, when what comes through in all the evidence from the period
is that it was one of the most extreme experiences any community
could possibly undergo. Far from being peripheral, this voiding stakes

a strong claim to being placed at the narrative's nerve centre; indeed, many crucial aspects of the Kerala story such as the immense symbolic significance accorded to the Aruvippuram Pratishta and the chain reaction triggered by the Guru's actions across all the major communities of the region can scarcely be grasped without it.

Intercommunal Co-arising

Learning across communities is an everyday process in any multi-communal society, but what was witnessed in Kerala in the rapid emulation by other communities of the changes occurring within the Ezhava community cannot be grasped as an aspect of such everyday learning. Kunhappa tries to capture this phenomenon using the metaphor of 'shock treatment':

> This shock given at about the middle rung of the caste ladder (the Ezhavas) was transmitted upwards to the Nambudiri Brahmins and downwards to the lowest among the several castes below the Ezhavas. Social reformation all round was the result of this shock treatment. It produced very strong and effective movements of reform among all the castes, such as the Nambudiris, the Nairs, the Ezhavas, and the Pulayas, besides affecting other castes too.[63]

Although it was the Ezhavas that led the way with a self-administered 'shock treatment', it was only thanks to its 'other-dependence' (*paratantra*) on the other communities—the fact that all the *other* communities were intact and, therefore, could, by default, still lend to the Ezhava community its outline form—that it managed to persist as 'a community' in the course of its self-voiding without entirely disintegrating. What remained of the community, once it had been divested of its substance, was only the pure *form* of community sustained by all the other 'still substantive' castes and communities. By the time the community returned to substantiality from its self-voiding, the very mode of its determination had in turn been inverted: *the 'context' of intercommunal relations that had previously determined it had itself been recontextualized and subordinated as a secondary moment of the community's own dialectic of contraction-expansion.*

To assert that the entirety of the prior intercommunal context was itself recontextualized does not imply that every trace of the earlier practices was eradicated. What it does mean is that the prior world of intercommunal relations as a meaningful hermeneutic totality with a given disposition of gods and rituals, affinities and aversions, obligations and proscriptions, underwent a dissolution to make way for a re-inscription of communities within a thoroughly transformed horizon of relationality. The analytical question this raises in our context is: Through what categories can we grasp this transformation of an inert multiplicity of communities into a dynamic web of self-aware intercommunal relations? How did communities that were transacting across boundaries as mere entities transcend their entityness and recover the truth of their relationality? *It is in confronting this question that metaphysics interposes itself as necessity.* History, sociology, anthropology, and the other social sciences have certainly catalogued for us the plurality of communities, their contest for resources, their cross-cutting enmities and alliances, their mutual perceptions and prejudices, but they have offered us no clue to the emergence of a dynamic of awakened intercommunal relationality.

To put the matter in Madhyamika terms, Kerala's social transformation occurred as the 'dependent co-arising' of its multiple communities, and any explanation of this co-arising would, therefore, necessarily have to think *relationality* and *emergence* together. From the Madhyamika standpoint, if we were to stop with the mere assertion of relationality between a pre-given set of communal entities, we would not be properly seized of the doctrine of *pratitya-samutpada*, in which relationality (*pratitya*) and co-arising (*samutpada*) are indissociable. The positing of pre-existent substantive entities, which are only subsequently brought into mutual relation, runs counter to the very essence of pratitya-samutpada, in which it is always relationality that is primary, the entities being only secondary nodal points in criss-crossing relational pathways. In any constellation of communities, it is, therefore, not enough to point to their mutual dependence; it is only when relationality is presupposed as *anterior* to their entityness that they can also be conceived as *co-arising.*

The Eclipse of Representation

If, in light of what we have asserted about intercommunal relationality, we turn to extant narratives of the communal transformation in Kerala, we uniformly run into a blind spot in their accounts of the period of Ezhava insubstantiality. The problem here has to do not with this or that particular depiction of the community but with *a deadlock of the representationalist problematic itself*—that is to say, of the 'abstract concept' adequating itself to the 'concrete reality'. This is not because the concrete phenomenon in question is so complex, so far in excess of our abstractions, that no conceptual apparatus could possibly grasp it, but the precise opposite: representation dissipates here in a blur of disputations because there is no longer any community with a set of positive attributes which abstraction could adequate itself to. To put it differently, it is the so-called concrete entity of the community that itself turns abstract with self-voiding. What is left as a remainder in 'reality' is a community with its form still intact but divested of any substantive content whatsoever.

The emergence of this paradoxical 'concrete abstraction' in reality also points to the representational limits of empiricism, as also of any resort to the way reality appears to the everyday consciousness of the individuals involved. Every attempt to hew closely to the so-called real persons, entities, and actions comprising such an event by directly soliciting categories from those involved turns into a pseudo-concrete exercise, the outcome of which bears little resemblance to what transpired in the interim between communal dissolution and its re-substantialization. When representation does finally emerge after its dissipation in concrete-abstraction, it can reconstitute itself only as a social/spiritual duality—seen to this day in the irreconcilable split in portrayals of Narayana Guru: he is either *advaitin or* social reformer, and every effort to translate one into the other or to stitch together a composite picture quickly turns into an artificial academic exercise failing to attract any adherents. In a sense that is more than merely 'rhetorical'; the real Narayana Guru is neither the one nor the other but the gap between these two incommensurable perspectives.

The true problem here is not how to bridge the gap separating the advaitin and social reformer versions but rather how this gap came to be in the first place—to conceive this gap in its becoming. The incommensurability itself is irreducible and cannot be surmounted by a more 'synthetic' mode of representation because they are both necessarily partial attempts to come to terms with the representational void from which they emerged. This is why although there is partial truth in both halves, their summation does not add up to the whole; what such a summation always misses is the void that was *generative* of the two dimensions as distinct, and which persists today as the absent point of their convergence. Representational 'totality' here would, therefore, have to include *three* elements: the advaitin, the social-reformer, plus the void of their incommensurability that undercuts the self-sufficiency of both the preceding narrative solutions. And it is precisely this *third* element that keeps Narayana Guru socially alive today not only as an object of veneration but also as a subject of contestation.

This predicament of representation is correlative to the extreme reflexivity of a community sundered from its *differentia specifica* in its mutation into the pure *form* of community *qua* community; it is this representational eclipse that the various narratives in their differing ways have tried to suture into a chronologically ordered flow. For the Vedantin, Narayana Guru belongs in an Advaitic lineage going all the way back to Shankara; for the historian, he led a 'social reform movement' aimed at ridding his backward caste of irrational beliefs and superstitions; for the sociologist, his aim was a progressive 'Sanskritization' and adoption of Brahminic forms of worship so as to gain unqualified acceptance for his community as 'Hindu'; for the communist, his efforts were directed at conscientizing the masses so as to lift them up from their false caste consciousness to the properly historic class consciousness. The reason for this mass narrative avoidance is not far to seek: Within the chronological order common to all of them, what place could there possibly be for the 'nothing' of the void?

From a metaphysical standpoint, however, it is crucial that this void be kept front-and-centre because it is precisely the self-induced extremity of this condition that gave rise to convulsions in all the other communities leading to their own internal transformations. *Such a reconfiguring of the entire web of communal mutuality is relationality coming to self-awareness in its passage from the other-dependence (paratantra) of entities to their collective dependent co-arising (pratityasamutpada).* From this vantage point, the question of whether the Aruvippuram Pratishta and the famed rejoinder really did occur chronologically prior to all the consequences of self-voiding is secondary. What does seem to have been crucial was the collective need for a 'scene' that could make the whole whirligig of events cohere—as if the 'working-through' of the trauma of communal self-voiding *had* to find its echo in the midnight scene of the pratishta and the simultaneous juxtaposition of two words that could not previously be thought together: 'Ezhava' and 'Shiva'.

Plainly then, the incident's historicity is a minor part of the story; its contemporary resonance cannot be read as an 'effect' produced in the standard historical manner by the prior 'cause' of the event's facticity. However, the point here is not to deny its veracity as history but to try to understand why a midnight incident in an obscure village should be given a *significance nonpareil* in the collective memory. And the answer to this puzzle is to be sought not in the chain of historical causality but in a different mode of determination in which effects *precede* cause. What we are confronted with here is a case of the 'cause' that is in turn caused by its effects: the pratishta is not a first cause that determined the community's future course, but a moment marking the paradoxical birth of the collective subject of the Kerala event *after* its effects were already being felt across the social landscape. Without the 'caused cause' of the pratishta, the 'effects' themselves would be a bric-a-brac of occurrences that could not cohere into any kind of meaning. The pratishta as a past that was never necessarily present-in-itself as 'history' registers the birth of the collective subject of the Kerala event in one community's abyssal encounter with the void of its own non-substantiality.

The central fallacy of those who would like to reduce the Kerala transformation to a set of 'caste reforms' lies in the belief that it would somehow have been possible to make a direct transition from the 'pre-Aruvippuram life-world' to the new 'reformed life-world' by-passing the temporal loop in which the effects preceded the cause. The Aruvippuram Pratishta is not a moment in forward-flowing chronological time; rather, its retroactive condensation of a community's collective experience of self-voiding is to be located in a temporality in which the scene's entire effectivity derives from this 'looping back' as a cause paradoxically caused by its effects. As apocryphal, the pratishta will, therefore, always be truer than the 'real' event in all its facticity: no set of economic, political, or cultural factors in their 'complex interaction' with one another can account for the encounter condensed in the pratishta, which lies outside the entire chain of historical causes and effects.

The thrall to a linear narrative form has, therefore, left us with a double effacement of the metaphysical underpinnings of Kerala's social transformation: it cannot bring itself to acknowledge either the representational eclipse that lies at the heart of the transformation nor, as a consequence, the wholly unintended effect of the pratishta's psycho-social efficacy. The pratishta is memorialized in the way it is *only* because it was never the object of a deliberate choice: it owes its significance as a 'founding event' solely to its standing as the scene of a dharmic act shorn of all *telos*. It is, therefore, thoroughly misleading to speak of the pratishta as having been deliberately undertaken by Narayana Guru to 'refine the spiritual condition of the people', to 'awaken the people to their own subjectivity',[64] or to otherwise teleolize it, no matter how elevated the motive.

Here we touch upon the central paradox of the pratishta scene: its entire performative power would have dissipated, had it deliberately been enacted as a transgression against the Master's prohibition. Neither in any of Narayana Guru's own works nor in the innumerable tales and legends surrounding his memory is there any trace of defiance or appeal to the colonial or the Brahmin Master—a fact completely overlooked by champions of the 'subalterns' who now wish to claim the Guru as one of their own. This feature also enables us to precisely specify what separates the Kerala event from the 'reform movements': the latter's betrothal to a Master-figure—either in the mode of emulation as in the efforts of the Brahmo Samaj and Arya Samaj to Protestantize themselves, or in the mode of defiance as in the Dravida Kazhagam's fiery displays of impiety towards Brahminic rituals and practices. One is, therefore, tempted to read the placement of the Aruvippuram Pratishta at the head of a linear chronology as a kind of defense mechanism: better to preserve one's narrative coherence by clinging to the idea that it was a gesture of heroic 'resistance' on the part of the downtrodden subaltern than to accept the unsettling truth that the pratishta was not a message of 'defiance' addressed to anyone at all. Better the comforting thought that we are always 'resisting' some power centre that determines us from afar than the terrifying prospect of taking full possession of our autonomy.

We have occasionally resorted to the expression 'subject of the Kerala event' here as if there were some sort of active collective agency at work, but who precisely was this 'subject' that first underwent the communal self-voiding? Upon closer examination, it turns out that the very notion of an 'Ezhava community' that underwent 'reforms' shows itself to be shot through and through with inconsistency. When compared with the Ezhavas as they are presently constituted, the community which was then referred to by that name was a miniscule proportion of the total population. The prominent Ezhava leader C. V. Kunjuraman is once said to have exclaimed:

> Community? Oh God! The very word community was unheard of among the Ezhavas. Those with and without status are to be found among all communities but that doesn't explain the way things were among us. We were fragmented into all kinds of lineages: chattans, oolans, pandas, pambilis, illams, kollakarans.... Ezhavas belonging to one lineage were considered a separate caste and forbidden from entering into marital relations with other Ezhavas...[65]

What Kunjuraman does not seem to sufficiently appreciate here is that the fragmentation he bemoans can only be perceived a posteriori once the Ezhavas had been forged into 'a community', and that what is today known as the 'Ezhava caste' is an entirely retrospective construction that brought within its fold a multiplicity of previously dispersed communities (Ezhavas, Thiyyas, Thandans, Pandichons, Panickers, Ezhavathis, Channars, Chovans, and so forth), not all of whom were even engaged in the same 'caste occupation'—so that there was never the 'Ezhava caste' that first existed, then 'reformed itself'. It is not enough to assert that the collective self to which the community 'returned' was not the same self that underwent the voiding; rather, the communal self to which it 'returned' was constituted in the very movement of its 'returning-to-itself'. It was the 'returning' that gave rise to the self to which the return returned. The communal self here has no substantial actuality whatsoever: it only emerges as a retroactive effect of the process through which the conditions that had previously determined communality are in turn subordinated as a subsidiary moment of the intercommunal dialectic.

A drastic conclusion imposes itself here. The Ezhavas as a community do not pre-exist the voiding; it is the voiding that retroactively generated the community. Not only was the community that undertook the passage through self-voiding not the community that returned from it; the paradox proper to communality is that it is self-voiding that retroactively revealed the self that underwent the voiding. The Ezhava communal self as a pre-existing entity that was put through the paces of its transformative tribulations turns out to be the purest of illusions.

Backwater Illuminations

And now to return to Martin Heidegger via the Kerala event. Might this event help us shed any new light on the great thinker's political blunder? Can it in any way help us see how the very philosopher who warned us against mistaking ontic entities for the ontological truth ended up discerning in Nazi barbarism a salvific force for modern man? What precisely went wrong with his worthy goal of realizing in ontic practice the ontology laid out in *Being and Time*? Is the move from Dasein's resoluteness as 'fate' to the collective resoluteness of a people assuming its 'destiny' innately fraught with fascist peril? Heidegger's illustrious student Karl Lowith records the following response of his former professor when it was suggested to him that his enthusiasm for Nazism sprung from the very essence of his philosophy: 'Heidegger agreed with me without reservations and spelled out that the concept of "historicity" was the basis for his political engagement.'[66]

'Historicity' for Heidegger belongs to the very being of Dasein and is an umbrella concept for existential categories like 'anticipatory resoluteness', 'ecstatic temporality', 'being-towards-death', and 'potential-for-being' that lift Dasein out of its everydayness. In the midst of its habitually induced ontic inertia, Dasein is made aware of the press of the ontological by the *angst* that surfaces occasionally from within. Through the experience of *angst*, authentic Dasein confronts the truth that all being is a being-toward-death: this existential terminality is what makes its temporality and freedom concrete. And it is through the resulting 'anticipatory resoluteness' that Dasein's 'thrownness' is made transparent to itself, and the existential possibilities in light of which Dasein can undertake its 'existentiell modification'[67] are disclosed. Through 'resoluteness', Dasein extricates itself from dispersion in 'everydayness' and returns to itself. Historicity is rooted in the ecstatic temporality that surfaces in anticipatory resoluteness.

Resoluteness reveals past possibilities based on Dasein's specific mode of self-projection towards the future, and serves as the ontological ground for ontic commitment. Since Dasein's actuality inevitably falls short of the potentiality that is revealed through resoluteness, 'guilt' is inherent to its being. Far from being solipsistic, however, 'resoluteness brings the self-right into its current concernful being alongside what is ready-to-hand, and pushes it into solicitous being with others'.[68] This 'concernful being' is what Heidegger calls 'care', and it is the concatenation of angst, care, and guilt that turns Dasein's non-identity with itself into a source of creativity. However, this creativity—even when accompanied by heightened social consciousness—remains at the level of the individual. It is only with Heidegger's notion of 'destiny' that the plane for resolve shifts from individual to community.

The lack of any specific ethico-political content to the category of 'destiny' has often invited the charge of 'empty formalism' from Heidegger's critics; however, when Heidegger asserts that destiny 'is how we designate the historicizing of the community, of a Volk',[69] his aim is not to supply any sort of prescriptive politics, it is only to specify the condition of possibility for any authentic political engagement. Without some concept akin to 'destiny', the community would be entirely at the mercy of unrelenting contingency impinging on it from without. To characterize the very notion of 'destiny' as 'crypto-fascist', the way many of Heidegger's liberal critics have done, is, therefore, to also rob communities of any autonomous capacity for self-relating, leaving them only with Chakrabarty's sad residual tasks of 'modifying' and 'unsettling' universal history. These liberal critics are certainly correct to pinpoint the notion of *Volksgemeinschaft*[70]—the ethno-national community that would realize itself through the medium of the state—as the source of Heidegger's Fascist temptation. What they are loath to acknowledge, however, is that liberalism is itself wedded to an idea not far removed from Volksgemeinschaft: the state as 'national community' to whose imperatives every other form of community must bend.

The problem with Heidegger's notion of 'communal destiny' then is not any 'proto-fascism' intrinsic to it, but in its failure to grasp 'historicizing' as *a co-historicizing not only of Dasein-with but of Mitsein-with*. The central theoretical loophole here lies in the failure to extend the 'being-with' that is integral to Dasein to the level of Mitsein—*as Mitsein's being-with other Mitsein*. At the level of Dasein, Heidegger is emphatic that 'others are encountered environmentally'[71] as habitat and not as present-at-hand, but this environmentality is not extended to Mitsein's encounter with other Mitsein. Heidegger fully acknowledges that just as 'Dasein comes to realize that beyond Dasein-with and Dasein-in ... it must become Dasein-for'[72] (its ownmost possibilities), Mitsein too must become a Mitsein-for; *what is missing, however, is any recognition that Mitsein can become Mitsein-for only as Mitsein-with*. Therein also lies the source of Heidegger's practical political blindness: not in the idea of 'destining' as such, *but in his inability to think a co-destining with European Jewry*.

This can be seen clearly in the category of 'resoluteness', with which Heidegger tries to bridge Dasein and Mitsein: 'Resolve is a distinctive mode of Dasein's disclosedness.... Resolve, as authentic Being-one's-Self, does not detach Dasein from its world, nor does it isolate it such that it becomes a free-floating "ego".... Resolve brings the Self right into its concernful Being-along-side what is ready-to-hand and pushes it into solicitous Being-with-others.'[73] Here once again, being-with-others is implicitly posited as a unitary Mitsein, which then slides imperceptibly into the 'national community' of Volksgemeinschaft.

The category of 'resolve' presents other problems that are covered over in Heidegger's assertion that 'resolve, as authentic being-one's-Self, does not detach itself from its world.'[74] It is not clear what Heidegger means when he uses the word 'detach' in this way unless he is stating what is in any case impossible: a cutting off of all links with the world. On the other hand, if 'resolve' is not to fall into the decisionism of a 'choice' between alternatives that leaves the subjective position of the choice-maker intact,[75] it will have to make room for some form of 'detachment'. The movement of resolve cannot be one of returning to the self-sameness of the being that undertook the resolve. As in the Kerala event, that to which resolve returns must come to be constituted in the very movement of that resolve.

This aporia in Heidegger's concept of 'resolve' is also reflected in his discussion of tradition. When he talks of the possibilities opened up by 'the heritage', he is not denying that these possibilities are already present in Dasein's thrownness; what he is asserting is that they can only be discerned in the 'running ahead of itself' of Dasein's anticipatory resoluteness.[76] 'Destiny' is Mitsein's 'running ahead of itself' that is disclosive of its potentiality-for-Being, and Mitsein's historicizing makes its 'heritage' available as possibilities that it can take over. In Mitsein's historicizing, the 'there' of its thrownness is made transparent to itself, and it is through this opening up that tradition's possibilities are disclosed to it. Tradition then is not simply delivered over to Mitsein for the taking; it has to be reclaimed in resoluteness. What Heidegger overlooks here, however, is that Mitsein's destining is always already a co-destining; for tradition's possibilities to disclose themselves, Mitsein's (co-)destining must, therefore, ontologically be preceded by Mitsein-with.

At the level of Dasein, Heidegger is extraordinarily attentive to its non-coincidence with itself: as we have seen, it is through the *angst* of non-coincidence that an awareness of the ontological is intimated to Dasein, necessitating a *separation* from the inertial everydayness of 'the they' before it can assume its being-toward-death. Mitsein, however, is automatically assumed to be unitary, and aside from for the formal assertion of its historicity, the precise modality of the unfolding of Mitsein's destiny remains under-specified in Heidegger.

For a disclosure of its ownmost possibilities, however, Mitsein too must pass through its moment of separateness, but this separateness is not that of entities distinct from one another because of some specific 'difference' as perceived from the standpoint of the non-engaged external observer. As far as the communities themselves are concerned, any such 'difference' is operative only as a second-order difference: their very 'difference' is differently perceived from the standpoints of the different communities. Furthermore, any such 'difference' between communal entities is always redoubled as an internal self-difference within each, so that 'separation' here is not a withdrawing or pulling away from the other but a separation from this very separation from the other, and the full assumption of the community's own self-difference.

An Ontological Politics?

And so we arrive back to the question with which we began: Can ontological truth be translated into politics? Can politics ever root itself in an ontological foundation, or does politics necessarily imply an opacity as to its ontological ground? Conversely, does insight into ontological truth necessarily lead to error in the ontic realm—which is how Heidegger justified himself in the wake of his disastrous political engagement? Must a privileging of ontology inevitably culminate in an amoral politics? Is there a 'proto-fascist' danger lurking in the very subordination of the political to the ontological? Should one then simply abandon Heidegger's distinction between being and beings?

The answers to these questions depend crucially on how the relationship between ontology and politics is conceived. Liberal critics have sought an expeditious exit from this problematic by setting aside the whole question of ontology, seeking instead to enlarge the field of the political by expanding the notion of rationality beyond the merely instrumental. Habermas, for instance, explicates a conception of communicative democracy by specifying a set of normative conditions for undistorted communication. Rorty wants to strictly mark off a private arena of irony and whimsicality from a public domain where the proper means for promoting the common good are collectively deliberated upon and implemented. Efforts like that of Habermas and Rorty approach the political by simply sidestepping the ontological. But the question of just what we mean when we posit entities such as 'community', 'state', 'nation', 'religion', and so on has not thereby gone away. From the standpoint of ontological difference, it *is* possible to distinguish between an ontological politics that brings about a transformation in the very horizon of meaning within which entities are disclosed, and an ethical or religious politics that remains circumscribed within a given meaning horizon. In this sense, an ontological politics is a politics that can neither wish away the question of being by 'ethicizing' it, nor resolve it precipitately by resorting to a hypostatized entity called 'community'.

And it is precisely in confronting this question of ontological politics that the Kerala and German experiences present radically contrasting pictures. As noted earlier, from the perspective of the Kerala event, there are two crucial pieces missing in Heideggerian ontology: a notion of Mitsein-with as correlative to Mitsein-for; and a necessary moment of self-separation in the 'resolve' that precedes the disclosing of tradition's possibilities. For Heidegger, as we have seen, the bridging concept between the domains of ontology and politics is 'historicizing' through which ontological truth is actualized in the ontic realm of politics. And—at least for a brief period in the mid-1930s—Heidegger mistook Nazism to be the form of politics that answered to the exigencies of the age of technological nihilism and through which the ontological structures spelt out in *Being and Time* would receive their ontic fulfilment. It is in his search for such a *direct* translation of ontology into politics that Heidegger makes his fateful turn to the state as carrier of ontological truth. This, together with the two missing pieces already mentioned, yielded the *Fuehrer* as the historical embodiment of the resoluteness of the 'German national community'. The autonomy of the Volk that Heidegger had initially set out to safeguard is in this way haplessly surrendered to the very institution that poses the single greatest threat to it. 'Errors' such as these are, of course, always owned up after they have wreaked their irreparable havoc, and Heidegger was no exception in this respect.

Now, insofar as every politics presupposes some understanding of being and its relation to beings, politics *cannot but* be implicitly ontological. What this implies is that rather than summarily dismissing the very priority of ontology over politics as misguided, we ought to pay close attention to the precise manner in which the ontological takes precedence over the political in the two contrasting cases before us. In Germany, an *explicit* metaphysical transformation of politics was aimed at, ending up in the nightmare of the Holocaust; in Kerala, there was a genuine metaphysical transfiguration of society, but not as the intended effect of a goal-directed decision. Narayana Guru himself remained scrupulously distanced from any activity that might be considered overtly political, even as Kerala's traditional order was crumbling all around him. The political in Kerala was never the object of a *direct* metaphysical programme the way it was in Germany; what metaphysics accomplished in Kerala was to open up a fragile space beyond the determining reach of universal history, within which an autonomous politics of intercommunality could unfold.

Unlike in Germany, there was no effort to 'fuse' metaphysics and politics; on the contrary, *the gap between the two was steadfastly retained* in Kerala's version of ontological politics. Resisting any wholesale metaphysical usurpation, politics remained a distinct sphere in which the agonistic play of community interests could unfold; crucially then, the role of metaphysics in Kerala's transformation was not only to buffer its politics from the clasp of universal history *but equally to insulate politics from metaphysics itself*. Implicit in this separation was the awareness that while there can be a 'directly' ethical or religious politics, there cannot be a determinate political programme derivable directly from an ontological foundation. What the Kerala experience teaches is that metaphysics *can* clear a space in which an autonomous politics can be provisionally sheltered from universal history; what it *cannot* do is rid politics of its constitutive agonism.

This does not in any way imply that there is no place for the state; however, under no condition can intercommunal dialectics cede to the state the role of overarching structural principle. Historically in Kerala the self-voiding of the Ezhavas was followed not only by all the other communities reconstituting themselves; its intercommunal space also expanded to host a new quasi-community of the Left comprised of people from all communities *and* it managed to produce a succession of responsive governments led by both political fronts, which implemented democratic measures in land reform, food distribution, health provision, and educational access. Robin Jeffrey, the Australian political scientist who has studied this social transformation at great length, arrives at the conclusion that 'most of Kerala's "favorable" outcomes have resulted less from government policies than from the popular demand that has extracted such policies'.[77] Entirely absent, however, was the Teutonic temptation, operative at least since Hegel—and all too evident in Heidegger—to view the state as a quasi-spiritual 'self-conscious ethical substance'[78] in which 'freedom enters into its highest right'[79] so that a *Volk* may realize itself.

Notes

1. Jacques Derrida, *Margins of Philosophy*, translated by Alan Bass (Chicago: University of Chicago Press, 1982), 22.

2. As George Steiner has put it, only half tongue-in-cheek, 'When he says that Western history may well turn on the translation (the right apprehension) of the verb "to be" in a pre-Socratic fragment, Heidegger is being deadly serious.' George Steiner, *Martin Heidegger* (Chicago: University of Chicago Press, 1987), 39.

3. J. Habermas, 'Work and Weltanschauung: The Heidegger Controversy from a German Perspective', translated by John McCumber, *Critical Inquiry* 15 (Winter 1989), 445–55.

4. Paul de Man, whose anti-Semitic rants had just come to light.

5. Dipesh Chakrabarty, *Provincializing Europe: Postcolonial Thought and Historical Difference* (Princeton: Princeton University Press, 2000).

6. Chakrabarty, *Provincializing Europe*, 18.

7. Chakrabarty, *Provincializing Europe*, 6.

8. Chakrabarty, *Provincializing Europe*, 20.

9. Chakrabarty, *Provincializing Europe*, 254.

10. Chakrabarty, *Provincializing Europe*, 239.

11. Chakrabarty, *Provincializing Europe*, 19.

12. Chakrabarty, *Provincializing Europe*, 68.

13. The concept of 'life-world' as the totality of a meaningful hermeneutic habitat is originally Husserl's and roughly parallels Heidegger's unwieldy 'being-in-the-world'.

14. Chakrabarty, *Provincializing Europe*, 68.

15. Chakrabarty, *Provincializing Europe*, 253.

16. Chakrabarty, *Provincializing Europe*, 20.

17. Chakrabarty, *Provincializing Europe*, 70.

18. Chakrabarty, *Provincializing Europe*, 250.

19. Ferdinand Tonnies, *Community and Civil Society*, translated by Jose Harris and Margaret Hollis, edited by Jose Harris (Cambridge: Cambridge University Press, 2001).

20. Chakrabarty, *Provincializing Europe*, 4.

21. Chakrabarty, *Provincializing Europe*, 248.

22. Chakrabarty, *Provincializing Europe*, 254.

23. James Phillips, *Heidegger's Volk* (Stanford, California: Stanford University Press, 2005), 6.

24. Phillips, *Heidegger's Volk*, 6.

25. Phillips, *Heidegger's Volk*, 6.

26. Phillips, *Heidegger's Volk*, 6.

27. The emerging consensus in 'Heidegger studies' is that there are three distinct phases of his thought: the early phase of the existential philosophy of Dasein laid out in *Being and Time*; a middle phase where the emphasis shifts to 'the history of being' and its epochal disclosures; and a last phase of withdrawal into reflections on poetry, language, and the doctrine of 'letting be' as a way of countering the will to power and its technological nihilism. Some have interpreted this trajectory as stemming from Heidegger's realization that the existential starting point of *Being and Time* was too subject-centered to illuminate the meaning of Being, and that this accounts for the subsequent shift from the voluntarism of the 'resoluteness' expounded in *Being and Time* to the near-fatalism of the 'releasement' elaborated in his last phase. From our perspective, however,

it is the problematic of Mitsein that proved to be the central theoretical deadlock of *Being and Time*, which the turn to the 'epochal disclosure of being' enabled Heidegger to evade, never to be picked up again. In the wake of his egregious political blunders in the 1930s, he was probably wise to sidestep the thorny business of Mitsein, but what gets lost in the shifting of responsibility for being onto an epochally disclosed modern subjectivity and its innate nihilism is the constitutive tension of *Being and Time* itself.

28. Phillips, *Heidegger's Volk*, 7.

29. Steiner, *Martin Heidegger*, 153.

30. Phillips, *Heidegger's Volk*, 13.

31. Heidegger distinguishes between the two by using the word *Geschichte* for the former and *Historie* for the latter.

32. Miguel de Beistegui, *Heidegger and the Political* (London: Routledge, 1998), 14.

33. Steiner, *Martin Heidegger*, 91.

34. Phillips, *Heidegger's Volk*, 32.

35. Martin Heidegger, *Being and Time* (New York: Harper Perennial, 2008), 32.

36. Heidegger, *Being and Time*, 436.

37. Martin Heidegger, *An Introduction to Metaphysics*, translated by Ralph Manheim (New Haven, Connecticut: Yale University Press, 1959), 37–9.

38. de Beistegui, *Heidegger and the Political*, 17–19.

39. Heidegger, *Being and Time*, 437.

40. de Beistigui, *Heidegger and the Political*, 91.

41. Heidegger, *Being and Time*, 326.

42. Phillips, *Heidegger's Volk*, 16.

43. Heidegger quoted in de Beistigui, *Heidegger and the Political*, 115.

44. de Beistigui, *Heidegger and the Political*, 17.

45. de Beistigui, *Heidegger and the Political*, 18.

46. de Beistigui, *Heidegger and the Political*, 19.

47. M. K. Sanoo, *Narayana Guru Swami Jeevacharitram* (Kottayam: National Book Stall, 1986), 473.

48. Udaya Kumar, 'Writing the Life of the Guru: Chattampi Swamikal, Sree Narayana Guru, and Modes of Biographical Construction', in *Biography as History: Indian Perspectives*, edited by Vijaya Ramaswamy and Yogesh Sharma (New Delhi: Orient Blackswan, 2009), 58.

49. N. Kumaran Asan, *Brahmasree Narayana Guruvinte Jeevacharitra Samgraham* (Trivandrum: Asan Memorial Committee, 1973 [1915]), 31. This essay was originally published in the Malayalam journal *Vivekodayam*.

50. V. R. Krishna Iyer, 'Prolegomenon to a Biography of Narayana Guru', in *Narayana Guru* by M. K. Sanoo (Bombay: Bharatiya Vidya Bhavan, 1998), xvii.

51. K. V. Subramanyam, *Sahodaran Ayyappan Jeevacharitram* (Aluva: K. V. Subramanyam, 1973), 6.

52. Moyarathu Sankaran, *Ente Jeevithakatha* (Calicut: P.K. Brothers, 1965), 53.

53. Bill McKibben, 'The Enigma of Kerala', *Utne Reader*, no. 74, (March-April 1996), 106.

54. M. N. Srinivas, *Caste in Modern India and Other Essays* (Bombay: Media Promoters & Publishers, 1988 [1962]), 34.

55. Murkot Kunhappa, *Sree Narayana Guru* (New Delhi: National Book Trust, 1982), 27 (emphasis added).

56. K. Sreenivasan, *Sree Narayana Guru* (Trivandrum: Jayasree Publications, 1989), 55.

57. Sreenivasan, *Sree Narayana Guru*, 28.

58. Sreenivasan, *Sree Narayana Guru*, 54.

59. Murkothu Kumaran, *Sree Narayana Guru Swamikalude Jeevacharitram* (Varkala: Sree Narayana Dharmasangham Trust, 1999 [1930]), 148.

60. Both Shiva and Sharada are currently worshipped at Shivagiri.

61. Kunhappa, *Sree Narayana Guru*, 29.

62. A. S. P. Aiyer quoted in A. Ayyappan, *Social Revolution in a Kerala Village: A Study in Culture Change* (Bombay: Asia Publishing House, 1965), 135.

63. Kunhappa, *Sree Narayana Guru*, 24.

64. P. K. Balakrishnan, *Narayana Guru Samahara Grantham* (Kottayam: National Book Stall, 1954), 125.

65. Puthuppally Raghavan, ed., *C.V. Kunjuramante Thiranjedutha Krithikal* (Thiruvananthapuram: Kaumudi Public Relations, 2002), 124.

66. K. Lowith, 'Last Meeting with Heidegger', translated by Lisa Harries, in *Martin Heidegger and National Socialism*, edited by Gunther Neske and Emil Kettering (New York: Paragon, 1990), 157–9.

67. Heidegger, *Being and Time*, 312.

68. Heidegger, *Being and Time*, 312.

69. Heidegger, *Being and Time*, 436.

70. *Volksgemeinschaft* was the term used by the Nazis to designate the 'German national community' and which Heidegger also uses on occasion. See Martin Heidegger, 'Political Texts: 1933–1934', *New German Critique* 45 (1988), 98.

71. Phillips, *Heidegger's Volk*, 17.

72. Steiner, *Martin Heidegger*, 100.

73. Heidegger, *Being and Time*, 344–6.

74. Heidegger, *Being and Time*, 345.

75. What Heidegger had in common with the Nazis was not the latter's racial biologism but a shared understanding of 'the Germans' as 'a nation' that

had to be reinvigorated, and whose collective subjective position had been reduced to that of a people humiliated in the Treaty of Versailles concluded after World War I.

76. 'The resolve in which Dasein comes back to itself, discloses current factical possibilities of authentic existing, and discloses them in terms of a heritage which that resolve, as thrown, takes over. In one's coming back resolutely to one's own thrownness, there is a hidden handing down to oneself of the possibilities that have come down to one, but not necessarily as thus having come down.' Heidegger, *Being and Time*, 435.

77. Robin Jeffrey, *Politics, Women, and Well-Being: How Kerala Became a Model* (New Delhi: Oxford University Press, 2001), 227.

78. G. W. F. Hegel, *Philosophy of Mind* (Oxford: Clarendon Press, 1971), 263.

79. G. W. F. Hegel, *Elements of the Philosophy of Right*, edited by Allen W. Wood (Cambridge: Cambridge University Press, 1991), p. 275.

4

THE POLITICS AND METAPHYSICS OF INTELLECTUAL PRACTICES

Ashis Nandy and U. R. Ananathamurthy
in Conversation

EDITED AND ANNOTATED BY VINAY LAL

The following dialogue took place at the second meeting of the Backwaters Collective in Varkala in the summer of 2012. Its inclusion in the first volume of the proceedings of the Collective has been precipitated by the sudden and greatly lamented passing of Ananthamurthy in August 2014. Every attempt has been made to retain as much of the flavour of the original as possible, even if, on occasion, the syntax is a bit peculiar; if a few liberties have been taken in editing this conversation, it has been solely with the intention of bringing clarity to arguments that might otherwise be obscure.

Ananthamurthy and Nandy forged a close friendship over the last few decades, and each has occupied a distinct place in the intellectual life of contemporary India. Though Ananthamurthy wrote only in Kannada, barring a few short pieces penned in English, his interventions in important debates and his role as head of a number of national institutions, including the Sahitya Akademi (Academy of Literature), rendered him into a public figure and made him widely known to English-speaking readers. The positions he staked were not always understood and, like Nandy, he came in for ample criticism from both the left and the right. It is at his behest, for instance, that the Government of Karnataka officially changed the name of Bangalore to Bengaluru on 1 November 2006, opening him up to the charge that he was a nationalist and Kannada chauvinist. In a short lyrical piece entitled 'Ooru and the World', Ananthamurthy wrote quite plainly that 'most people of Bangalore are unaware of even the existence of Bengaluru'. He goes on to share his dream 'of a time when those who admire the wanderings of Joyce's hero Daedalus also open their eyes to the rich Dalit world that Kuvempu's character Nayigutti leads us into'.[1] Shortly before his death, Ananthamurthy was mired in another, more disturbing, controversy that moved the state government to furnish an armed police guard at his residence. Alarmed at the prospect of Narendra Modi's electoral triumph that would catapult him to the office of the Prime Minister of India, Ananthamurthy had, in an 'emotional moment' as he was to later say, declared that he would in the eventuality of a BJP victory buy himself a one-way train ticket to Pakistan. Upon the BJP's resounding victory, the foot soldiers of Hindu nationalism began to pound ferociously at his door. However, in some respects, all of this was tangential to the life and achievements of a writer who described himself as a Gandhian socialist. As a recent collection of his essays, *Rujuvathu*, translated into English by his former student and long-time friend and associate N. Manu Chakravarthy, so amply demonstrates,[2] Ananthamurthy had an extraordinary command over the entire history of Kannada literature and an easy versatility with literature in Sanskrit, other Indian languages, and world literature. He had the gift of the storyteller who knew both the 'frontyard' and the 'backyard' of India's intellectual and literary traditions. Many of his readers still know him as the author of the short but searing novel, *Samskara*, while others swear by stories such as 'Suryana Kudure' ('Stallion of the Sun').[3] But I think I shall remember him most by his piece which was prompted by news reports in the early 1980s about men and women in the village of Chandragutti who every March would offer naked worship to a Goddess in fulfilment of a vow. Isn't it profoundly moving, Ananthamurthy asks in 'Why Not Worship in the Nude? Reflections of a Novelist in His Times', that a woman's naked body is 'neither aesthetic nor erotic for the worshippers. And can that happen anywhere else in the world? A naked body is sacred for them'.[4]

Controversy has also followed Ashis Nandy at every turn of his intellectual life. It is doubtful that Nandy would characterize himself as a Gandhian socialist; indeed, it is uncertain how he might be described, and he has variously been styled a cultural psychologist, political sociologist, social theorist, postcolonial intellectual, and cultural critic, though an intellectual street fighter appears to be a description that would fit him well.[5] His little book, *The Intimate Enemy: Loss and Recovery of Self under Colonialism* (1983), is now standard fare in postcolonial courses and easily the best known of his works in the West. In India, however, Nandy has been rather more prominently associated with intellectual positions that many of his critics have attacked as romantic, regressive, anti-modernist, and anti-humanist. What is quite certain is that many of the positions he embraced, which once appeared to be outlandish and indefensible, such as his unflinching critique of secularism, his espousal of what he called 'critical traditionalism', or his devastating indictment of the entire discourse of development, have over the course of the last few decades become part of the common sense of a self-reflective intellectual life. There are still purveyors of ideas, to be sure, who dismiss Nandy as 'a master at repackaging elite prejudice as counter-intuitive insight and paradoxical wisdom',[6] but we can perhaps with some profit and amusement recall that India is also the place where, in the wake of the demise of the Soviet Union and the dismantling of the 'Iron Curtain', the communists eagerly rushed to claim the myriad statues of the leaders of discredited and highly authoritarian regimes. Nandy's world view is perhaps best captured in his own words, as in the short note appended to his most recent collection of essays, *Regimes of Narcissism, Regimes of Despair*, where he outlines the concerns that have guided him over half a century of political and intellectual life:

> The first is to acknowledge and listen to those silenced or ignored by an iniquitous, arrogant global knowledge system; the second is to look at politics and society through the prism of persons and their selves, to ensure that the human is not overwhelmed by impersonal institutional structures and the so-called larger movements of history; and the third is to explore within cultures—as encrypted in everyday life of ordinary people—to identify possible means of resistance to the mega-projects of the state and of ambitious, apparently

space-and-time-defying movements and ideologies claiming privileged or superior knowledge and rationality.[7]

More than anyone else, Nandy has been singularly instructive about
the possibilities of a dissent that cannot be captured or conveyed in
the languages customarily associated with dissent.

***

U. R. Ananthamurthy (URA): Since I am older than Ashis, let me
have the advantage of saying some things first. I have always felt that
when Ashis Nandy is there, I am going to hear something unexpected,
something I've not thought of until now. You can tell him anything
and then he opens out and then he agrees or disagrees with you. In
short, a dialogue with him is always possible, and I am finding that
in this whole group, such a dialogue is possible with everyone; and
now all the participants at this conference have become such good
friends with each other, teasing one another.... When people begin to
tease each other, it is a sign that we have succeeded in being a community, a community that one wants to belong to. And this would not
have been possible in any university now: I have been Vice Chancellor
of a university,[8] and I know well how they are run. This [convivial-
ity] has become possible in this group and I feel really grateful. We
should meet again and then go deep into this question that we did not
really face up to—a question about the personality of Narayana Guru,
who was a kind of an *Avadhoota* [an enlightened being, one who is
beyond ego-consciousness] and also an activist. That is not true of
Ramana [Maharshi] as it is of Narayana Guru.[9] There is something
very special in this. Is it because Narayana Guru came from one of
the lower castes? He became an activist also. You know he had that
kind of compassion, along with a great awakening of the mind. This
is a great combination, I tell you, especially when I think of other
religious leaders, and nowadays the religious leaders are all land grab-
bers. [Laughs gently.] They are a desperate lot. We've been speaking
about action and thought, and the question has been raised whether
thought isn't action here. When you are in troubled times, you think
of people like Narayana Guru; at times, he does not feel political at
all, but of such a one who was not political at all, it could be said
that he was more political than anyone else. The communist party

won elections because of Narayana Guru's work in Kerala. The lower
castes in Kerala are very different from the lower castes in Karnataka,
for example; politically they were radical. It is only the Communist
Party that has ceased to be radical. [Again laughs.] Narayana Guru's
thought can still make you radical. There is a strange kind of relationship between action and thought here; practice is not something
that you go to texts of foreign origin for, and Narayana Guru may
not have read the great texts of modernity. You know when Narayana
Guru meets Gandhi,[10] for me the most striking part is this: Narayana
Guru, a Shudra, asks this Vaishya, 'Can you speak Sanskrit?' And
then Gandhi asks him, 'Guru, would you wear khadi?'[11] That's a great
exchange for me between the two. Many possibilities were opened by
this exchange; truly this is a very international place.

About my visit to the Sivagiri Ashram, I found it very disappointing
that the Guru is represented by a very big statue. If I were part of your
community, I would quarrel with you. How did you allow a statue of
Narayana Guru to be put there? It's a white statue which doesn't look
like Narayana Guru at all; so there is some decadence also. We should
really be talking of great moments and of new openings, and then
of certain kinds of decadence setting in. When people were talking
about religious consciousness, they all just talked about it; but it is
there in operation here and we should be able to address questions of
this kind. Let me talk about what had happened when I was working
in Kerala; I was here for four years. There was one lecturer, most likely
not from a lower caste but rather upper caste, but he was very active in
the Sasthra-Sahitya movement.[12] He would come to his college, which
was run by SNDP Yogam [Sree Narayana Dharma Paripalana Yogam,
or the Sree Narayana Trust], and make fun of 'your cement Guru'; you
see there are cement statues of Narayan Guru installed everywhere,
and the college wanted to punish him and they wanted my approval
as Vice Chancellor. I said an apology will be enough in this case and
the matter can be thus settled. The community representatives went
to the Governor and said Ananthamurthy is anti-backward class. I was
not, but I had to face all this; and I could face all this because I was
infused somewhere by Narayana Guru's spirit, which is above everything else. One could take shelter under something that is bigger than
what is the practice; that is why I said, if the practice is faulty, you
should have something within that community with which you can

criticize the practice. His spirit stands for philosophy, action, politics, and also social reform. All these questions could have been examined in greater depth, and perhaps in the next conference we should be doing that, addressing ourselves to immediate questions—the questions that might strike a housewife, not just philosophical problems, but our own problems about our own creativity and of our own time. Also, when we use comparative categories, and I wish it was done today when we were discussing Jnaneshvar and the Guru,[13] we can bring in much more of Indian thought. I think we could have discussed Shankaracharya and Narayana Guru, and in what way the two are different, because Shankaracharya didn't go in for any action of that kind, but Narayan Guru did—he was a literalist of Advaita. That's why I said in my opening remarks, I used this phrase from Yeats who called Blake a 'literalist of his imagination',[14] and Narayana Guru was a literalist of Advaita, much more than anyone else. These are I think very special topics for us, much more so than very speculative things. I am not against speculation, but I would like that to be built into a certain fabric of the here and now. And then I would say what Ashis had mentioned, 'Which Indian thinker should I go to?' I think Indian thinking begins with that kind of engagement. That engagement is possible with Narayana Guru.

Ashis Nandy (AN): I think that's an excellent beginning because indirectly Ananthamurthy has emphasized a part of the story that we have not, or which has been weak in our exercise. During the course of this meeting, over these last three days, we have been rather sensitive to the issue of metaphysics of politics and public life, but we have been less sensitive to the politics of metaphysics, and I don't think any metaphysics of politics is complete or even possible without sensitivity to the politics of metaphysics.

URA: That's what I said, religion is politics in eternity.

AN: Yes, I absolutely agree. I want to be very clear about this, I don't want to beat around the bush; we have known each other for some time. Some of you [at this conference] I know over three meetings, and some of you I am meeting for the first time; but at least in this kind of a seminar, which is a continuing effort, we should be free enough to say anything. I personally think that the best turn Professor Hegel could have done to the southern world—Asia, Africa, and

Latin America—is not to have been born. [Laughter around the room.]
He is not only a racist, but he provides a non-racist justification for
a progressivism of some kind which has been devastating and took a
huge toll on human lives and has been a major source of disruption
in our societies. I hold him personally responsible. Marx's racism:
everybody knows about it, but it basically comes from left-Hegelian
thought. That's the justification. In fact, in the case of someone like
Kant, who was actually a practicing racist, his thought reflects that
racism less. Nobody works on this contradiction, nobody works on
Hegel from this point of view: while Hegel in his life was not a racist,
in the sense in which Kant was, but his work makes the most hand-
some contribution to the destruction of cultures and threatening the
cultural survival of countries in the southern hemisphere.[15] This is
the first point that I wanted to make.

The second point I wanted to make is this: that if you look at the
papers presented here, you will find no reference or very little reference to works by people who have worked on politics of knowledge—
and there have been people of this kind—and that politics is
important. I don't mean to say that we have to do what you might call
intellectual profiles of them, but at least let's take into consideration
people who have tried to grapple with the issue here and there over
the last hundred and fifty years. I'm not saying that we have to think
only of those who are contemporaries. Some papers have tried to do
it, but only with respect to those who we would think of in any case;
I would have liked at least one or two papers that are trying to probe
some intellectual traditions which we have not heard of—about some
figures who have something to say about the politics of metaphysics,
who have shown some sensitivity to it, who would help us to fight the
kind of metaphysics and its politics that we are confronting.

URA: Actually there is a critique of Shankara: if you are an Advaitin,
you can conveniently have two realms: one is the *Loukik* realm where
Advaita doesn't apply, and it is a *Paramarthik satya* [absolute real-
ity]. Shankara made this—Paramarthik satya—possible you know.
Hence, India could tolerate any injustice in its own society, because
Paramarthik satya is different; so you can easily slip into it. There
is this politics in certain kinds of Vedantic thought. You know this
is the politics of Shankara's Vedanta. Whereas the same Advaita is
taken by Narayana Guru and [he has] not done that. This again is very

interesting. That's why I started with the story of the Chandala. It's a very great incident for me. All Brahmins tell the story of Shankara being enlightened when he meets a Chandala but there is a moment in Shankara's encounter when he agrees with the Chandala that he doesn't know true reality and he accepts the discourse from the Chandala's viewpoint. But the storyteller tells us that it was Shiva who came in the form of Chandala, and Narayan Guru says, 'No, no, no ... it was a real Chandala, it is that Shankara saw Shiva in the Chandala.'[16] This is another kind of politics.

AN: Hmm ... hmm, lovely ...

URA: It is also the kind of politics he did ... taking the same concepts ...

AN: I think ordinary people are aware of this, aware of this kind of story which I have been hearing from my childhood. I tried to say it to somebody but I didn't complete it. Shankaracharya once fell into a well and when one of his students rushed to help him out of it, the other student stopped him, saying that it is all Maya—the well is Maya; Shankara is Maya; we are Maya. Hearing this, Shankara shouted, 'You fool, throw a rope first and then talk of it.'[17] I think these are actually ordinary people's philosophy; fragments of ordinary people's philosophies, and we have made no effort to tap them.

URA: To tap them in our discourse.

AN: That's right ... that's right ... that's right. Because the everyday life, 'Loukik', is naturally dualistic and Shankaracharya recognizes this.

URA: Yes ... yes.

AN: Everybody sings his *bhajan*, 'Bhaja Govindam Mudhamate',[18] but that bhajan itself is a dualist bhajan, there's no doubt about that ...

URA: I have no doubt about it either, because he has made room for it: there is the ultimate Paramarthik satya where the self disappears and there is a world where you can do without everyday reality. Has that hurt India? That is what I want to ask. Has it made us sort of easy people? Do we accept anything easily? If it's a Paramarthik satya ... I don't have to worry about it. Whereas I find in the West you know there was a problem about this kind of thinking. I like a lot of the West because they are troubled by this kind of thinking. However, this appearance and reality becomes a very important thing for many

Indians. There is a word which I use in Kannada and it is still being used, I use the word *Bhode* ... Bhode is the word I use for the Indian mind which accepts anything, which says yes to anything, and which doesn't require any enquiry. Bhode also means noble and very big. One assumes big words, you know, and then one gets lost in some kind of a metaphysics which doesn't bite into any realities and hence I think a critique of it is very necessary in terms of actual everyday experience. The quotidian experience has to be brought into that.

AN: I also want to draw the attention of the group—and I'd like its reaction to this assertion—to the fact that we have been hesitant to venture irresponsible statements here and I don't know why that should be so. We are not telling you to write your final versions of your paper here. But I would have really liked to have heard more adventurous statements, frankly, if you want to work at the margins of metaphysics and margins of politics. I mean you are at the margin in any case—at least in a group like this where half of whom are not philosophers. As far as I am concerned I cannot even spell the names of most of these German philosophers. [Laughs.] But let's leave that aside. I think that the real problem that we are facing today in India—and even globally—can be summed up basically as a set of three constructions; these are philosophical problems, and I shall very quickly enumerate them because these matters are very close to my heart. One, we see all over the place, a kind of encroachment of concepts or ideas which didn't hegemonize a particular domain ... and ultimately get identified with the entire domain and you cannot enter that domain without invoking that concept. For example, even in social sciences, indeed all the way from the social sciences to newspaper editorials, you do not hear the phrase 'social change' any more, it is 'development'.

URA: Yes, yes. [Nods in evident agreement.]

AN: There was social change before the idea of development came.[19] Development is a very new idea, for the first time used in its present sense in 1949 by the great professor and philosopher, Harry S. Truman. My respect for him is not so unbounded, howsoever great he may have been, that I consider that any concept that he might have generated to be that valuable and that permanent in social knowledge. But I don't see any effort to get out of the stranglehold and the result is this, that today, even in the southern hemisphere, even in the countries which have suffered from large scale destruction of life support systems of the poor and the powerless—countries like Brazil, for example, and the whole Amazon basin—there is no concept of thinking outside development. Such is the politics of knowledge in our times that whatever alternative concepts or modifications are suggested, human beings always add an adjective and make it softer. So I have heard of Rural Development, Alternative Development, Ethno Development, et cetera, unending number of things ... Inclusive Development, nowadays, and Sustainable Development.[20]

URA: Ashis, we have forgotten the word *Sarvodaya*.[21]

AN: Yes. [They both laugh gently.]

URA: In the whole development [discourse], what we lost is the concept of Sarvodaya, completely lost it; nobody speaks of it, as a matter of fact, our Prime Minister should go and talk about Sarvodaya to Americans because they need Sarvodaya, but we don't talk about it. You know, we have lost that courage which Gandhi had, you see.

AN: So how do we recover—how *do* we recover—this space, how can we say that social change has a number of approaches, development is only one of them, even development with capital 'D', but there is also Sarvodaya, and how do we get back to the simple concepts of everyday lives which have been hegemonized and have shrunk, shrunk to almost obscurity. That's one challenge. I would suggest that there also is a tendency—the politics of metaphysics also works in this way—I have given it a name also, I call it 'Split Legitimacy'. You will notice that the sacrosanct concepts and evaluative categories of our times have all been relieved of their responsibility and those who pursue these also are relieved of their responsibility. I will give you an example to make it clear: if you discover penicillin, if you are Sir Alexander Fleming, everybody applauds you as a discoverer of the first antibiotic. You get the Nobel Prize, which he got. But, who discovered Zyklon B, the gas that killed the inmates of the concentration camps, an estimated one and half million people? It will be 'the Nazis', 'Third Reich', 'the military industrial complex', 'modern capitalism': everybody is responsible except the actual name.[22] There are no names of those who worked on developing the gas, no name

of the scientist who discovered 'Zyklon B', only the institutions are
blamed. Only institutions are blamed. This is very clear in science
but it also true of a large number of cases of Satanism in our times.
And I do believe that it is our responsibility as a part of this Politics of
Metaphysics to have equitable distribution, symmetrical justification
of agency, attribution of agency. Let's call it symmetrical attribution
of agency. If you applaud Fleming for his discovery of Penicillin, you
must also identify the persons or scientists who discovered Zyklon B.
I would like to know this: who discovered Napalm?[23] It is very difficult
and I have some ideas of who discovered it; I was curious about it for
twenty years, and only when I was in Berlin, I accidentally found that
there were some clues to a biographical account of one of the scientist
friends of Einstein. But this is the way it goes, nobody knows who is
the discoverer of Napalm.[24]

URA: Which is the third? You wanted to make three points.

AN: Ah, ok. I will very quickly make this last point. The third is better
known now but I think there is a new kind of space-time translat-
ability which has emerged in the global public culture over the last
250 years. Let me put it this way. Prior to that, if you look at earlier
descriptions of countries like India and China, these are seen as exotic
places. Peculiar? Yes. Strange practices? Yes. Fearsome? Yes. Magical?
Yes, but, they were *different* entities, they were a cultural presence.
They were also seen as ancient civilizations, with a distinctiveness of
their own. As late as Voltaire, this is true; Voltaire considered Chinese
civilization to be the most civilized. China is for him the most civilized country in the world. It was after the 'discovery' of the Americas
that we have to think of three major things: the slave trade, colonialism, and the two global wars. All this happened after enlightenment
values had seeped into European society. So, the kind of marauding
conquest which was endorsed by the church became more and more
difficult—the kind of direct marauding style in which the Spaniards
and Portuguese specialized, for instance. In its place came a new kind
of thing where these differences between cultures, geographical differences, became pronounced. Somebody was mentioning about this
vertical plane and lateral plane. Here in our group, who was that?

Guest: Sir, he was an outsider, from the [Sivagiri] Ashram.[25]

AN: *Acchha.* It could be used in a different way: that which was in the horizontal plane was converted and was transposed to the vertical plane as a chronological thing. So, that which was strong, exotic, or different became actually the past of Europe. We were also like this. This is human development, as of now. So they are today like us and tomorrow if they read the right textbooks diligently, then they will progress. They will crawl their way up the inclined plane of history: I use that term, 'inclined plane of history', at the top of which stand other civilized societies which are advising you how to climb it [the inclined plane] better, because they have already reached there. So they are naturally consultants to us because they know what we are better than we know ourselves! Because they have been us sometime in the past and have transcended that phase. So, they are experts on our contemporaneity. We are their past, and they are also experts on our future—because they are living it out. We have to reach it in the future!

URA: Great ... [laughs].

AN: So, this is the situation, this is also part of the politics of metaphysics. And I think I find it very difficult to discover writers, who are free from this, in some sense. A couple of days ago someone was grumbling about these articles. What's his name? Perry Anderson had written these pieces,[26] and I told this person what Ananthamurthy told me once when Salman Rushdie wrote that nothing interesting has come out in the literature of any Indian languages—literally nothing of worth except in English.[27] And he told me that I am not worried because he had written it in the *New York Times*. If he had written it in the *Times of India*, I would have been worried. I like that, I like that. We shouldn't be worried about [such matters] because this is the way they all look, they may not say it often. But [these sentiments] are always there. Anyhow, these are the three points I wanted to make.

URA: You know after the Khrushchev period, the Russians invited me to a conference of their foreign literature institution which had published my novel. And everyone was talking and there was this person who came in rather dramatically, he was a Russian writer and he began to sing a song and then all the others bent their head down.

He asked, 'Why do you bend your heads down? Didn't we all sing it in praise of Stalin? Me and you?' He said something like that. I was very moved by his speech and then he sang the whole song. However, with that they were ashamed and then they asked me to talk, and I thought of Hegel. I said there is an anti-Hegelian statement in India, in my language; it's totally anti-Hegelian, this is Purandara Dasa [that I am speaking of].

AN: It is?

URA: Purandara Dasa,[28] he is a dasa, he went from home to home, singing; he has this poem, you have to look at this one line. I asked them to write down this line and then look at it. 'Uttama Prabhutwa lolalotte'; 'lolalotte' is a meaningless term. We use 'lolalotte' for—'there's nothing'. 'Uttama Prabhutwa', they are two Sanskrit words, 'Uttama Prabhutwa lolalotte'; Hegel thinks of some Uttama Prabhutwa coming out of this. But for Purandara, he lived at the time of Vijayanagara empire when there was a 'Uttama Prabhutwa' in a sense. And he says, 'Uttama Prabhutwa lolalotte'. And look at the strategy. The first two words are Sanskrit and the third is a childish term. Putting these three together itself is an *enactment* of 'lolalotte' for 'Uttama Prabhutwa'. I said if you writers write this line on your flag and say: to think that any Prabhutwa can become an Uttama—is also 'lolalotte'. That is the Marxian Dream that you will go higher and higher and reach a utopia. Or even if it is 'Uttama', it is 'lolalotte'. It means both. In this way the words are combined: if the Prabhutwa *is* Uttama, it is 'lolalotte'. To think that Prabhutwa *can become* Uttama is also 'lolalotte'.[29] You know, that was a certain kind of mind which I find in folk songs, this is a song that the folks [common people] would sing. This is being anti-Hegel, you see.

AN: So, before I give the microphone back to Ananthamurthy for his last word—we decided we would talk for twenty minutes—I will give my last word. Namely, that we owe no obligation to anybody. This venture is not sponsored by any university or state. It is not sponsored by anybody who will hold us accountable for wrong footnotes or missing footnotes. So, at least don't come and tell me that you have done something perfectly. I would be suspicious about such perfection. Please send that paper to an international journal. I would be delighted; it belongs there. Please, for us, write what you did not want to write earlier or could not write earlier, did not have a chance to write, and might be embarrassed to show to all your friends.

URA: [Laughs heartily.] Who said it, you know Krishna could not be revealed to the naked Gopis because they held their sarees with their teeth? So drop it from your teeth. It was you who said it?

Guest 2: Yes, and she [one gopi] complained that that there was a thirty second delay in my calling and your coming. Krishna said, 'no', because there was a thirty second difference between it leaving your hands and the saree leaving your teeth.

Guest 3: So can we consider the formal dialogue concluded and start the open discussion?

Guest 4: I just wanted to throw out this question that given that we were in the proximity of Narayana Guru and of course there were a couple of very deep engagements with Narayana Guru's work and so at the end of these three days, I am wondering what exactly does Narayana Guru mean for us in terms of the basic question with which the conference took off, which was the relation between metaphysics and politics. I mean, what exactly does he embody? I mean, just off the cuff, I can imagine the fact that he is somebody who was a thinker and a social worker, somebody who actually was working in the social arena, there's some obvious answer there, but as to what he embodies in terms of the answer to the questions that we have been asking—in fact in some papers there was the non-relation between the metaphysics and politics and in some papers there was the coming together of the two. But what exactly does Narayana Guru stand for—for us? That's not clear to me.

URA: It is simple. Here is a case where metaphysics itself was politics. Without being a conniving kind of politics. It was not that—but it *was* politics. And Shankaracharya's was another kind of politics. Okay? So we need to examine it. In Narayana Guru, his Advaita became politics. I was trying to tell Ramu[30] all this, here is Advaita in action.

Guest 5: I would ask, if his metaphysics was politics, in that case, what was the originary position, if there is such? Should the originary sensibility be political or should it be metaphysical? And will the originary position be a limitation on 'development'?

URA: I would like it to be metaphysics. Personally, I would like it to be a deep philosophical thought—so deep that it begins to make changes around me, in my own life and all around me. That's what I would like. It's not having an origin in politics. If there is origin in politics then there will be a British empire.

Guest 6: But, regarding your distinction between Ramana Maharshi and Narayana Guru. So what did you mean by that?

URA: You know in my nature, I am more moved by Narayana Guru. I feel more sympathy towards him. But Ramana, I don't know much. I also told you a story which Vinda Karandikar[31] wrote which is also very much to the point here. I think I have shared it with some of you. Vinda has a poem, he is a great Marathi poet. Here is the great Marathi saint poet Tukaram. Tukaram is in a market and is walking and Shakespeare comes from the other side. Shakespeare immediately recognizes Tuka and says, 'Tukaram, I am so happy, I met you. You have seen god, you have seen god standing on a brick', and then Tukaram says: 'No, no, what is my achievement? You have seen the whole world, you have the entire knowledge of the world. You are greater than me', and so the discussion went on. And then Shakespeare once again affirms that Tuka has described the complete metaphysics of man. At this point, there is the sound of a bell. It appears that Tukaram was very afraid of his wife, who would get very irritated if he didn't come home in time for the meal, and so then Tuka says, 'I may be what you say but I have to go home.'[32] So, who is considered a domestic-world man and who is more spiritual? This is Vinda Karandikar. In my own times a fellow poet conceiving a poem like this—this is a great thought for me.

(The discussion went on for another hour ...)

Notes

1. U. R. Ananthamurthy, 'Ooru and the World' [2006], translated from the Kannada by Bageshree S., in *Multiple City: Writings on Bangalore*, edited by Aditi De (Delhi: Penguin Books, 2008), 63–7.

2. *Rujuvathu: Selected Essays of U R Ananthamurthy*, edited and with an introduction by N. Manu Chakravarthy (Bengaluru: Prism Books, 2014).

3. U. R. Ananthamurthy, *Samskara: A Rite for a Dead Man* [1996], translated by A. K. Ramanujan (2nd ed., Delhi: Oxford University Press, 1979);

for a translation by Narayan Hegde of 'Suryana Kudure', see N. Manu Chakravarthy, *U. R. Ananthamurthy Omnibus* (Gurgaon: Arvind Kumar Publishers, 2008), 138–62.

4. See *Rujuvathu*, 187–211, especially 197.

5. For a lengthier introduction to Nandy's world view, see *Dissenting Knowledges, Open Futures: The Multiple Selves and Strange Destinations of Ashis Nandy*, edited by Vinay Lal (2nd ed., Delhi: Oxford University Press, 2013). Christine Deftereos, *Ashis Nandy and Cultural Politics of Selfhood* (New Delhi: Sage Publications, 2013), is the first full-length study of Nandy's writings.

6. S. Anand, 'The Nandy Bully', *Outlook* (11 February 2013), available at: http://www.outlookindia.com/article/The-Nandy-Bully/283765 (accessed 27 March 2015).

7. Ashis Nandy, *Regimes of Narcissism, Regimes of Despair* (New Delhi: Oxford University Press, 2013), 197.

8. Ananthamurthy served as vice chancellor of Mahatma Gandhi University, Kottayam, Kerala, from 1987 to 1991. He was also chancellor of the Central University of Karnataka, established in 2009, from 2012 until his death in August 2014.

9. Ramana Maharshi (1879–1950) is generally viewed as among the greatest figures in the modern history of Indian spirituality. He is commonly characterized as an Advaitin, but the following conversation, recorded by one of his disciples in the 1930s, suggests why Ramana would most likely have disavowed such a description:

> Devotee: Does Sri Bhagavan advocate *advaita*?
>
> Ramana Maharshi: *Dvaita* [dualism] and *advaita* [non-dualism] are relative terms. They are based on the sense of duality. The Self is as it is. There is neither dvaita nor advaita. I am That I Am. Simple Being is the Self.

See Munagala Venkataramiah, *Talks with Sri Ramana Maharshi: On Realizing Abiding Peace and Happiness* (reprint ed., Thiruvanamallai: Sri Ramanasramam, 2013).

10. Gandhi and Narayana Guru met only once in March 1925, on the occasion of the Vaikom [Vykom] satyagraha, at the residence of A. K. Govindadas near the Guru's ashram at Sivagiri in Varkala, Kerala. Most of Gandhi's biographers have had little to say about their encounter; a notable exception is Joseph Lelyveld, who recounts their meeting in *Great Soul: Mahatma Gandhi and His Struggle with India* (New York: Alfred Knopf, 2011), 191–2. The editor's preface to this volume offers a somewhat more detailed account of their encounter and the modes in which one might interpret it.

11. Portions of the conversation are reported in M. K. Sanoo, *Narayana Guru: A Biography*, translated by Madhavan Ayyappath (Bombay: Bharatiya Vidya Bhavan, 1978), 188–9.

12. The Kerala Science Literature Movement came into existence five decades ago and seeks to bring science to the people, enabling them to use science as a tool of social revolution [see www.kssp.in, a bilingual site in Malayalam and English]. The movement has aimed at making available scientific literature in Malayalam and spreading awareness of scientific thinking. Its relationship to the masses has not yet been fully analysed: though the idea that scientific creativity and experimentation are not the preserve of elites is of course laudable, some within the movement, inspired by the ideas of scientific communism, are also moved by the notion that the Indian masses are especially superstitious. Another similar movement, which originated in Chennai in the early 1980s but has since generated autonomous branches in a number of Indian cities, including Varanasi, is the Patriotic and People-Oriented Science and Technology (PPST) movement.

13. The reference here is to Jnaneshvar, the thirteenth-century *bhakta* and poet who is credited as the founder of Marathi literature; his two-volume commentary on the Bhagavad Gita, the *Jnaneshvari*, written when the author was but twenty years old, is one of the classics of Indian philosophical and devotional literature.

14. In *Ideas of Good and Evil* (3rd ed., London: A. Bullen, 1907), William Butler Yeats described Blake as a 'too literal realist of imagination, as others are of nature'. Blake was keen that poetry and the visual arts depict symbols in their natural state.

15. Hegel has been pronounced as the father of modern racism in a number of works, among them Karl Popper's *The Open Society and Its Enemies* (Princeton: Princeton University Press, 1950). However, though the racism of Kant and Hegel has been discussed here and there in the literature over the last several decades, only now do we witness more systematic attempts to grapple with the question of race in their works. See, for example, Jonn M. Millensen, ed. and trans., *Kant and the Concept of Race: Late Eighteenth-Century Writings* (New York: SUNY Press, 2013); Robert Bernasconi, ed., *Race: Blackwell Readings in Continental Philosophy* (Oxford: Basil Blackwell, 2001); and Robert Bernasconi and Sybol Cook, eds, *Race and Racism in Continental Philosophy* (Bloomington, Indiana: Indiana University Press, 2003).

16. The Sanskrit sources for the story of Shankara's encounter with the Chandala are ably described by Govind Chandra Pande, *Life and Thought of Sankaracarya* (Delhi: Motilal Banarsidass, 1994). The gloss on this

story by a contemporary Indian philosopher, S. Radhakrishnan, is of some interest: 'There is a story that when Sankara, in spite of his non-dualism, asked an outcaste to clear the way for him, the outcast who was God himself asked: "Do you wish my body to leave your body, or my spirit to leave your spirit?" If democracy is to be seriously implemented, then caste and untouchability must go.' See his *The Brahma Sutra* (London: George Allen & Unwin Ltd, 1960), 163.

17. Many such stories have been told about Shankara, his disciples, and the play on *maya*. A. K. Ramanujan, a revered teacher and interpreter of Indian literature, and perhaps the world's foremost authority on Indian folktales, was himself extremely adept at telling stories. He says of one of the teachers of Shankara's school that he had 'convinced his disciples that the world was an illusion, only the transcendent was real. They were convinced; they were dazzled. Just then a mad elephant rushed into their midst, uprooting trees, wreaking havoc. The teacher was the first to see it, and he got up in a hurry and began to run for his life. The disciples, still in a daze, called out to him, "*guruji, guruji*, all this is *maya*, the elephant is only *maya*! Don't run!" The guru, not stopping for a second, said, "It's true. The elephant is *maya*. But my running away is also *maya*," and he ran away'. See 'Where Mirrors are Windows: Towards an Anthology of Reflections', in *The Collected Essays of A. K. Ramanujan*, edited by Vinay Dharwadker (Delhi: Oxford University Press, 1999), 32–3.

18. The 'Bhaja Govindam' is an eighth-century composition that, even as it may be viewed as the summation of Shankara's adherence to Advaita Vedanta, also suggests that he himself abided by the *bhakti marga* [the path of devotion to God]. It enjoins the spiritual aspirant to worship Govinda (*bhajagovindam bhajagovindam/govindam bhajamudhamate*), but this is followed at once by an almost impatient admonition: 'Oh fool! The rules of grammar will not save you at the time of your death' (*samprāpte sannihite kāle/nahi nahi raksati dukrakarane*). The spiritual aspirant of this story is savaged as a 'fool' (*mudhamate*): as described by T. M. P. Mahadevan, the bhajan is likely to have been occasioned by Shankara's chance meeting in Varanasi with an aged scholar and venerable pandit who was teaching the rules of Sanskrit grammar to his pupils by rote, whereupon Shankara advised him not to waste time on arcane rules of grammar and be focused rather on the direct experience of God. See his *The Hymns of Sankaracarya* (Delhi: Motilal Banarsidass, 2002), 33.

19. Nandy has argued this point in various ways over the course of the last three decades. One of his clearest and most succinct articulations of this argument is to be found in his highly influential but controversial essay,

'The Politics of Secularism and the Recovery of Religious Tolerance' (1990), which commences with the following statement: 'A significant aspect of post-colonial structures of knowledge in the third world is a peculiar form of imperialism of categories. Under such imperialism a conceptual domain is sometimes hegemonized so effectively by a concept produced and honed in the West that the original domain vanishes from our awareness. Intellect and intelligence become IQ, the oral cultures become the cultures of the primitive or the preliterate, the oppressed become the proletariat, social change becomes development.' See *Mirrors of Violence: Communities, Riots and Survivors in South Asia*, edited by Veena Das (Delhi: Oxford University Press, 1990), 69. For a more full-blown discussion of the 'imperialism of categories' in a related idiom, see Vinay Lal, *Empire of Knowledge: Culture and Plurality in the Global Economy* (London: Pluto Press, 2002).

20. For a similarly withering critique of the ideology of 'development', see Majid Rahnema, 'Development', in *The Future of Knowledge and Culture: A Dictionary for the 21st Century*, eds Vinay Lal and Ashis Nandy (Delhi: Penguin Viking, 2004), 71–7.

21. Sarvodaya is 'the welfare of all', and is sometimes translated as 'universal uplift'; the idea is associated with Gandhi, who coined the term when he rendered John Ruskin's *Unto This Last* into Gujarati, and later with Vinoba Bhave, among others. Gandhi has described in his *Autobiography*, translated by Mahadev Desai (2nd ed., Ahmedabad: Navajivan Publishing House, 1940 [1927]), 220–1, how he came upon Ruskin's book and what he understood by the teachings that he rendered with the term sarvo-daya: the good of the individual is contained in the good of all; the labour of the barber, teacher, lawyer, farmer, or indeed anyone else has equal value; and 'a life of labour, i.e., the life of the tiller of the soil and the handicraftsman is the life worth living'.

22. The point is well taken and not commonly realized. Consider, for example, this description of how Zyklon B came to be used as the preferred instrument of killing at Auschwitz: 'In June 1941 Himmler ordered [Rudolf] Hess to prepare to use Auschwitz for the Final Solution of the Jewish problem. Instead of inefficient carbon monoxide, Hess introduced a pesticide known as Zyklon B, which was made under license from I. G. Farben by two German firms, Tesch und Stabenow of Hamburg and EGESCH of Dessau, an I. G. Farben affiliate. On 3 September 1941, the gas was first tried out on nine hundred prisoners, most of whom were Russian prisoners of war. The experiment proved to be a "success". Thereafter Zyklon B was used to kill Jews for a period of thirty-four months. Estimates concerning the number of Jews

killed at Auschwitz vary from 1 million to 2.5 million, with the lower figures being the more likely.' See Richard L. Rubinstein and John K. Roth, *Approaches to Auschwitz: The Holocaust and Its Legacy* (Atlanta: John Knox Press, 1987), 154. This account correctly credits Hess with having 'introduced' Zyklon B at Auschwitz but we are none the wiser about its invention. A scholarly article about German chemical warfare adds other details about Zyklon B's use as a pesticide and trial runs, so to speak, on Soviet prisoners of war, but it similarly throws no light on its inventor. See Edmund P Russell III, '"Speaking of Annihilation": Mobilizing for War Against Human and Insect Enemies, 1914–1945', *The Journal of American History* 82, no. 4 (March 1996): 1505–29.

23. The word 'Napalm' is derived from naphthenic acid and palmitic acid; these two constituents of a gelling agent, in combination with petroleum, produce an incendiary device that generates heat of between 800 and 1200 degrees Celsius, causing severe burns, asphyxiation, and death. Its most extensive use, until the Americans virtually made the Vietnam war synonymous with Napalm, was in the fire-bombing of Japanese cities in World War II, and the most enthusiastic advocate of Napalm bombing was the sadistic American general, Curtis LeMay.

24. A recent scholarly article describes the discovery of Napalm as part of the legacy of Louis Fieser, an organic chemist at Harvard who is described as having done fundamental research on steroids, cancer prevention, and much else. Like many other American scientists, he was willing, during World War II, to lend his expertise to research that might help produce a more deadly arsenal of weapons. See Dieter Lenoir and Thomas T. Tidwell, 'Louis Fieser: An Organic Chemist in Peace and War', *European Journal of Organic Chemistry* 4 (February 2009): 481–91. Nandy's point, of course, is scarcely contradicted by this information: we all recognize Fleming as the inventor of penicillin, but who has heard the names of those associated with the invention of Zykon B or Napalm?

25. The ashram of Sree Narayana Guru: most of the sessions at the conference were open to the wider public and to the residents of the ashram.

26. The reference here is to a series of articles by Perry Anderson on the partition of India, Gandhi, Nehru, and Ambedkar that first appeared in the *London Review of Books* and were collected together as *The Indian Ideology* (Delhi: Three Essays Collective; London: Verso, 2013). Anderson is not even remotely a specialist on India, but his review essays on some dozen or two dozen books on history and politics in mid-twentieth century India are written with breathtaking nonchalance and confidence, as though he had been a student of Indian history his entire life. If an

Indian scholar had dared to piece together an overarching argument from say some ten books on Churchill, Britain's ignominious treatment of its colonies, and its cowardly resort to partition—in Ireland, India, Cyprus, and Palestine—to 'resolve' problems largely of its own making, and offered the conclusion that Britain's genocidal impulse is clearly to be seen in the Bengal famine of 1943, he or she would of course have at once been ruled out of hand. But it is precisely a similar tenor of argument that is to be encountered in Anderson's appraisal, where he takes upon himself the task of doing what Indians are evidently incapable of doing, namely brutally eviscerating the halo that has been placed around Gandhi, Nehru, and Indian secularism. From being a scholar of English history and Marxism, Anderson has over the years embraced nearly the entire world as his own intellectual fiefdom: this, too, is an entitlement from birth of the Western scholar, who as he advances in years feels capable of taking on the world. There is another imperialism at work here, but the Western scholar who is self-avowedly a Marxist is perhaps the least capable of that insight. The English historian, in particular, is seldom able to abandon the legacy of the empire on which the sun never set: witness, for example, the cavalier histories of Niall Ferguson.

27. Salman Rushdie and Elizabeth West, eds, *Mirrorwork: 50 Years of Indian Writing 1947–1997* (London: Picador, 1997).

28. Purandara Dasa (1484–1564) was a major composer of Carnatic music and an itinerant poet-saint who lived in the heyday of the Vijayanagar empire. He remains largely unknown to the English-speaking world; for a sampling of his songs, see William J. Jackson, *Songs of Three Great South Indian Saints* (Delhi: Oxford University Press, 1998).

29. In his lectures on the philosophy of history, Hegel gave it as his view that the Orient represented the childhood of man; the mind was most developed in Europe, reaching its apotheosis in Germany. Puranadara Dasa's anti-Hegelianism informs what might otherwise appear as obscure in his poem, 'Uttama Prabhutwa lolalotte'. Uttama Prabhutwa signifies great governance or statehood; 'lolalotte', on the other hand, is a term used by children to signify something that is bereft of meaning, something like nonsense verse. By placing 'lolalotte' in apposition to 'uttama prabhutwa', Purandara Dasa sought to convey his view that most claims to good government or more broadly the hegemony of the state were meaningless, just as bereft of meaning as 'lolalotte'.

30. Ramchandra Gandhi (1937–2007) was an Indian philosopher, besides being a friend of Nandy, Ananthamurthy, and several of the other participants in the Cochin conference. Ramu, as he was known affectionately to his friends, gathered around him students of Advaita, sojourners in truth,

and fellow explorers of India's traditions of philosophical enquiry as they pondered the ideas of modern-day figures such as Gandhi, Aurobindo, Vivekananda, Ramakrishna, and, in particular, Ramana Maharshi.

31. Govind Vinayak Karandikar, more commonly known as Vinda Karandikar (1918–2010), a Marathi poet, critic, and translator of great eminence, was conferred the Jnanpith award, the highest literary honour bestowed upon a writer in India, in 2003.

32. Dilip Chitre, Vinda Karandikar's equally eminent contemporary as (to use the old expression) a man of letters, gave it as his view that Tukaram was to Marathi what Shakespeare was to English. The poem in question is called 'To see Tukaram, Shakespeare Came Over', and its concluding lines run thus:

> Shakespeare said, 'Why!, Because of your words,
> that "Inexpressible" itself, played in the soil'
>
> Tuka said, 'My friend, in vain is all word-play.
> Everyone has to go, his separate way.
> On different ways, there are different thorns;
> but along with the thorns, one meets Him again.
> ... Now, listen, listen, there tolls the temple bell;
> the shrew at home: is waiting...'

See *The Sacred Heresy: Selected Poems of Vinda Karandikar*, translated from the Marathi by G. V. Karandikar and edited by Dilip Chitre (New Delhi: Sahitya Akademi, 1998).

5

'A MARRIAGE MADE IN HEAVEN'?
How Metaphysics Transforms Politics:
A Case Study[1]

JULIUS LIPNER

In an article entitled 'Whose Imagined Community?', Partha Chatterjee makes the following comment:

> In my reading, anti-colonial nationalism creates its own domain of sovereignty within colonial society well before it begins its political battle with the imperial power. It does this by dividing the world of social institutions and practices into two domains—the material and the spiritual. The material is the domain of the 'outside', of the economy and of statecraft, of science and technology, a domain where the West had proved its superiority and the East had succumbed.... The spiritual, on the other hand, is an 'inner' domain bearing the 'essential' marks of cultural identity. The greater one's success in imitating Western skills in the material domain, therefore, the greater the need to preserve the distinctiveness of one's spiritual culture. This formula is, I think, a fundamental feature of anti-colonial nationalisms in Asia and Africa.[2]

Whether this idea applies as a generalization is not clear to me, but, remarkably, it was anticipated with respect to the Indian situation in an important Bengali text written towards the end of the nineteenth century. At the end of Bankim Chatterji's famous religio-political novel, *Ānandamaṭh* (first published serially from 1881–2, and then in book-form, with significant changes, in 1882), the mysterious Healer is giving advice to the sage Satyānanda, who is disheartened at the apparent failure of his campaign to drive out the foreigner, in effect, the British, from his land.

'The true Hindu rule of life (*prakṛtahindudharma*)', declares the Healer,

> is based on knowledge, not on action. And this knowledge is of two kinds—outward and inward (*bahirbiṣayak o antarbiṣayak*). The inward knowledge is the chief part of the Eternal Code (*sanātandharma*), but unless the outward knowledge arises first, the inward cannot arise.... For a long time now the outward knowledge has been lost in this land, and so the true Eternal Code has been lost too. If one wishes to reinstate this Code, one must make known the outward knowledge first. Because the outward knowledge no longer exists in this land ... we must bring in the outward knowledge from another country. The English are very knowledgeable in the outward knowledge, and they're very good at instructing people. Therefore we'll make them king. And when by this teaching our people are well instructed about external things, they'll be ready to understand the inner. Then no longer will there be any obstacles to spreading the Eternal Code, and the true Code will shine forth by itself again.[3]

The parallel between the two statements is clear: Partha Chatterjee's material or 'outside' empirical domain and Bankim Chatterji's 'outward knowledge' on the one hand, and Partha Chatterjee's spiritual or 'inner' domain and Bankim Chatterji's 'inner knowledge', which enshrines the distinctive Eternal Code of the Hindus, on the other. In both cases, the former domain acts as a foil for the latter, and this results in the precipitation of patriotic, political action. Or we can put it differently: in the colonial metanarrative represented here, it is the metaphysical that underlies and catalyses the political (where by 'metaphysical' is meant a sphere or undergirding reality that is essentially trans-empirical). In this study, I wish to analyse how this dynamic was played out in one important modern Indian context.

The following statement appeared on 14 June 1908 in an (English) article entitled 'The Bed-Rock of Indian Nationalism – II', in the influential and militant Calcutta weekly, the *Bande Mataram*.

> The different world religions representing different world cultures that have already found a habitation in India will remain here always, form elements of the common national life, and contribute to the evolution of the composite culture of modern India [Christianity and Islam have been mentioned earlier]. The Hindu culture, however, on account of its age and its superior numerical strength, will always form the ground work of this composite Indian culture and civilisation. The dominant note of Hindu culture, its sense of the spiritual and universal, will, therefore, be the peculiar feature of this composite, Indian nationality.
>
> The new movement which seeks to embody the ideals and aspirations of this nationality, is, therefore, an essentially spiritual movement. And the type of spirituality that it seeks to develop is essentially Hindu. Its key-note is the essential unity of God and man.... [T]aken by himself, man is a toy of time, a play-thing in the hands of death; but when viewed in relation to God, he is a spirit, a soul, an *atma*, eternally pure, free, and self-realised, as the Supreme Spirit, the Over-Soul, the *Paramatman* himself.

Politically, a 'majoritarian' view underlies this passage in terms of a metaphysical bias towards the traditional 'Hindu' doctrine of *Advaita* or 'non-duality' that had come progressively to influence the thinking of the Bengali intelligentsia from the early nineteenth century on, largely through the writings of the reformer Rammohan Roy (1772?–1833).[4] As a statement of political intent, this position was to undergo some revision in a more egalitarian vein before it could be endorsed constitutionally some four-and-a-half decades later. Nevertheless, in the passage quoted, the *lakṣaṇas* or marks of Advaitic teaching stand out clearly. Let us note them: the 'essential unity [= *ekatva*] of God [= the Supreme Reality or *Brahman*] and man'; 'man's' dual nature at the empirical level—materially a 'play-thing' of time and death (the chief characteristics of *saṃsāra* or the cycle of rebirth), but spiritually a soul, an *ātman*, ultimately one with the *Paramātman* or 'Supreme Spirit', as—in the well-known Advaitic phrase—'eternally pure, free, and self-realised' [= *nityaśuddha-mukta-buddha*].[5]

Here again, we see a two-tiered conception at work incorporating a reference to a metaphysical realm of spirit manifesting in the empirical realm through a certain type of polity. The relationship between the two realms is described in terms of the doctrine of advaita or underlying non-duality (how this relationship is ultimately resolved is another matter). In traditional Hindu philosophical theology, Advaita became a prominent school of thought among others in a movement called Vedānta that looked mainly to three textual sources for religious inspiration—the Upaniṣads, the *Brahma Sūtra*s and the Bhagavad Gītā.[6]

In the present context, Advaita, variously modified as a precursive doctrine for social and political change, took nearly a century to establish itself as the preferred metaphysics in the minds of such influential Hindu proto-nationalists and nationalists as Swami Vivekananda (1863–1902), Aurobindo Ghose (1872–1950), and M. K. Gandhi (1869–1948). But first it had to undergo an important shift of emphasis at the hands of Bengali social reformers active earlier in Calcutta, the administrative and political hub of British India. The ideal human type for Vedānta in general and Advaita in particular, as endorsed by Advaita's great philosopher-theologian Shankara in the eighth century C.E., is the *saṃnyāsin* or renouncer, who looks askance at socially engaged action, preferring to withdraw from the world. It is Rammohan Roy, however, lauded as the progenitor of social reform and the modernist mind in nineteenth-century Bengal, who is credited with initiating the shift among the Bengali intelligentsia from the renouncer to the (male) 'godly householder' (*brahma-niṣṭha-gṛhastha*) as the ideal human agent for the times. As noted earlier, Rammohan sympathized philosophically with the Advaita world view,[7] but in a tract published in 1826, he defended his new ideal 'using arguments and quotations from Manu which he had already used in previous tracts'.[8] It was the (male) householder, rooted spiritually and gnoseologically in Brahman, contended Rammohan, who was best equipped, socially and ethically, to meet the challenges India faced from the ferment of new ideas pouring in via British rule.

The householder was 'socially' equipped to meet the modern challenges that faced him because he was *in* the world, and therefore committed to it. He had a family to support, and, as likely as not, a business to run or a job to maintain (in such fields of activity as publishing, teaching in schools and colleges, government bureaucracy, and so forth) in the capitalist economy that had begun to flourish under British auspices (we must remember that the ideal householder for Rammohan belonged to the middle-classes—the so-called *bhadralok*). He was compelled to interact and to network. The saṃnyāsin—both the saṃnyāsin of later Advaita as also of Shankara's cogitations—opted out of the hectic mix of relational action that was so constitutive of everyday life, and ideally remained detached from the socially engaged world.

And the householder was 'ethically' primed to engage with modern society because the social engagement of his everyday existence necessarily implied the formulation of a realistic ethic with which to interact with the world. It is here that the ideal of self-denying activity in everyday life (*niṣkāma karma*) promulgated by the Bhagavad Gītā, a text ensconced in Book 6 of the Mahābhārata, and a crucial resource for Vedānta, played its part, not by demanding, in this new interpretation, a complete abandonment of worldly desire or the fruits of action, but by providing the scriptural authority for prioritizing as one's proper dharma (cf. the *sva-dharma* of Gītā 3.35), the public good (= the *lokasaṃgraha* of Gītā 3.25) over and above personal gain. As the discourses of the pioneers of the Tattvabodhini Society in Calcutta in the early nineteenth century declare, there was still scope for concupiscence in marriage and acquisitiveness in business.[9] The Gītā's ideal of *niṣkāma karma* now underpinned an ethic of qualified self-interest. Though this would take time to develop intellectually in bhadralok circles, the idea was that by reinterpreting his 'own *dharma*' (sva-dharma) to mean not so much the particular duties of caste and stage-of-life (the *varṇāśramadharma* of yore), but a new, universal dharma of active, balanced good-will towards all, the householder could fulfil his destiny by being *in* the world, but not *of* it in some worldly, self-serving sense. This crucial, indigenous, insight was Rammohan's original contribution to the new ethic of a modernizing Bengal among the intelligentsia of his times, notwithstanding his open admiration for Jesus as the ethical exemplar for humankind.[10]

At the heart of this combination of Vedāntic metaphysics and the core-ethic of the Gītā lay a revolutionary paradigm that developed in time, both in Bengal and wider afield in the subcontinent, into a blueprint for social, and eventually, political action. This paradigm sought to blend a twofold discipline: (a) in accordance with Vedāntic teaching, a mental *ascesis* that aimed at a progressive dismantling of the unreconstructed 'experienced-self' or *ahaṃkāra* (with its ego-centric image of a grasping, relational 'I') with a view to achieving a new, reconstructed subjectivity that was characterized by a realization of its profound unity with an underlying Higher Self (Paramātman), and (b) an ethical discipline, derived from the Gītā (and, on occasion, also from other authoritative Hindu texts with a similar didactic message), of altruistic outreach that would reinforce this new realization of self, if by 'altruism' is meant acting intentionally for the benefit of some 'other' or the common good, without thereby primarily intending benefit or gain for oneself. This was, I believe, the key context for the resurgence of the Bhagavad Gītā as a spiritual resource among the English-educated elite in the nineteenth century, first in Bengal, and subsequently, in other parts of the subcontinent.

Note that in the eyes of the practitioner, the self of the quotidian 'other' was also to be reappraised concomitantly with the ongoing deconstruction of the practitioner's old sense of self, the overall objective being to arrive at a new perception of subjectivity—for both practitioner and 'other'—that would result in socially and politically regenerative action. How this Vedāntic–ethical model—which I shall dub the 'altruistic model (or paradigm)'—actually translated into social and political action in *fin de siècle* India, at the hands of several key practitioners, we shall enquire into presently.

Let us note first that this model could assume two modes. In what appears to have been its more dramatic mode, the metaphysical component informing the relationship between the spiritual and empirical realms was monistic or Advaitic in character; its chief features have been mentioned above. However, in the apparently less dramatic form of the paradigm, the metaphysical component was still Vedāntic (in that it was couched largely in Upanishadic terms), though here the relationship between the two realms was seen not as Advaitic but as theistic; this relied on an alternative interpretation of the Upaniṣads.

In both cases, the new episteme was at work. In the Advaitic mode, the practitioner sought to rehabilitate his own as well as the

perceived subjectivity of the 'other' in terms of a kenosis of self
that in the final analysis would be based on a realization of non-
duality (or intimate identity—hence 'advaita') between not only all
selves (or *jīvātmans*) but also all differentiated being. This, as we
shall see, could generate a powerful incentive for social and political change. In the case of the theistic mode, the practitioner sought
to reconstitute both his own sense of self and that of the perceived
'other' on the basis of a new relationship between the two that was
informed ideally by an intense awareness of union with a perfect,
provident, and personal God (*Īśvara, saguṇa Brahman*) who indwelt
all reality and whose wish was to bring about the welfare of the
whole cosmos and the divinely appointed end of every stratum
of being.

Both kinds of practitioner invoked an other-regarding ethic as the
means to realize their (neo-)Vedānta-inspired goal, an ethic derived
in some way, as we have noted, from the Gītā (and like-minded texts).
This included control of the senses, a meditative turn of mind, the
dismantling of selfish forms (and norms) of behaviour, and so on—all
accredited features of the *yoga* of action (karma) found in traditional
readings of Hindu ethics. But the new (bhadralok) *karmayogī* was also
encouraged to acquire qualities, in addition to the traditional virtues of
self-control, honesty, truth telling, forbearance, and so on, that would
equip him to meet the fresh challenges taking shape, socially, eco-
nomically, and politically, under an increasingly consolidated British
paramountcy—qualities such as the acquisition of business acumen,
a moderated desire for economic success, and a sense of one's social
and economic worth. And both kinds of practitioner regarded the
(godly and male) householder (*gṛhastha*) as the individual best suited
to accomplish this, for it was the householder, and not the renouncer,
who clearly wielded the most influence in the diverse social contexts
of the times.

There was a strong element of patriarchy to this turn of mind, no
doubt; but it called for an altruistic ethic nonetheless in so far as the
prime objective was to seek the common good, even at the expense
of serving one's personal interests. Thus, whether the reconstruction
of the social other was to be done in the more philosophically selfless terms of Advaita or in terms of a more expansive sense of self
as recommended by the theistic option, the altruistic paradigm came

into play in both cases. The old order was passing away and a new had to be devised. No doubt too, this would be achieved through a conceptual dialogue with Western ideas, but the fundamental vehicle of reform would be indigenous, namely what we have called the altruistic paradigm, and it is to the diverse enactment of this paradigm that we now turn.

Post-Rammohan, one can detect how this model was being informed conceptually, especially with regard to its theistic version, in a remarkable series of discourses that have been preserved for posterity in a booklet entitled *Sabhyadiger Baktṛtā* ('Members' Addresses'), published by the Tattvabodhini Sabha (or Society, founded in 1839 by Debendranath Tagore, 1817–1905) in Calcutta in 1841.[11] 'These discourses (*vaktṛtā*) offer us a precious glimpse at the articulation of modern Vedānta in the decade after Rammohan Roy's death, when the task of reinterpreting Vedānta for the modern era was only just getting under way.'[12] The following passages (in my translation) give a brief flavour of the ideas that were being disseminated.

True worship (*sākṣātupāsanā*) of Brahman arises from control of the senses and from accepting the teaching of the Vedic and Vedāntic scriptures, because it is only through this kind of worship that Brahman is known and liberation achieved.... The merciful Lord (*dayābānparameśvar*) does not create anything in vain. Living beings (*jīb*) arise because desire (*kām*) was created; humans protect themselves from each other because anger (*krodh*) was created; creatures (*prajārā*) occupy themselves in doing their proper tasks because fear was created; wives, children, friends and relatives are cared for because infatuation (or attachment, *moha*) was created, and so on: if you consider things in this light you will realize that the senses lie at the root of carrying out worldly living (*saṃsār-nirbbāha*). And the opposing virtues of modesty, forbearance (*kṣamā*) and so forth were created to check an excess of desire, anger and so on.

Therefore, most respected members, spend your whole lives in fostering forbearance, sincerity, kindness, righteousness (*dharma*), truth and so on, in behaving correctly by controlling desire, anger, greed,[13] attachment, pride etc., and in seeking out the true teaching of the Vedānta and other scriptures; by this you will attain happiness in this life and final liberation in the next (from the First Address).... In so

far as there is no desisting from hankering after things, life continues
apace. Farmers and skilled workers, hoping for greater wealth, and
having produced a great deal of the finest foodstuffs, fruits and so
forth on the one hand, as well as various kinds of the most splendid
clothing on the other, duly dispatch these to various lands through
merchants themselves desirous of greater riches, the result being that
we sit here in this one place, enjoying to our great satisfaction so many
kinds of things arriving from so many countries.... And from among
such individuals who benefit the country by attaining wealth, riches,
fame and so on, they are the wise and happy ones who seek the wealth
and riches solely for the benefit of the country (from the Eleventh
Address).[14]

A pragmatic ethic, it is true, but also professedly an other-regarding
one through a reformulation in new circumstances of what was perceived to be the wisdom of the past (namely the Vedānta). The 'bells
and smells' of the liturgy of image-worship (pauttalikpūjā) of the time
of the various sects, and those aspects of this liturgy's self-serving,
supplicatory ethic, were to be abandoned in favour of a purified faith
and a puritan ethic that looked to the greater good. And to follow this
course of action, both one's own self and that of the other had to be
related afresh. Thus, to avoid lusting after the wives of others, the latter were to be viewed now as one's mother, or sister, or daughter; one's
business rival was also, in this new scheme of things, one's brother;
the man or woman in the street (irrespective of social status) was also
one's compatriot, and so on. On the basis of this newly constituted,
self-effacing conception of an enlarged human family, a nation was
now in the making, inchoately at this stage no doubt, but in so far
as the process had begun, also inexorably; there could be no turning
back.

A watershed text in this regard, mainly but not only for Brahmo
theists, was Debendranath Tagore's Brahmo Dharma, published in
1850 as a treatise in two parts, comprising 295 Sanskrit verses in all,
and accompanied by a commentary prepared by the author himself
in Bengali. Part I was more metaphysical in character and treated of
the nature of the divine being, while Part II dealt mainly with how
the enlightened householder should live his life.[15] We can give no
more than a glimpse into Debendranath's thinking in this text, but on
the Supreme Being that produces, sustains, and indwells all finite

being, Debendranath could write in his Bengali commentary as follows:

> The Supreme Godhead is but one (*parabrahma ek-mātra*). He is motionless, yet He is faster than the mind. None of the senses can apprehend that Supreme Godhead who continues to elude them (*agragāmī*) [vr. 36 of the text as a whole, or vr. 2 of Part I, Chapter 5].... He is hard to know; having entered secretly into every being, He abides in the soul (*ātmāte*), and dwelling in [its] most inaccessible places, becomes its intimate companion (*nityahayen*) [vr. 52 of the text as a whole, or vr. 5 of Part I, Chapter 7].... Just as the birds protect their young by covering them with their wings, and so safeguard them from various dangers, even so is this whole world covered and pervaded by the Supreme Lord (*parameśvar*), and constantly safeguarded. He is the Great King of the world, our Father, Protector (*pātā*) and Friend. His rule (*śāsan*) extends in all directions, and his love (*prem*) is manifest everywhere [vr. 35 of the text as a whole, or vr. 1 of Part I, Chapter 5, my translation].

And on the relationship one should cultivate with this deity and the way of life this engenders, Debendranath declares:

> One should not become a renouncer (*sannyāsī*), having abandoned relations with members of one's family, viz. mother, father, brother, sister and wife, children and so on. For these relationships have been instituted by the Gracious Lord (*mangalsvarūpīśvar*). One should not cut them off; one should rather safeguard them by becoming a householder [*gṛhastha*; vr. 159 of the text as a whole, or vr. 2 of Part II, Chapter 1].... One's older brother is like one's father, the wife and son are like one's own body (*śarīr*), one's servants are like one's own shadow, and one's daughter is most deserving of kindness. For this reason, even if provoked by these individuals, one should not get angry, but should rather always bear up with patience [cf. vr. 164 of the text as a whole, or vr. 7 of Part II, Chapter 1].... Living in a forest or abandoning speech is not the mark of a sage (*muni*). Ponder over what concerns yourself (*āpanār biṣay*) in private: 'Who am I?', 'What is my relationship with this body?', 'What is my relationship with this world?', 'Where have I come from?'.... 'For what reason do I abide here?', 'Where will I go in the end?' [cf. vr. 186 of the text as a whole, or vr. 2 of Part II, Chapter 4].... If one is devoted to God with all one's heart (*sarbāntaḥkaraṇe*), one becomes a friend to oneself [cf. vr. 195 of the text as a whole, or vr. 11 of Part II, Chapter 4]....

After having fully satisfied in the appropriate way the needs of all
the dependents to whom one is obligated, one should be charitable
to (*dān karibek*) the stricken and distressed needy and suffering. Nor
should one exclude oneself from pleasures and enjoyments (*bhog-
suke*) ... And envy no one [cf. vr. 228 of the text as a whole, or vr. 1 of
Part II, Chapter 9].... Regard the wife of another as your mother....
And regard everyone else with the same love (*prīti*) with which you
love yourself [cf. vr. 252 of the text as a whole, or vr. 8 of Part II,
Chapter 11].[16]

One could quote from the Bengali commentary of many more verses,
but perhaps enough has been done to give an accurate idea of what
Debendranath had in mind in this important work. The Sanskrit
verses in the treatise as a whole, eclectically selected by Debendranath
to give guidance to the practitioner and on which he provides his
Bengali commentary, were gleaned from a variety of indigenous texts;
these include the authoritative Vedāntic Upaniṣads (the principal
source for Part I), the Mahābhārata (including the Gītā), the Manu
Smṛti, and a number of other *smṛti* works.[17] It is worth observing
that though in today's terms Debendranath's instructions may be
regarded as patriarchal, sexist, and very 'bourgeois' indeed, in the
Hindu context of the times, his recommendations were both socially
and religiously innovative in that they purported to transcend caste
and sectarian differences; equally important, it was emphasized that
they derived from Hindu tradition itself. All Debendranath claimed
to do was to so collate and order the texts that they could speak
for themselves (with a little help from his commentary). In the event,
they required the cultivation of a new perspective of 'the other' in
terms of an ethical magnanimity that *explicitly* and, to all intents
and purposes, coherently, placed the greater good of the wider community first. To accomplish this, if it was not necessary to seek to
dissolve the individuated self (jīvātman) in terms of a 'thin subjectivity', namely a reconstituted awareness of identity with the 'other'
as required by Advaita, the practitioner was certainly called upon to
radically reassess everyday I-consciousness in favour of a 'thicker' and
still-transparent subjectivity that realized its integrated oneness with
the Supreme Lord, who was a friend, helper, and protector, within a
context of active benevolence towards all. And the ideal practitioner in
this scheme of things was no longer the renouncer, but in the wake of

Rammohan's activist paradigm-shift, the self-denying (male) house-holder. This householder now became the disciplined practitioner or karmayogī par excellence (though it was only later, when Bankim Chatterji [1838–94], the pioneering novelist and social commentator, was at his creative peak, that this particular term, now enlarged by Bankim to include women, came into its own[18]). It was this newly envisaged paradigm, first broached in the discourses of the early members of the Tattvabodhini Sabha and then developed further in Debendranath's *Brahmo Dharma*, that inspired such reformist think-ers as Keshab Chandra Sen and Aksay Kumar Dutt to promulgate their particular brands of social and other agency.[19]

As the nationalist movement gathered momentum in the latter half of the nineteenth century, the altruistic paradigm was increas-ingly implemented in the political context. It was Bankim again who made a special contribution in this regard by helping embed the para-digm, with particular emphasis on its theistic form, especially in the educated Bengali consciousness, not least through the ideology of his last three novels, *Ānandamaṭh*, *Debīcaudhurāṇī*, and *Sītārām* (all pub-lished within the last decade or so of his life). As is well known, the need for a cultivated discipline of self-denial (*anuśilan*), as endorsed by the Gītā, that could work in the service of the common good, espe-cially to alleviate the sufferings of the oppressed and needy, is a salient theme in one way or another in each of these stirring narratives. And emblematic of the consciousness that grew with this discipline was the famous hymn, *Bande Mātaram* ('I revere the Mother'), which was inserted into the first of these novels, *Ānandamaṭh*, and which gave the militant journal from which we quoted towards the beginning of this essay its name.[20] The hymn helped to both iconize and politi-cize the land—in the first instance, the land of Bengal, but in due course, the 'Motherland' that was to become the political entity that was India. Both geographical configurations were to be served by patriots, in terms of a self-denying ethic that would defend the indig-enous community from hostile intent.

Let me state at this juncture that I am not interested in pursuing here the theological implications of the altruistic paradigm. There may well be a Supreme Reality, inherently *saguṇa* or *nirguṇa*, namely with or without essential attributes—call it Brahman or what you will—that underlies the multiplicity of this world, and with which union in one form or another is our ultimate spiritual end. In regard to this, for our purposes I maintain what has been described by others as a 'pragmatic agnosticism'. I am interested, rather, in what I call the 'functional' or 'instrumental metaphysics' of the paradigm, namely its capacity to generate a certain course of action in and for the intended welfare of the quotidian world.

In a fairly recent work,[21] Andrew Sartori has argued, in a section entitled 'The National Church', that throughout the nineteenth century in England there was a common concern among various intellectuals who were national figures (for example, John Seeley, John Henry Newman) to discern the role of religion through institutional structures such as the Anglican Church, as essential for reasserting—in the face of counterblasts by Dissenters of one sort or another—'the integrative social role of the Visible Church as the embodiment of human community and the antithesis of atomic individualism'.[22] In Britain, this had implications for creating a fresh perspective on what the nation, as a collective with a particular history, might be. The body politic, now animated by the solidarities and spiritual guidance of institutional religion, was to become a reflection—if not an extension—of the anti-secularist dimension of the Church, and in the process incorporate the advances of science which, if divorced from the leavening agency of the Church, tended towards a dangerous, crass, and undercutting materialism. If aligned, however, with the social project of the Church, science would take its rightful place as a bulwark of true religion.

Nineteenth-century Hinduism did not have an institutional, centralizing counterpart to this Visible Church. What acted significantly in this role, however, for Hindu India, first in nineteenth-century Bengal, and then in other segments of the subcontinent—and this is one of the main propositions of this essay—is what I have dubbed the altruistic paradigm. It was this paradigm, deployed theistically or Advaitically, that functioned analogously to the Visible Church of England, as an important agent for bringing about integrative change in Indian (admittedly, mainly Hindu) society.

As the nineteenth century progressed, and one social or political activist after another embraced the paradigm and implemented it according to circumstances of time and context, the paradigm was able to engender a variety of fresh applications among the Hindu elite. This it could do in the main for two reasons: (*a*) it had a spiritual/religious (namely Vedāntic) framework that was pliable enough to evoke, through its various adaptations, (*b*) *indigenous* cultural associations in terms of recognizable patterns of thought and action. In other words, both structurally and psychologically, the paradigm had historical and cultural roots in what came to be formulated as a (neo)-Hindu identity. Following are three salient examples, from later in the century in contrast to our earlier illustrations, which clearly had far-reaching effects, socially and/or politically.

We start with the Bengali, Swami Vivekananda (1863–1902), whose influence was seen as emanating chiefly from the operational centre of British rule at the time, namely Calcutta, notwithstanding his travels in India and abroad. It is uncontroversial to say, I think, that Vivekananda is acknowledged as one of the architects of the neo-Hinduism that emerged to confront the modernist challenges of the late nineteenth century.[23] Equally well known is the fact that Vivekananda professed an Advaitic outlook to found his social and proto-political agenda. At the core of this agenda was an ethic that Vivekananda derived from the famous Upanishadic dictum, *tat tvam asi* ('That you are'; cf. the *Chāndogya Upaniṣad* 6.12.1-3, and so on). Here, by means of a number of illustrations, the sage Uddālaka Āruṇi gives instruction to his son Śvetaketu about the inner, sustaining Self of all being, concluding again and again with the declaration, '*tat tvam asi, śvetaketo*', 'That you are, Śvetaketu'. Vedāntins have traditionally read this apparent identity-statement in various ways. Vivekananda adopted an Advaitic or non-dual interpretation; what is interesting is the way he finds a social ethic in Uddālaka's teaching. He says,

> Behind everything the same divinity is existing, and out of this comes the basis of morality. Do not injure another. Love everyone as your own self, because the whole universe is one. In injuring another, I am injuring myself; in loving another, I am loving myself. From this also springs that principle of Advaita morality which has been summed up in one word – self-abnegation.[24]

Again,

> There are moments when every man feels that he is one with the universe, and he rushes forth to express it, whether he knows it or not. This expression of oneness is what we call love and sympathy, and it

is the basis of all our ethics and morality. This is summed up in the
Vedanta philosophy by the celebrated aphorism, Tat Tvam Asi, 'Thou
art That'. To every man, this is taught: Thou art one with this Universal
Being, and, as such, every soul that exists is your soul; and every body
that exists is your body; and in hurting anyone, you hurt yourself, in
loving anyone, you love yourself.[25]

This is a clear example of the Advaitic application of the altruistic
paradigm: through the specificity of the decidedly Hindu tat tvam asi
ethic, the practitioner is encouraged to identify at the deepest level
of self with the other, so as to effect, by appropriate selfless action
(vide the use of 'self-abnegation' at the end of the first passage), a
new order of society that by implication transcends the discriminative
differences of caste, gender, and other divisive circumstance. In its
traditional Vedāntic interpretation, this dictum had no reference to
an engagement with society—a social ethic—that stressed the cultivation of a common humanity; rather, it was invariably interpreted to
reveal how the individual's ātman or core-self was related existentially
to the Supreme Self or underlying ground of all being. Vivekananda,
however, interpreted the dictum as a summons that would inspire its
hearers to unite for a common cause that liberated the whole collective from oppression, or rather the multiple oppressions—cultural,
religious, political—of British rule. This goal was to be achieved in
this world rather than in some future utopia. The method that would
bring this about—Vivekananda's newly formulated discipline of yoga
with its attendant practices (articulated through a dialogue with western ideas of equality, progress, secularism, rationality, science, and so
on)—we cannot delve into here. Certain it was that Vivekananda in
his conception of religion wished to depart from a spirituality that was
immersed in doctrines and creeds, that could not come to terms with
the discoveries of modern science, and that incorporated an idea of
society that made it a function of traditional socio-religious practices
(for example, caste and sectarianism) to such an extent that it fell easy
prey to modern (European) positivist and materialist critiques.[26] Only
the selfless mentality generated by the neo-Advaita he formulated
could act as the antidote, for it was an Advaita that set one free from
the thrall to the petty ego of everyday life and from the traditional
practices of varṇāśrama dharma. But to say this is to affirm that the
altruistic paradigm was to be adhered to in a new form.

Our second example is taken from the life of M. K. Gandhi, who, this time for overtly political reasons, brought the same paradigm to bear through his doctrines of *ahiṃsā* (non-violence) and *satyāgraha* or 'truth-force'. S. K. Saxena describes the thinking behind the Mahātmā's plan of action well, clearly highlighting its Advaitic rationale:

> To suffer is to fraternize. True, the ego here ceases to serve as a foothold. But the loss is at once a release; and the 'sufferer' feels anchored and enriched in his realized identity with others.... [S]o far as we are really identical in being, when anyone is purified through prayerful suffering the good in others too tends freely to surface.[27]

In other words, the practitioner of this new politics is to efface the ego within the embrace of a greater self through a kind of Advaitic vision that encompasses society as a whole. This can be accomplished through a disciplined solidarity that strips the other—especially the rejected other (for example, the 'untouchable')—of contingent differences such as caste, gender, and so forth. It was this rationale— Gandhi's belief in and felt identity with humanity's universal oneness, irrespective of creed, gender, or ethnicity—that fuelled his altruistic campaigns for Indian *svaraj,* whether by means of fasting, marches, or other forms of nation-building activity. So he could say: 'I believe in *advaita.* I believe in the essential unity of man and for that matter of all that lives. Therefore I believe that if one man gains spiritually, the whole world gains with him and, if one man falls, the whole world falls to that extent.'[28] And again: 'I believe in the rock-bottom doctrine of Advaita and my interpretation of Advaita excludes totally any idea of superiority at any stage whatsoever. I believe implicitly that all men are born equal. Untouchability has to be rooted out completely, so that the fundamental principle of Advaita Hinduism may be realised in practical life.'[29]

Once again, we see how the altruistic paradigm, this time embedded in the circumstantial applications of such action-concepts as ahiṃsā and satyāgraha, and based purportedly on an Advaitic metaphysic, propelled Gandhi to seek a polity that transformed society from within for the betterment of all, especially for those who for long centuries had had their very humanity questioned through social filters that were neither egalitarian nor communally integrative.[30]

Our third example is taken once again from the writings of Bankim Chatterji. As a successful novelist and social commentator during the final decades of the nineteenth century, Bankim wielded considerable if diffuse influence on the thinking of especially younger Bengali intellectuals of the time. In a curiously syncretistic statement amalgamating the theistic and Advaitic elements of the altruistic model, Bankim sets out to give the basis for effective action in (Indian) society for the welfare of all its members in his important work, the *Dharmatattva*.[31]

> The Hindu God.... pervades everything (*sarvabhūtamay*); it is He who is the inner Self (*antarātmā*) of all things. He is not the material world, being different from it, but the world exists in Him alone.... He is present in everyone. He is present in me. In loving myself, I love Him, and in not loving Him, I fail to love myself. And in loving Him, I love every human being. In not loving every human being, I have failed to love Him and myself.... So long as I do not grasp the fact that the whole world is myself, that the universe is not different from me, I have not acquired knowledge, or *dharma*, or devotion (*bhakti*) or love (*prīti*). Therefore love for the world lies at the very root of Hindu *dharma*, and there can be no Hinduness (*hindutva*) without this indivisible, non-separate, universal love.[32]

No doubt this is meant to combat Christian teaching regarding the basis of love for one's neighbour—the implication is that Hindus have a more persuasive and inclusive template in their ethical–theological tradition for other-regarding action—but the terminology underlying the metaphysics of this statement clearly derives in important respects from Vedānta. We shall say more about the 'Hindu' character of Bankim's conception presently, but note that the two-tiered structure of this template remains intact: We have the metaphysical tier of an all-pervading and all-sustaining God whose nature is a wholly encompassing love, and the empirical stratum of a material world or universe which, through the prevenient presence of its intimate, undergirding divinity, I have to realize as 'not different from me' if I am to act towards the world in the appropriate manner; acting in this way constitutes right religion/action or dharma, and it is this that reveals what the otherwise elusive character of 'Hinduness' (or *hindutva*) might be. And there is no doubt that the inspiration for this self-denying ethic harks back to the Gītā.[33]

In the *Dharmatattva*, Bankim formulates in some detail his famous concept of *anuśilan* or the culture of disciplined action that must inform and motivate human relationships in the new society he envisaged for a Hindu India coming to terms with modernity, a concept he had already anticipated in the development of various narratival characters of the loose trilogy that constituted his final novels (mentioned earlier).[34] Elsewhere I have described Bankim's notion of *anuśilan* as

> the disciplined cultivation of our physical, mental, and aesthetic capabilities (*bṛttis*) in a spirit of proper love (*prīti, bhakti*)—in ascending order of priority—for ourselves, our families, the society and birthland in which we live, and the whole world of inorganic and organic being, all encompassed in and orientated to the love of God (*īśvar*)....
> But there must be a balance, a harmonization (*sāmañjasya*) of these loves; one cannot be emphasized at the expense of another. Western patriotism has done just this, viz. seeking the aggrandizement of one's own country at the expense of other peoples (hence colonialism); Hindus [in the past] have gone the other way: loving all creation at the expense of a proper patriotism and self-love (hence meekly accepting foreign rule). The *locus classicus* for the development of this integrated love, its theatre for a proper maturity, is not the life of the wandering renouncer or ascetic (*sannyāsī*), but society [with special reference to the householder]. For it is amid the relationships of society that self-love and other love, that love for one's country and love for the world as encompassed in love for God, can be properly articulated and perfected.[35]

Sartori argues that Bankim arrived at this notion of a harmonized society of non-individualistic, subordinated selves through a dialogue with the views of August Comte.[36] No doubt Comte had something to do with the shaping of it; it is well known that Bankim was considerably influenced by Comte's thought (among other Western thinkers). Nevertheless, it was to Hindu insights that Bankim turned in the *Dharmatattva* to ground his conception of the world and the source from which it derives (not least to the Upaniṣads when he characterizes this source as essentially *sat, cit,* and *ānanda,* or 'being/truth, consciousness and bliss/joy'): 'Those who are engaged in reforming [our] faith should keep in mind that just as God is essentially being/truth [*satsvarūp*] and consciousness [*citsvarūp*], so is He essentially bliss [*ānandasvarūp*]. Thus, unless the aesthetic capabilities [*cittarañjinībṛtti*] become the norm and means [*bidhi ebaṅg upāy*] for the disciplined cultivation of all the others, no reformed faith [*saṅgskṛta dharma*] can survive'.[37]

For Bankim, the teachings of the Upaniṣads have been injected and—in respect of the aesthetic of joy (*ānanda*, somewhat lacking in the Upaniṣads)—been developed in the religion of the Purāṇas to produce a synthesis, which when duly purified of Purāṇic excesses, is fit to become the national faith (*jātīya dharma*) of India.[38] The social organism that results is thus truly homebred, notwithstanding its refinement by way of Comtean (and other Western) principles.

In all the examples given in this essay, Advaitic or otherwise, the practitioner was encouraged to embark in general on a course of spiritual and moral discipline [based on a philosophical stance that regarded the quotidian or ego-self (ahaṃkāra) as ultimately an impediment to the realization of one's true subjectivity] that would reconstitute the 'other' as the target for self-denying social and/or political action (the 'other', in theory, including not only one's compatriots, but also one's nation-in-the-making, namely the 'Motherland', and, indeed, the colonial oppressor himself or herself). The practitioner acted in the role of a karmayogī—a designation derived from the Gītā that has come to characterize at its best the activism of Hindu participants in the Indian nationalist movement: a participation that was visionary, disciplined, and selfless.

One notices a sort of paradox inherent in the implementation of our paradigm: a kenosis or at least attenuation of one's own self (either by way of Advaitic sublation or through a purification of the ego where the theistic mode was concerned) so that the 'other' may find a new identity through a reconstructed, 'bestowed self', as for example, a subject for emancipation from caste or gender discrimination, or a compatriot in the cause of svarāj, or even as an oppressor who through his or her shared humanity with the oppressed could after due change of heart become a liberator.

One also notices two other features of this historical paradigm: (*a*) its revisionary pretensions, and (*b*) its ostensible Hinduness. Let us briefly consider each in turn.

In its historical applications, the altruistic paradigm invariably turned to past Hindu teachings to create both structure and content.

Thus within its traditional two-tiered structural template of the 'transcending spiritual/metaphysical' applied to the 'determining empirical', the actual content of the model varied in terms of recognizable indigenous cultural norms that in the first instance derived their fundamental inspiration from Vedāntic teaching (at least within the time frame that we have discussed in this essay). This Vedāntic bias was then modified further by ideas and practices that reflected the specific context of the *persona* of the practitioner. We have seen how this was so (for example, Vivekananda's tat tvam asi ethic, Gandhi's appeal to Advaita as a socially leavening and politically transformative force through his action-concepts of satyāgraha and ahiṃsā, and so on). But such a course of action necessitated a revisionary gaze on the past. Or to put it differently, past norms had to be recapitulated in terms of the pressing social and political exigencies of the present. And in the process the past was idealized, reconstituted, transcreated, so as to be transformed into a suitable medium for addressing present concerns. Let me give an example from Bankim's influential novel, *Ānandamaṭh*.

Bankim sets the narrative in Bengal, about a hundred years before the novel was written, at the time of the great famine of 1770 and its aftermath. Associated with this famine were the activities of bands of itinerant renouncers ('*sannyasis*' and '*fakirs*'), who by their great numbers could be troublesome to various authorities in the region: particularly, the big Hindu *jamidars* or landholders who were deputed to collect revenue, and the two groups to whom they answered—the now largely titular local Muslim rulers and the British of the East India Company, between whom the apportioning of this revenue was a major bone of contention (not to mention the local population of the region's villages, who were regular victims of the itinerants' predatory need for food, and so forth.). As I write in the 'Introduction' to my translation of the novel:

The Bengal of that time presented itself [in Bankim's authorial gaze] as contested ground. Who was in charge of this space, authorised to rule? The British had been granted the *dewanee*, that is, the rights to collect revenue. But as Bankim makes a point of saying in the novel, 'In 1770 Bengal had not yet fallen under British sway'.... Perhaps the Muslims were in charge then?.... [But] Mir Jafar [the erstwhile ruler of Birbhum, where the novel is set] and his colleagues were

not in effective control of the region, at least from the point of view
of the narrative. And as for the *santāns* [patriotic sons of the land] of
Bankim's *sannyāsī* rebellion, they had only just embarked on their
campaigns to oust their enemies; they were not the ruling power in
the land.... We are faced with the depiction of a ravaged, rudderless
Bengal which from the viewpoint of a purposeful history is virtually
a blank canvas, and as such a fitting template for the ideological construction that Bankim will attempt.[39]

This is the revisionary space Bankim has created to express the
message he wishes to convey about the patriot's goal in the contem-
poraneous situation under British rule (when the novel was actually
written), through the unfolding of the story, and it is this context that
determines narratively the sage Satyānanda's political statement
prefiguring the altruistic paradigm, quoted towards the beginning of
this essay. This could hardly pass for a historically 'objective' context;
rather, it was a revisionary imaginary that could act as the vehicle for
what the author wished to say.[40] Analogously—this would need to be
spelt out, of course—the other activists we have discussed, created or
implied a past that was at least seminally capable of sustaining in one
way or another their actualized insights of the present. Let us pass on
now to our second observation.

The reader may well have gained the impression that the formulations of the altruistic paradigm we have considered possess a restrictive
character, as if their scope were intended to apply to Hindus only,
to the exclusion especially of Muslim observers and participants in
the struggle for a socially and politically transformed India. Even
as apparently attentive an activist as Gandhi to Muslim hopes and
aspirations in the nationalist cause seemed blithely oblivious to the
repercussions of this seemingly exclusionary, or at least assimilative
(Hindu), stance.[41] But it need not have been so. As we have seen, each
implementer of the model implied or affirmed its intended universal
application (all the more so because of its altruistic claims). The mere
fact that there was a Vedāntic substrate to the articulation of each version need not of itself have come across as exclusionary. After all, no
idea, especially no idea intended to animate the quotidian, can avoid
the specificity of its originary context. But in each case not enough was
done to provide a countermanding rhetoric that clearly affirmed the
application's universalist aspirations in the Indian context, especially

in the light of the history of communal tensions in the subcontinent. With due effort, this would not have been difficult to achieve. The almost inexplicable presence of this rhetorical 'blind spot' in the presentations of the paradigm of the various Hindu activists played a significant role, I believe, in creating the impression that the project for social and political reform in India during and around the turn of the nineteenth century was essentially a Hindu one, and in the course of time this progressively helped form and alienate (especially) Muslim perceptions and participation.

I have argued elsewhere on a more general basis that Hindu tradition is inherently open-ended in terms of what I have dubbed its structural 'polycentrism'. Hindu polycentrism is a distinctive cultural phenomenon whereby a certain principle, idea, or precept is thought to express itself empirically in plural fashion, so that its originative force is distributed and compounded among a set of interactive polarities. Consider, for example, so-called Hindu polytheism, even within one sectarian tradition, that of ŚrīVaiṣṇavism. Here we have seemingly multiple deities: Viṣṇu-Nārāyaṇa, and his 'chief consort', Śrī-Lakṣmī. How to make sense of this? Elsewhere, in terms of polycentrism, I have described this kind of theistic approach as follows:

Viṣṇu-Nārāyaṇa manifests in various modes particular to time and place, e.g. as one *avatāra* or other, or as this or that *persona* through the image(s) resident in one temple or other, in accordance with his gracious will. The Goddess Śrī-Lakṣmī, the other person of the Godhead, has her own history and panoply of multiple manifestations. Yet the broad gamut of these secondary forms, which invariably have their own liturgies of worship, are expressions of the same Godhead, endorsing and reinforcing each other in a shared framework of divine salvific efficacy. Or, to put it more specifically in the language of polycentrism, the one transcendent invisible Godhead, itself composed of two personal centres in dialectical relationship, manifests concretely through individualized *personae* that function as interactive centres of shared grace and power within one and the same domain of ŚrīVaiṣṇava cultic practice...

It is a polycentric reality in that the 'divine' centres of the [extended] system—....with their own sometimes apparently conflicting cultic histories—are interpreted as actual expressions of the one ultimate Godhead, Viṣṇu-Nārāyaṇa. Further—and this is important—the ŚrīVaiṣṇava (stem-) system itself is but one centre among many in the extensive tracery of the Hindu banyan, drawing its distinctive life force from the shared environment of the whole.[42]

Similarly, the constructs of dharma, Veda (scripture), *tīrtha* (pilgrimage), and so on, as understood within the parameters of 'Hinduism', can all be interpreted as different facets of the same distinctive phenomenon of polycentrism.[43] In this light, the formulations of the altruistic paradigm might also be considered as representing an open-ended expression of Hindu polycentrism. Traditional Hinduism's tendency towards conceptual open-endedness allows for a more universalist formulation of the altruistic paradigm in the future than its erstwhile historical versions; it need not be an exclusionary construct.

As I see it, a salient theme of the Colombo Conference of 2010—the instigator of the Cochin Colloquium in 2011 from which this essay derives—was a stress on Hindu conceptual flexibility. In his address at Colombo ('From Buddha to Narayana Guru'), one of the inspirers of that Conference, Ashis Nandy, spoke as follows when commenting on a notable feature of Indian beliefs:

.... [T]here is an openness between the domain inhabited by humans and the domain inhabited by gods and goddesses, demons and asuras ['anti-gods']. The gods and goddesses enter our lives with ease and go out of our lives with ease as if it is part of their lives. The demons and the asuras also enter our lives with ease and go out with ease.... And that is also part of the tradition, this play with gods and goddesses, this play with your own belief systems.... This is absolutely vital because this play, this almost personal relationship with gods and goddesses, gives your identity a different kind of flexibility.

It is about one significant historical instantiation of this unique flexibility that this essay has been concerned—an indicator perhaps of our paradigm's continuing viability and adaptability. That the paradigm represents an oscillatory dialectic between spiritual and empirical elements need not be a drawback; on the contrary, the rhetoric of most if not all nationalist mythologies and histories contains a synergy of this nature.[44] That such a large part of the Indian nationalist narrative is also informed by a distinctive, accommodative *mentalité*, one feature of which we have explored in this essay, bodes well, it seems to me, for the ongoing transnational discourse about the formation and implementation, in different contexts, of democratic polity.

Notes

1. This is a revised version of the paper I read at the Colloquium in Cochin, 2011 that generated the publication of this book. I am grateful to the sponsors and organizers of the Colloquium for the opportunity to participate, and for the collegial discussion that followed my presentation.

2. In Gopal Balakrishnan, ed., *Mapping the Nation* (London and New York: Verso, 1996), 217.

3. Cf. Bankim Chandra Chatterji, *Ānandamaṭh*, or *The Sacred Brotherhood*, translated with an Introduction and critical apparatus by J. Lipner (New York: Oxford University Press, 2005), 229.

4. By a 'majoritarian view' I mean a view that privileges, in the process of political decision-making, the opinion(s) of those who are numerically in the majority against the opinion(s) of those who are numerically in the minority, simply by virtue of the fact that the former are numerically superior. The view is majoritarian here from the viewpoint of the Hindu bias envisaged, not from the viewpoint of the specific Hindu doctrine mentioned: Advaita has always been espoused by a minority of Hindus. On Rammohan's pioneering influence in this regard, see S. Cromwell Crawford, *Ram Mohan Roy: Social, Political, and Religious Reform in 19ᵗʰ Century India* (New York: Paragon House Publishers, 1987), and Brian A. Hatcher, *Bourgeois Hinduism, or The Faith of the Modern Vedantists* (New York: Oxford University Press, 2008); on Rammohan Roy's Advaitic cast of mind, see Dermot Killingley's still unrivalled doctoral thesis for the University of London, 'Rammohun Roy's Interpretation of the Vedānta' (PhD diss., University of London, 1977).

5. The (somewhat awkward) conjunction 'as' before 'the Supreme Spirit' towards the end of the passage seems intended to express identity with the Supreme Spirit, as in Advaitic teaching, rather than similarity (as 'in the manner of').

6. See J. Lipner, 'The Perils of Periodization, or How to Finesse History with Reference to Vedānta', in *Historiography and Periodization of Indian Philosophy*, edited by Eli Franco (Vienna: De Nobili Research Series, 2012), 145–70.

7. Cf. Killingley, 'Rammohun Roy's Interpretation of the Vedānta', especially Chapters 5 and 6.

8. Killingley, 'Rammohun Roy's Interpretation of the Vedānta', 234.

9. Cf. the tenor of the discourses of these members of the Tattvabodhini Society in Hatcher, *Bourgeois Hinduism*.

10. For Rammohan, it was Jesus' message and subsequent enactment (by his death) of love for neighbour ('Love thy neighbour as thyself')

that elevated him to the status of ethical exemplar, not the theological teachings found in the Gospels and subsequently concerning his person.

11. Hatcher introduces and translates this collection, 'which records twenty-one discourses delivered before the Tattvabodhinī Sabhā during the first year of its existence, 1839–40', in Hatcher, *Bourgeois Hinduism*, 5.

12. Hatcher, *Bourgeois Hinduism*, 5.

13. Namely *kāma*, *krodha*, and *lobha*, the three vices regarded by the Gītā (16.21) as the threefold gate to hell.

14. I am grateful to Marina Chellini of the British Library for making this rare Bengali text available to me. All translations from the Bengali in this essay have been made by the author (unless indicated to the contrary).

15. For Debendranath's role in the Bengal of the time, see D. Kopf, *The Brahmo Samaj and the Shaping of the Modern Indian Mind* (Princeton: Princeton University Press, 1979); see also Frans L. Damen, *Crisis and Religious Renewal in the Brahmo Samaj (1860–1884)* (Leuven: Department Oriëntalistiek Katholieke Universiteit, 1983), especially Part.1.2, and Hatcher, *Bourgeois Hinduism*, especially Chapter 2.

16. My translation, though I have been glad to consult that made by H. Sarkar in *Brahmo Dharma*, reprint (Calcutta: Sadharan Brahmo Samaj, 1992).

17. In *Brahmo Dharma* Sarkar provides a valuable service by identifying the sources of the various verses.

18. Bankim Chatterji made an important contribution by de-gendering the karmayogī ideal so as to include women, not least through his novel *Debī Chaudhurāṇī*; see *Debī Chaudhurāṇī*, or *The Wife Who Came Home*, translated with an introduction and critical apparatus by Julius Lipner (New York: Oxford University Press, 2009).

19. A similar paradigm, intended to implement values according to which the practitioner sought deliverance *from* the world as a *jīvanmukta*, namely 'an individual liberated while still living in time' (or equivalent) rather than social engagement *in* the world, was the more traditional ideal; for an analysis comparing Hindu and Buddhist paradigms in this respect, see W. L. Todd's doctoral dissertation, 'A Selfless Response to an Illusory World: A Comparative Study of Śāntideva and Śaṅkara' (PhD diss., Lancaster University, 2011).

20. *Bande Mātaram*, or rather its first couple of verses, is now, somewhat controversially, India's National Song (in contradistinction to its National Anthem), so that the memory of its historical political role endures. On the hymn in Bankim's *Ānandamaṭh*, see Lipner, *Ānandamaṭh*, especially

84–99 and 242–5; on the controversial nature of the hymn, see J. Lipner, 'Icon and Mother: An Inquiry into India's National Song', in *Political Hinduism: The Religious Imagination in Public Spheres*, edited by Vinay Lal (New Delhi: Oxford University Press, 2009), 96–121.

21. Andrew Sartori, *Bengal in Global Concept History: Culturalism in the Age of Capital* (Chicago and London: The University of Chicago Press, 2008).

22. Sartori, *Bengal in Global Concept History*, 129.

23. See, for example, Torkel Brekke, *Makers of Modern Indian Religion in the Late Nineteenth Century* (Oxford: Oxford University Press, 2002), Part I.

24. From a lecture entitled 'The Vedanta Philosophy', delivered before the Graduate Philosophical Society of Harvard University in March 1896; see *The Complete Works of Swami Vivekananda*, vol. 1, 15th edition (Calcutta: Advaita Ashrama, 1977), 364.

25. From a lecture entitled 'The Spirit and Influence of Vedanta', delivered at the *Twentieth Century Club*, Boston, in 1896; cf. *The Complete Works*, vol. 1, 389–90. I am grateful to my former doctoral student, T. Green, for directing me to these references. See also J. Lipner, *Hindus: Their Religious Beliefs and Practices*, 2nd edition (London and New York: Routledge, 2010), 386, note 13.

26. Tom Green's doctoral dissertation, 'Vedanta and Secular Religion in the Works of F. Max Müller and Swami Vivekananda' (PhD diss., University of Cambridge, 2011), provides a stimulating discussion of a number of these issues.

27. S. K. Saxena, 'The Fabric of Self-Suffering: A Study in Gandhi', *Religious Studies* 12, no. 2 (June 1976): 240–1.

28. From *Young India*, 4 December 1924 in M. Chatterjee, *Gandhi's Religious Thought*, (Basingstoke: The Macmillan Press Ltd, 1983), 104.

29. Quoted in J. T. F. Jordens, *Gandhi's Religion: A Homespun Shawl* (Basingstoke: The Macmillan Press Ltd, 1988), 114. I am grateful to Claudia Cope for directing me to these two quotations.

30. In both Vivekananda's and Gandhi's cases, as is well known, the Bhagavad Gītā played a crucial role for helping articulate the *niṣkāma* or non-self-serving ethic of their applications of the altruistic paradigm. Though it is the case that the examples we have discussed in this essay for implementing this paradigm have been drawn from the lives of men, a number of prominent women were also involved in nineteenth century India in promoting this project. We may mention, for example, the Englishwoman, Sister Nivedita (that is, Margaret Noble, 1867–1911), who accepted Swami Vivekananda and his thought as the guiding lights for her protracted stay and work in India.

31. The *Dharmatattva* (The Principles of *Dharma* or Right Religion), composed in Bengali, and published in 1888, is written in the form of a dialogue between a teacher and his disciple; this format is meant to give the teacher's instruction the weight of authority.

32. The extract from the *Dharmatattva* given above (author's translation) is taken from Chapter 21. The Bengali can be found in *Dharmatattva: Baṅkim Caṭṭopādhyāy*, edited by Brajendranāth Bandyopādhyāy and Sajanīkānta Dās (Calcutta: Baṅgīya Sāhitya Pariṣat, 1964).

33. The Gītā is mentioned or quoted in the great majority of the twenty-eight chapters of the treatise.

34. See, for example, Part I, Chapters 15–16, of Lipner, *Debī Chaudhurāṇī*.

35. See Lipner, *Debī Chaudhurāṇī*, 12; see also the *Dharmatattva*, especially Chapters 20–5.

36. Sartori, *Bengal in Global Concept History*, 129–35.

37. *Dharmatattva*, Chapter 27.

38. *Dharmatattva*, Chapter 27.

39. Lipner, *Ānandamaṭh*, 59–60.

40. Indeed, though the novel begins in 1770, with Birbhum under the nominal rule of Mir Jafar, Bankim could hardly have been ignorant of the fact that this ruler, whom he reviles in the story, had died in 1765! As Bankim states in a Notice prefacing his next novel, *Debī Chaudhurāṇī*, 'After *Anandamath* was published many wanted to know if there was any historical basis to that work.... Since it was not my intention to write a historical novel, I made no pretense about historicity'; see Lipner *Debī Chaudhurāṇī*, 39.

41. For a consideration of aspects of Gandhi's stance in this respect, see especially Nikky-Guninder Kaur Singh's and Daud Rabbar's contributions in *Indian Critiques of Gandhi*, edited by H. Coward (Albany: State University of New York Press, 2003). Gandhi could be rather naïve in his appreciation of the implications of a Hinduist stance. In response to the charge that Bankim's popular nationalist hymn, *Vande Mātaram*, was exclusionary, in favour of Hindu sentiment, he wrote in his weekly, *The Harijan* (1 July 1939): 'As a lad when I knew nothing of *Ananda Math* or even Bankim, *Vande Mataram* gripped me. I associated the purest national spirit with it. It never occurred to me it was a Hindu song or meant only for Hindus. Unfortunately, now we have fallen on evil days. All that was pure gold before has become base metal today.' Jinnah, the leader of the Muslim League, on the contrary, objected strongly to the song precisely on the grounds that it was an exclusively Hindu song.

42. See Lipner, *Hindus: Their Religious Beliefs and Practices*, 372–3.

43. See further, the 'Concluding Postscript', in Lipner, *Hindus: Their Religious Beliefs and Practices*, 371–5, and J. Lipner, 'On Hinduism and Hinduisms: The Way of the Banyan', in *The Hindu World*, edited by S. Mittal and G. Thursby (New York and London: Routledge, 2004), 9–34.

44. See, for example, David Brading's meticulous tracking of this synergy in the case of Mexico: *Mexican Phoenix: Our Lady of Guadalupe: Image and Tradition across Five Centuries* (Cambridge: Cambridge University Press, 2001).

Sastri has also concluded coherently to support the idea that Religion... *International Studies* 27–3, and I. *post.* On Hinduism and Hindutva, The Way of the Banyan, in *The Hindu World*, edited by S. Mittal and G. Thursby (New York and London 2004) a 200.b.5.
See, for example, I and Hindutva a minimum reckoning of this is very in the case of diverse. Meaning, *Hinduity Quarterly* of Gandhi on liberty and ... on common Practice in multiplicity Cambridge University Press 2001.

6

THE TRANSMUTATION OF METAPHYSICS AND POLITICS IN LITERATURE

N. MANU CHAKRAVARTHY

I

I had better state at the very beginning that my approach to, and understanding of, metaphysics and politics is largely shaped by a literary sensibility. As a student of literature, I correlate philosophical concepts and political ideas and categories with the lived experiences of individuals and communities that actually represent what we call historical realities. A literary sensibility has enabled me to understand abstract notions in concrete terms by locating them in the experiential realities of individual and community life and, at the same time, has helped me evolve abstract ideas from the quotidian realities of life. In other words, the organic relationship between ideas and concepts and actual experiences has shaped my intellectual preoccupations and concerns.

I also find it very important to state quite emphatically that I am not systematically trained in philosophy, either Western or Indian. My understanding of Indian and Western philosophy has been through the lessons learnt from my father and his works on the *Rg Veda*, *Rk Samhita*, and the Mahabharata, and, later on, from my teacher who taught me the Brahma Sutras and, of course, my intense reading of Daya Krishna, Jonardon Ganeri, and the works of Bimal Krishna Matilal, Karl Potter, and Roy Bhaskar, as well as the writings of Kant, Nietzsche, and Heidegger. But I am still an 'outsider' to the discipline of philosophy. So, in my essay, the references to metaphysics and politics, while drawing from philosophical texts and sources, are also based on how they find expression in literary works that situate them in various historical contexts. Moreover, all the contradictions, paradoxes, and dualities of life—in cultural, political, and economic spheres—are enacted in literary texts that, without advancing simplistic and reductionist ideological positions and solutions, compel us to comprehend the complex relationship between metaphysics and politics without overlooking the dichotomies of cultures and societies. In other words, for the creative process, metaphysics and politics are not mere epistemological and theoretical issues dealing with nature, empirical reality, and the spirit, but are essentially manifestations of the choices that individuals and societies make as regards their present and future. It is for this reason that the literary imagination integrates metaphysics and politics with ethics and morality, and, thereby, registers its own moral vision. Metaphysical reflections indeed have political implications just as political actions and choices engender metaphysical ideas and values. Literary texts—in the oral and written traditions—are open negotiations with the dialectical relationship that exists between philosophical and political concepts that influence history and the political exigencies of history that transform ideas and, even, alter their ontological nature. So questions of ontology become major complications and pose immense problems for the literary imagination, which eventually holds on to an ambivalent position as the only legitimate vision as regards human choices. To further this point, it only means stating that a complex literary experience comes through a negation of crippling, circumscribing abstractions—of philosophical and political concepts—that parade as Universal Truths, and is an encounter, and an endless confrontation, with concepts, notions, and categories that become dogmatic and tend to reduce the openness and transparency of systems of belief, faith, practice, and of epistemology itself. This is also the epistemological edifice of a rich literary text.

This essay is an attempt to come to terms with several crucial questions, debates, and tensions of knowledge and history that haunt Indian life at several levels in areas of politics, philosophy, religion, and spirituality. One only needs to turn to a few crucial literary texts from the Indian context where one can discern a profound convergence of epistemological, philosophical, and ethical issues that unfold the multiple dimensions of metaphysics and politics. It is also necessary to recognize the fact that discussions on metaphysics and politics move from epistemological planes to ethical realms and, hence, quite often, one recognizes a conflation of these apparently different fields.

II

At one level, philosophy as a discipline recognizes critical enquiry as an autonomous practice that is not dependent on ethical principles. Critical enquiry, with its own methodology and procedures, is separate from theological studies or moral concerns. In the Indian tradition, Vatsyayana stated that if critical enquiry (*anviksiki*) were to be a part of 'dharma', it would become another Upanishad dealing with the *soul's progress*. There was an insistence on the epistemological freedom of critical enquiry wherein 'means' were divorced from 'ends'. Rational enquiry was an instrument to be used to serve any end. This instrumentalist understanding of rationality, whereby ends justify means, could be seen in Kautilya too. (We shall see later how, borrowing from ancient traditions, M. K. Gandhi, as an insider, altered these notions in the modern context.) But what is interesting is that there is an internal dynamic in the philosophical tradition too, which makes the whole debate between epistemology and ethics quite complex. It has been recorded by scholars that the early Naiyayikas, for instance, argued that there was a link between rational enquiry and the final ends of life. The argument goes that by interrogating epistemology and by debating theory, one attains the highest goal of life. The *Nyayasutra* looks at the causal relations between knowledge and liberation. It is important to realize that there are contradictory positions as regards epistemology and ethics, with some separating the two while others see one overlapping the other.

All literary works do not engender unproblematic ideas and experiences in relation to ethics, politics, and metaphysics. There are indeed a number of works that—by their ideological positions and the values they endorse—create problems for those who attempt to integrate rationality with ethics. The politics of such works is indeed a contentious issue. It is also indicative of the fact that philosophical positions are not entirely free from amoral/immoral elements, and, at times, could even endorse fascist attitudes.

One text that raises such questions is Visakadatta's *Mudrarakshasa*.[1] In the sixth century A.D., Visakadatta wrote a play on the manipulations and manoeuvrings involved in politics. The text centres round Chanakya and his opponent Rakshasa, who (using all their rationality and other resources) demonstrate that the intellect need not obey ethical principles. Moreover, ethical values of loyalty and devotion are determined by the kind of dedication one displays towards the king and the political state. The play is a vindication of Chanakya's position that the ends would eventually justify the means. Today it is possible to read the play as a text of political theory that justifies all methods as necessary and legitimate as far as the consolidation of a political state is concerned. The seeds of modern nationalism, one could argue, have been sown in this period itself. Both Rakshasa and Chanakya, though their motives are different, use all kinds of tricks to outwit each other justifying everything in the name of the state—to lie, deceive, betray, and kill without any compunction. It is also interesting to note that the text itself justifies these by creating Rakshasa and Chanakya as totally selfless characters who indulge in deception for 'reasons of State'. Bakunin's treatise on the state as an immoral, cruel, and divisive entity that justifies all methods of deception 'for reasons of State' is anticipated in *Mudrarakshasa* in the sixth century A.D. itself. The point is that by forging the political entity of the state with ethical values of loyalty and devotion, a new 'metaphysics' of the brutal physical reality of the state is created by Visakadatta in his text. It is also curious to see the 'loyal and noble' Rakshasa talking of his virtue and purity as a Brahmana who has been polluted by the touch of the Sudra, the official who arrests him. It is not a coincidence that the impersonal state, which is a political construct, is nurtured by the reality of a caste and class consciousness that advocates features of purity in relation to pollution. The supremacy of the political state is embedded in a caste and class hierarchical structure of a social order. It is in this context that the 'metaphysical' *gunas* of Rakshasa and

Chanakya are upheld in the text—both are selfless and stand for the idea of purity. In this particular sense, the political is given an ethical dimension and individuals are given metaphysical qualities that mask the ugly feature of the physical reality of the political state. The reading of *Mudrarakshasa* in the contemporary context throws considerable light on the complex relationship between metaphysics, politics, and ethics. *Mudrarakshasa* uses history to construct ideas of politics, ethics, and metaphysics in an 'objective manner' (of being 'objective' about history, politics, and the reality of the state), that is, 'morally neutral'. The moral neutrality of the text signifies the dichotomy that exists between philosophy and ethics and metaphysics and politics, apart from foregrounding the fact that the past, in its construction of the state, did have ideas of nationalism with a strong centre where profound ethical questions were subservient to pragmatic political principles. It is for this reason that in the modern world we cannot romanticize and glorify the past and lead ourselves to believe that it is only the contemporary world that creates major civilizational crises.

One of the great paradoxes of the modern world is that it has given birth to intense moral positions (as far as the future of human civilization is concerned) even as it has promoted raging conflicts and engineered paralysing genocides in the name of religious and political ideology. What is fascinating is that these debates that emanate both from deeply religious and extremely secular positions that seem to contradict each other, quite often converge to raise moral questions about choices—made by individuals and communities—that are not really different in nature. Profound moral issues that emerge from divergent philosophical positions tend to erase binary opposites when they interrogate religious and political notions and practices, whether of the past or of the present. These interrogations offer reconfigurations of philosophical texts of the past necessitating a fundamental restructuring of our comprehension and understanding of what we unconsciously receive and accept as the past. We have to acknowledge the fact that such interrogations challenge conventionally constituted epistemologies and the ethical practices that stem from them. In a way, these contemporary interrogations ought to be understood as 'spiritual' negotiations with history that transcend the limitations of mere intellectual debates. In other words, moral interrogations serve to produce moral practices and actions. This is the distinction that B. K. Matilal makes between religious dogma and moral action. Matilal reads Indian epics and philosophical texts to extrapolate what he calls 'action-guide' dilemmas from them. In his essay *Moral Dilemmas and Religious Dogmas*, Matilal asks, 'Can an act be simply moral without being religious in any sense? ... Can some "religious" acts be amoral and immoral? Can we give up morality in this way for the pursuit of religion?'[2] Drawing from the Mahabharata, and from the Gita in particular, Matilal raises ethical–philosophical questions while recontextualizing the past; more importantly, he underlines the moral imperatives that the present must accept. Drawing from Rabindranath Tagore's story *The Lord's Debt*, Matilal posits the view that a 'truly religious man can transcend his so-called religious dogma and put moral concerns over narrowly religious ones'.[3] Matilal further maintains that

the great epics, apart from being the source of everything else, con-stitute an important component of what we may term as moral philosophical thinking of the Indian tradition. Certainly there exists a lacuna in the tradition of Indian philosophy. Professional philoso-phers of India over the last two thousand years have been consistently concerned with the problems of logic and epistemology, metaphys-ics and soteriology, and sometimes they have made very important contributions to the global heritage of philosophy. But except some cursory comments and some insightful observations, the professional philosophers of India have very seldom discussed what we call moral philosophy today. It is true that the dharmashastra texts were there to supplement the Hindu discussion of ethics, classification of virtues and vices, and enumeration of duties related to the social status of the individual. But morality was never discussed as such in these texts. On the other hand, the tradition itself was very self-conscious about moral values, moral conflicts and dilemmas, as well as about the difficulties of what we call practical reason or practical wisdom. This conscious-ness found its expression in the epic stories and narrative literature which can, therefore, be used for illuminating any discussion of moral philosophy in India.[4]

It is Matilal's contention that the social sciences, both in India and the West, have overlooked the significance of epics and other cultural narratives and discourses, without which the complex fabric of Indian social life cannot at all be understood. Matilal's conviction is that epics are not just heroic tales, but happen to be practical lessons in morals and dharma. He maintains that the *dharmasastras* give only a skeletal view of dharma, whereas the richness, complexity, and ambiguity of the concept of dharma are interwoven in the narratives at every stage and thus one cannot afford to ignore the evidence of the epic and narrative materials in India. Matilal states quite emphatically that 'if the sociologist ignores them, he ignores India, that is, the reality, the turmoils, the conflicts, the clashes, the protests and above all the forced rationalisations and the ad hoc solutions'.[5]

Such concerns with ethics/morals and the dilemmas of modern civilization lead to a reinterpretation of the meaning of metaphysics and even give it a quotidian dimension, which is to argue that in the ordinary, trivial, and mundane matters of everyday life, metaphysical dilemmas are to be comprehended by an acutely sensitive individual. Going by this, metaphysical issues are to be seen in conjunction with the physical realities of existence and not as other-worldly. Hence, metaphysics and politics spring from the temporal and not from eternal absolutes.

The dramatization of these philosophical issues and their accompanying moral dilemmas have been the major preoccupations of our creative minds, and in their works one sees the 'realisation' of philosophical concepts and moral precepts in the lives of individuals and communities. The living practices of societies form the moral imagination of our creative works. If scholars like Matilal try to extract moral philosophy from out of the Indian philosophical tradition, students of literature try to abstract moral imagination from the creative process.

Let me turn, then, to Raja Rao's *Kanthapura* (1938),[6] which may be described as a *sthalapurana*. Out of the small local *sthala* with all its mythologies—the *puranas*—the novel constructs the history of the entire nation. The country's freedom movement, with a great metaphysical truth guiding its spirit, is seen in the little acts of the common people of Kanthapura. Great *metaphysical notions* become *moral actions* in the choices that the *small, common* people of Kanthapura make. Even Moorthy, the protagonist, is not a person of heroic stature performing high and mighty deeds, but is an ordinary human being who becomes an embodiment of the great ideas that reach him, and the entire village, through Gandhi when he visits the place. The novel correlates philosophical notions and metaphysical ideas with the transformation of the village as a result of the choices that the simple folk of the village make inspired by Gandhian ideals. Kanthapura, with all its traditional beliefs in the caste hierarchy and the superior status of the Brahmin, witnesses incredible radical changes transcending many crippling social constructs. Metaphysics, in the context of the work, is part of the politics of the freedom movement, and ethical values emerge from the fusion of the two. In fact, the simple people of the village—women and men of all caste groups doing their respective jobs as designated by the caste system to begin with—embrace the *Truths* disseminated by Gandhi and unconsciously transcend the boundaries of a decadent traditional order.

Raja Rao's work dissolves the binary opposition between the oral and the written, myth and history, and the 'local' and the 'national'. The metamorphosis that Kanthapura undergoes is amazing considering the fact that most of its residents are illiterate. The values and the vision of an ethical life that come to them are in the form of *Shrutis* and not as *Shastras* that one comes across in books. The community '*harikatha*' spreads metaphysics and politics to the entire village, while ancient legends carry modern histories in their being. It is the individual experiential, existential element of 'being' becoming the 'Being' of a great historical phase that the work captures. What is of extraordinary significance for us today is that questions relating to the status of women and the inhuman condition of young widows emerge in the novel as major moral dilemmas and not as sociological details, leading to the birth of a new consciousness in the community. Women confined to their kitchens and forced to do menial jobs emerge as ethically and politically conscious members of a society. The radicalization of the consciousness of the pariahs, the Muslims, and the women goes hand in hand with the emancipation that the Brahmin experiences when liberating metaphysical and political ideas sweep across Kanthapura. And what is astounding is that the nation is realized only through the *samudaya*, the community, experientially and existentially and not as an abstraction. Raja Rao is the inheritor of Tagore's moral position that rejects nationalism as an illegitimate construct. It is also absolutely necessary to see *Kanthapura* capturing the manner in which metaphysical and political notions and ideals are *actually realized* by the community, if only to understand how the literary imagination depicts the dialectical relationship between metaphysics and politics.

The simple folk of Kanthapura find themselves coming under the influence of two powerful figures who speak in two rather different idioms transmuting the ontological nature of the entire community. One speaks the language of meditation, spiritual transcendence, and detachment. This figure is Sadhu Narayan (actually Sri Narayana Guru the spiritual preceptor) who, even after having renounced the world, blesses Moorthy who has launched a political struggle against the British. In him the spiritual elements are integrated with the political. The other figure is Mahatma Gandhi, who gives Kanthapura a radical political consciousness but blends it with the spiritual or metaphysical quality of ahimsa—that political revolt must always be guided by the spiritual element of non-violence and sacrifice. Even Rangamma, the enlightened woman who enters the political move-ment, acknowledges the fact that it was Sadhu Narayan who taught her the meaning of meditation. Rangamma tells the others that it is the principle of meditation she derived from Sadhu Narayan that has given her tremendous strength—Sadhu Narayan and Mahatma Gandhi merge into each other, which is, literally and metaphorically, the blending of metaphysics and politics. If Narayana Guru brings renunciation, meditation, spirituality, and metaphysics into politi-cal action, Gandhi transforms politics into metaphysics—especially through ahimsa. In the novel, when Sadhu Narayan talks of renun-ciation as necessary for the soul, Moorthy, without striking a note of contradiction or opposition, invokes Gandhi and talks of *Truth is God*, and therefore, remarks that he should continue with his fight against the colonizer for that is the Truth he cannot abandon. In the midst of a historical struggle, in the context of a raging temporal issue, the moral imagination of literature conflates metaphysics and politics. It is equally important to realize that this is done not in the vague and amorphous area of a Nation, but in the little, physical space of a *grama* (village), where consciousness blossoms through Shruti (the wisdom of the oral tradition). Consequently, the creative process rejects nationalism and the authority of the Shastras (the hegemony of the dominant written tradition). In fact *Kanthapura*, as a sthalapurana, does not convert mythical figures into historical entities, but internal-izes them to draw moral principles. If Narayana Guru's lessons on meditation give spiritual strength to the commonest of the common people, Gandhi's reflections enable them to negotiate with forces of history without ever legitimizing violence as a means of liberation. Renunciation and political activism reflect each other. For Moorthy, what is paramount is Gandhi's reading of the Gita, in which Gandhi does not recognize Krishna as a historical figure and as a force advocating violence as inevitable, but as a consciousness urging Arjuna to take to arms for the simple reason that he was the one who had initiated the entire process and, hence, had no right to talk of ahimsa when the war was on. For Gandhi, Krishna's admonition was based on the fact that it was not ahimsa that really mattered to Arjuna, but only the sentimental reason that he had to kill his *bandhus* (relatives or kith and kin). The Gita, according to Gandhi, when properly realized, determines the ethical nature of the struggle and the future of the land. Metaphysical dilemmas, and spiritual and political conflicts are resolved only through uncompromising ethical choices that individuals and communities make, even while facing the threat of extinction. *Kanthapura*, as a fictional narrative, is an articulation of this vision.

III

Eminent philosophers have always questioned reductionist positions regarding ontology, especially when issues of identity—philosophical, religious, socio-cultural, and political—surface in the realm of epistemology, and at crucial historical junctures when philosophical positions do influence and determine cultural and political choices and are, therefore, not to be examined outside the pressures and conflicts created by the complex processes of history. In the Indian context, important literary minds have, as always, given concrete political and historical locations to philosophical debates, especially when they gain concrete manifestations through religious and political debates and conflicts. The intense struggle to reconstruct, recontextualize, and reimagine the past has been at the centre of the imagination of literature. Quite often one comes across literary texts wherein philosophical questions and debates become overwhelmingly central, compelling the reader to question the very nature of literary imagination. But such apparently extraneous elements that enter works of art lend rich philosophical and ideological dimensions to the works, apart from drawing attention to the crises that have engulfed the community. Rabindranath Tagore's *Gora* (1910) and *Ghare Bhaire* (*The Home and the World*, 1919) are two outstanding brilliant works that take upon themselves the full burden of confronting ontological and political questions that were the driving forces behind the nationalist movement.[7] In *Gora* and *Ghare Bhaire* are foregrounded the major debates of the times that shaped the religious and political imagination of those who were at the thick of the freedom struggle. As all significant literary works do, the two works *realize* ideological debates through the fundamental existential and experiential states of individuals and communities drawn into the various centres of conflict. One sees in the two works a complex juxtaposition of metaphysics and politics confirming the basic position that eventually moral principles firmly disallow any kind of dichotomy to be created between them.

In his very perceptive analyses of Indian philosophy, Daya Krishna shows that ontological issues are exceedingly problematic and one cannot really make categorical statements about what constitutes the essential nature of the Indian philosophical tradition. He argues that with many conflicting, and often contradictory, positions built into the Indian philosophical framework, it is not possible to talk of a single origin or a singular determining concept as far as Indian philosophy is concerned.[8] For that matter, the construction and meaning of Vedanta itself cannot be conclusively fixed. Daya Krishna draws upon various kinds of evidence to show that one cannot talk of texts of authority and schools of philosophical thought while dealing with the multiple ideas and issues that come into the Indian philosophical tradition. Referring to the three figureheads of Indian philosophy, Sankara, Ramanuja, and Madhwa, Daya Krishna shows that the three acharyas did not refer to the same texts while stating their philosophical positions. In other words, the foundational texts were different for each one of them. He further argues that even notions of spirituality and *moksha*, as one of the *purusharthas*, are not central to the Vedantic tradition. Hence, there is no single authority for the Indian philosophical system. What marks an Indian religious or philosophical identity and what determines one's origins, as far as individuals and communities are concerned, ought to be understood as open, inconclusive, and arbitrary issues never to be finally settled. The extension of this position is that in socio-cultural terms, an Indian identity cannot even carry notions of purity and untouchability. Matilal argues that this is the major reason why both *reformists* and *purist traditionalists* who try to restructure the Indian philosophical tradition, and thereby, the Indian past, cannot really be accepted by those who are fully aware of the contradictions, dualities, and counter positions, and discourses that have always been a part of Indian philosophy.[9]

At the historical level, Gandhi, in *Hind Swaraj*, while confronting various kinds of arguments and positions as regards the religious past of precolonial India and the future of a politically independent India rejects the ideologies of purity and pollution constructed by traditionalists and the idea of a strong centralized nation.[10] Gandhi's metaphysics and politics cannot accommodate religious and political absolutism of any kind. Tagore, who wrote his great work *Nationalism* in 1917, argues vehemently that the modern nation state of the West, if it ever became the political model of a free India, would annihilate the spirit that had sustained and nourished the many communities of Indian society.[11] For Tagore, India had always been a land of communities and societies and never a nation. Even while reflecting on the barbarity of colonial rule, Tagore repeatedly mentions that the major problems of India were social and not political and economic. Tagore argues for a 'spiritual unity' that would bring about a 'regulation of social difference'.[12]

In *Gora* and *Ghare Bhaire* one sees religious/spiritual, metaphysical/political positions recreating and reconstructing one another such that the origins of each as a separate entity are gradually erased, making it impossible even for those who advocate exclusivist positions to hold on to their imagined original principles. Gora, the protagonist of the novel, is awakened into a new reality and a different state of being when all his ontological beliefs collapse. And amidst these raging philosophical and political debates, the vital imagination of literature does not gloss over the plight of those who are *voiceless* and the utterly *disempowered*—for instance, the pathetic condition of the Muslims, a minority community in so many fundamental ways. Both the works position the Muslims to evoke profound moral problems that none with a conscience can ignore or overlook. Binoy in *Gora* and Nikhil in *Ghare Bhaire* symbolize the enlightened consciousness and the disturbed conscience of those for whom the spirit of humanism, touched by love and compassion, matters more than larger amorphous

abstractions revolving round notions of racial superiority and political freedom. Ideas of religion, spirituality, and the nation become
redundant and irrelevant when one comes face to face with the dismal
state of existence of the poor and the oppressed. Tagore's great works
challenge the Vedantic tradition and the reformist Brahmo Samajists
for whom the fate of the impoverished millions is hardly a matter of
concern. Tagore's works resolve the dichotomies between metaphysics and politics only through ethical choices and practices. And, it is
this deep preoccupation with human destiny that makes Tagore refute
the overarching nature of the Swadeshi movement, for it is a sentiment and a practice that the wretched of the earth cannot embrace.
Swadeshi is, as the two works reflect it, a luxury that only the middle
class and those above can afford to practise. Tagore holds on to his
vision that modern theories of politics and economics cannot bring
redemption and salvation to humankind. His civilizational vision
does not ignore the realities of human existence and experience. His
universalism finds expression in the metaphors he uses—*vasudhaiva
kutumbakam, viswaneedam, eka needam* ('the world is a single family',
'the world is a single nest'). But it is important to underline the fact
that the metaphors emerge through a rigorous rejection of metaphysics, religion, spirituality, and politics as exclusive categories having
no bearing on one another. It is by being rooted in the physical world
embracing all its multidimensional realities that one transcends its
crippling contradictions. And, it is by acknowledging the essential,
actual, physical truths of all human beings that one attains an all-
encompassing universal consciousness. Tagore's works contest all
vague abstractions about the past, present, and future of India, which,
for him, is in a very real sense *chinmayi* (the truth of consciousness)
and not '*mrinmayi*' (the geographical or territorial fact).

IV

Post-Independence India has continued to stretch all the debates of
the colonial period and, in most cases, has roused them to a fever-
ish pitch. One also witnesses a secularization of issues that, in
conventional terms, stayed within the framework of the religious
and the spiritual. At the same time, secular and political questions
have occupied domains that were previously foreign. Modern India

coexists with its traditional self unleashing strange contradictions and unimaginable tragic dualities for the individual and the community. The dichotomies of modernity have only enhanced the oddities of the traditional past making it virtually impossible for one to adopt a course of action that resolves all dualities and dissolves all contradictions. On the contrary, one is a witness to a certain choice—even a moral choice—only shaping greater contradictions and anomalies, converting such ethical action into a parody. Moral choices of individuals and communities appear to be whimsical and irrational in a context that dehumanizes all.

U. R. Ananthamurthy's *Bharatipura* (1973) gathers into its core all the tensions and ambiguities of a culture that, right from the dawn of independence, has had to deal with hybridity as an inevitable choice made by a nation in transition.[13] If Raja Rao's *Kanthapura* is a sthala-purana, Ananthamurthy's *Bharatipura* is a *desha itihasa* (history of the nation or national history) and, at the same time, a sthalapurana. The sthala, the local, and the *desha*, the nation, coexist in a state of opposition, as do tradition and modernity and the religious and the secular. What metaphysics and politics would a literary imagination construct while trying to capture a reality abounding with such disparate and recalcitrant elements ushered in by modern history? More importantly, how would a modern literary text mirror the moral anguish and emotional trauma of those sensitive individuals who, while choosing what they consider to be an ethical action, get deeply implicated in the complex structures of a society that converts everything into an anachronism? It is in attempting to answer these questions that one arrives at the complex meaning of a text like *Bharatipura*.

Jagannatha, the protagonist of the work, represents the hierarchies of caste and class of a traditional society that is moving into modernity. All the legacies of the past are carried on into the present, which releases new socio-economic and political energies into the community. It is in a feudal village that the modern, Westernised Jagannatha attempts to break the oppressive caste structure that has flourished as a *natural order* for centuries. Carrying all his notions of secularism and liberalism, Jagannatha wants to give self-respect to the Holeyas, the untouchables, of his village. Metaphysics and politics integrate in the choices that Jagannatha makes—first, to lend self-respect to the

Holeyas by making them touch the *Saligrama*, the consecrated stone, that the Brahmin worships, and, secondly, by forcing them to enter the temple, a symbol of upper caste hierarchy. The metaphysics and politics of the novel weave the Gandhian principle with the modern rational mode of action. The novel uses a Gandhian idea and combines it with a modern mode of action that borders on being 'violent' and 'brutal'. Gandhi's mode of gentle persuasion, supposed to lead the upper caste to a state of 'self purification', is forcefully conjoined with the modern approach of shaking the upper caste out of their state of complacency and sense of superiority rather violently. When Jagannatha forces the issue, the exact opposite of what he intends to achieve happens. The Saligrama gains a greater sanctity and the temple becomes more formidable. An ethical action is reversed, totally dehumanizing all those caught in the site of struggle. Jagannatha appears to be monstrous while the Holeyas emerge as utterly dehumanized creatures incapable of realizing their humanity. What is one to make of the moral imagination of a work like *Bharatipura*?

There have been many interpretations of the text. Many have seen it as reactionary, status-quoist, and retrograde for there is no redemption, no salvation for anyone. Others have recognized it as a major work that reflects all the dichotomies of modern India. My argument is that the complex realistic and allegorical nature of the work has to be conceptually interpreted going beyond mere sociological categories. And this is where the social sciences, in general, have failed to grasp the nuances of the literary text and thereby the subtleties of Indian social reality. (Matilal makes it clear that Max Weber and Louis Dumont fail to understand the enormous subtleties of the Indian society for they rely only on sociological details and do not turn to rich allegorical narratives[14]). Bruno Latour, in his text *'Pandora's Hope':* *Essays on the Reality of Science Studies*, sees Jagannatha's moral action as iconoclastic and regards it as anti-fetishism.[15] Latour, as a social scientist, is preoccupied with aspects of empirical reality and fails to comprehend the cultural realities of a social order embedded in states of contradiction and ambiguities. *Bharatipura* is about the choices an individual is compelled to make as a conscientious human being unmindful of the consequences. There is a double-bind at work here. Not to act in a situation that demands an 'ethical action' is a decision made in bad faith. However, tragically, the consequences of an ethical action turn out to be dehumanizing—given the dualities of the social reality—leading one to doubt the very basis of an ethical principle. This is the tragic fate, the existential predicament of an individual in a socio-cultural context ridden with unmanageable dualities. None can escape accusations and cynical remarks at such historical moments. This has been Gandhi's fate too. One cannot ignore the multiple dimensions of an allegorical text—rooted as it may be in the 'real' historical context—that attempts to dramatize the tensions of an entire socio-cultural order that is multilayered. The metaphysics and politics of *Bharatipura* highlight the dilemma of a globalizing world that refuses to let go of its traditional order. In fact, *Bharatipura* is a rich attempt to establish a transaction between Gandhi, Ambedkar, Lohia, and the extreme rationalists and secularists all of whom meet at the crossroads. *Bharatipura* is truly and openly ambivalent in its understanding of metaphysics and politics.

V

One cannot talk about the moral imagination of literature and its relationship with metaphysics and politics leaving out an area of experience and knowledge that has troubled the conscience of individuals who have contested the masculine nature of the state. Right from the epics to modern texts, the literary imagination has had a deep preoccupation with masculinity and its bearing on human existence and the social order.

In the Mahabharata, when Draupadi questions the authority of Yudhishtira in offering her as a bet in the game of dice, none in the Kaurava camp, including Bhishma, the *pitamaha* (venerable father figure), and Drona, the acharya, has an answer. There is no voice of wisdom that meets her question. Matilal argues that if Indian epistemology had confronted Draupadi's question seriously, the implications would have been radically different as regards the making of social laws and customs and the understanding of the status of women in Indian society.[16] The state as an instrument of brutal and oppressive reason has always negated the feminine principle and this has been a major area of contestation in discussions on metaphysics and politics. The Ramayana, too, has been subjected to such interrogations in all discussions on dharma and the ethics of action. Gandhi addressed this concern with great passion and eventually gave expression to his preoccupation through the religious-cultural symbol of the *Ardhanareeshwara* (androgynous, in the Indian tradition representing Parvati and Shiva).

The moral imagination of literature makes this issue a vital aspect of its being. *Kanthapura* by foregrounding women transcends the masculinity of history. *Gora* and *Ghare Bhaire* throw up women protagonists like Sucharita, Lolita, and Bimala ensuring that the feminine spirit and consciousness are part of the evolving nature of the world. *Bharatipura* moves into areas of the feminine principle by subtly depicting the sad predicament of mothers, wives, and daughters-in-law oppressed by a patriarchal order.

The fertile moral imagination of literature is enhanced by its deep preoccupation with the feminine principle even as it deals with all the overwhelming forces of masculinist history. It is not at all surprising that a philosopher like Daya Krishna, even while discussing the complexities of the *Rg Veda*, turns his attention to the hideous nature of the Indian socio-cultural order that has disregarded the spirit of the woman. The erasure of the feminine spirit is a matter of shame.

Metaphysics and politics, and all epistemological issues for that matter, cannot be complete without the feminine element being central to their enquiries. Metaphysics and politics cannot be regarded as universal in content and spirit if they were to exclude women as crucial centres of knowledge and experience. It is in fully acknowledging the value and meaning of the feminine spirit that literature extends its range of vision in relation to history, metaphysics, and politics.

Notes

1. Vishakadatta, *Mudrarakshasa*, translated by M. R. Kale (New Delhi: Motilal Banarsidass, 1965). The present essay has been shaped by a fairly intense reading of diverse texts, commentaries, and analyses that draw attention to the rather recalcitrant nature of the Indian philosophical tradition. Pioneering works have appeared over the decades challenging the attempts of those scholars who have tried to posit the idea of a homogeneous, unified tradition as regards Indian philosophy. The thrust of this essay comes from thinkers who offer valid contestations from different perspectives to such postulates.

2. B. K. Matilal, *Ethics and Epics: The Collected Essays of Bimal K. Matilal*, edited by Jonardon Ganeri (Delhi: Oxford University Press, 2002), 5. There are scholars who have attempted to uphold the contradictions and paradoxes that are embedded in Indian philosophical systems. Mention must be made of G. N. Chakravarthy (*Rk Samhitasara* [New Delhi: Sahitya Akademi, 1998]; *The Concept of Cosmic Harmony in the Rg Veda* [Bangalore: Nagasri Book House, 2005]; and *The Philosophy of History in The Mahabharata* [Mysore: Geetha Book House, 2005]); Karl Potter (*Presuppositions of India's Philosophies* [Englewood Cliffs New Jersey: Prentice-Hall, 1963]); Debiprasad Chattopadhyaya (*Lokayata* [New Delhi: People's Publishing House, 1981]); Jonarden Ganeri (*Artha* [New Delhi: Oxford University Press, 2006]); and Roy Bhaskar (*Meta-Reality* [New Delhi: Sage Publications, 2002]). All these texts figure indirectly in the essay, though they have played a prominent role in influencing the intellectual positions stated therein.

3. Matilal, *Ethics and Epics*, 13.

4. Matilal, *Ethics and Epics*, 22.

5. B. K. Matilal, 'Elusiveness and Ambiguity in Dharma-Ethics', in Matilal, *Ethics and Epics*, 39.

6. The edition used here is Raja Rao, *Kanthapura* (New Delhi: Orient Paperbacks, 1981). My essay is not centrally located in the major discussions on Indian philosophy. It is essentially an exercise rooted in the tradition of literary and cultural criticism. As many sensitive philosophers and social scientists have always noted, fables, mythologies, epics, and narratives of literature have been important markers of social and historical epochs and, therefore, have to be studied as crucial cultural expressions. It would not do for philosophers and social and cultural historians to regard them as mere negotiations of imagination. The aspirations, dualities, and contradictions of communities and the conflicts they engender constitute the core of literary imagination. The essay draws from Indian literary texts from the early twentieth century to almost the end of it while trying to show how philosophical questions and debates emerge through the political and cultural struggles of communities confronting historical changes. It is through the experiential realities of societies and individuals that metaphysics and politics have to be understood as basic elements of human life. The attempt in the essay has been to do that.

7. The editions used are the following: *Gora* (New Delhi: Rupa, 2005) and *The Home and the World* (New Delhi: Rupa, 2011).

8. See Daya Krishna, *Indian Philosophy: A Counter Perspective* (New Delhi: Oxford University Press, 1991) and *Contrary Thinking* (New York: Oxford University Press, 2011).

9. B. K. Matilal, 'Moral Dilemmas and Religious Dogmas', 'Moral Dilemmas: Insights from Indian Epics', and 'Elusiveness and Ambiguity in Dharma-Ethics', in *Ethics and Epics*.

10. M. K. Gandhi, *Hind Swaraj*, edited by Anthony Parel (New Delhi: Cambridge University Press, 1997).

11. Rabindranath Tagore, *Nationalism* (New Delhi: Penguin Books, 2009).

12. Rabindranath Tagore, 'The Cult of the Charka' and 'Crisis in Civilization', in *Words of Freedom* (New Delhi: Penguin Books, 2010).

13. U. R. Ananthamurthy, *Bharatipura*, translated by Susheela Punitha with an introduction by N. Manu Chakravarthy (New Delhi: Oxford University Press, 2010).

14. Particularly in 'Elusiveness and Ambiguity in Dharma-Ethics', in *Ethics and Epics*.

15. Bruno Latour, *'Pandora's Hope': Essays on the Reality of Science Studies* (Cambridge, Massachusetts: Harvard University Press, 1999).

16. 'Moral Dilemmas: Insights from Indian Epics', in *Ethics and Epics*.

7

MOVING IN THE DOUBLE BIND
Reconfiguring Indian Reflective and Creative Traditions Today

D. VENKAT RAO

Whenever freedom is no longer determined as power, mastery, or force, or even as a faculty, as a possibility of the 'I can' ... the evocation and evaluation of democracy as the power of the *dēmos* begins to tremble. If one values freedom in general, before any interpretation, then one should no longer be afraid to speak without or against democracy.

—Jacques Derrida[1]

Thought will be transformed only through thought that has the same origin and determination.

—Martin Heidegger[2]

Philosophical anthropology requires configuration of cultural difference. How do cultures differ from each other? How do they articulate this difference? (Needless to say, unifying and differentiating categories like anthropology and culture themselves are already rooted in a particular cultural thought about thinking and living as such in general.[3]) European intellectual history distinguishes and demarcates its identity in the name of a unique spirit, its ability to nurture questioning as the piety of thought,[4] its self-conscious and self-critical reflexivity, its universality, its ability to birth the science of rationality, purvey democracy to the world, and achieve all these in the thinking of the human as such.[5] Such is the autobiographical narrative of European sovereignty. This narrative continues to be hegemonic even in determining cultural differences.[6] We are all variously caught in the webs of this narrative even when we risk configuring the cultural differences of 'India'.

The future of philosophical anthropology, contends S. N. Balagangadhara, depends on the questions that we forge about man from our 'backgrounds'.[7] (It may be said in passing that Balagangadhara thinks that Indian reflections on the self are not entirely human-centred.) In response to such a call, though not entirely on the lines of his enquiry, this chapter ventures to speculate on Indian cultural difference. As what is thought is contingent upon the ways and modes in which it is thought, this enquiry focuses on the epistemic status of communicational modes (and forms) that have retained privileged status in Indian cultural formations over millennia. While outlining the nature and work of the preferred mnemocultural modes of Indian cultures, this chapter offers a sketch of the nurtured dispersals through which these modes sustained and flourished historically and the rupture they suffered in European epistemic violence. While reflecting on the epistemic–existential implications of these embodied modes (against the implicit background of the European narrative of the self), the chapter puts forward a reflective-pragmatic teaching and research project, which, it is hoped, will contribute to re-kindle and reorient thinking about our singular inheritances in the intellectually destitute postcolonial Indian context.

I

Reflective and creative compositions in Indian cultural formations preferred speech and gestural modes, musical–recitational and performative forms over millennia. Oral–gestural compositions showed indifference to writing even when this technique and technology was available. What is most intriguing in our context is that such phenomenal persistence of the embodied modes (speech and gesture) has not provoked any significant thought so far from the experience of changing communicational modes or systems. Why was there, for instance, such a cultivated indifference toward writing and recording systems even after writing became available in antiquity (by the time of Panini at least)?[8] Although there were no injunctions against writing (such as: thou shall not inscribe), why was writing slighted for centuries?

But more curiously, even when writing has made decisive inroads into Indian cultural practices, why is it that vocalic utterance, acoustic elaborations of compositions, and embodied performatives continue to regulate creative reflective work even to this day? This question gains even more significance when one notices that the Indian scribal output surpasses all the archives of ancient and medieval Europe put together at least by a thousand times.[9] Why is it that even after writing or literacy has come to prevail, they have not generated repositories and their custodians—that is, centralized archives[10] and archons—not gathered and regulated the reflective and creative energies of *kavis* (poets) and *śāstrakāras* (composers of śāstras) and others for centuries? Why is it that writing and literacy have not paved the way for a unified or normative law and a universalizable theoretical discourse (called philosophy) as they were supposed to have done in European cultural history? Why is it that the science of interpretation—hermeneutics, a science essentially based on *written* documents—has had no place in Indic reflective traditions? To my knowledge there is no single work in the Indian context that tracks the effects of writing on Indic reflective and creative traditions;[11] there is no account that tells us, as is claimed in the European context, whether and in what way Indic consciousness (if there is such a thing) was affected by the incursion of writing and literacy.

This extraordinary phenomenon—the persistence of acoustic, recitational, and performative force in composition and in dissemination—even after the proliferation of scriptive modes and indeed through them requires extended study and reflection. The phenomenon impels us to undertake at least two tasks: (*a*) receive and respond to the acoustic and performative currents in the most extended ways possible in our changed communicational contexts (which extend from oral to digital modes and more importantly, resuscitate and reorient the surviving embodied and enacted cultural forms of memory; (*b*) above all, develop reflective theoretical accounts based on the experience of locally generated acoustic and scribal compositions, or, in a word, mnemocultures. As can be noticed, these tasks are oriented towards practical and reflective goals; these tasks, however contradictory this claim might appear in what follows, can be undertaken today only in the context of the colonially established institutions like the university.

Speech and gesture articulate memory-traces. Scribal culture and its subsequent avatars (print and mimeograph) attempt to reduce them for the purposes of externalized articulation in tangible (lithic) forms. Yet the persistence of these alithic forces of the sign indicates that they can escape the reductions of the scribal power; they survive in the intimacy of the body, blurring the border between the enacted, embodied and externalized, and objectified memories. Writing and its extended avatars (print, image, digital creations) are irreducibly disembodied and externally retained (from the codex to database forms) articulations of memory. The legacy of literacy in the related form of scribality, law, and property continues to have a hold on the archive in general even (more) to this day. Gesture and speech, bare elemental forces of the hand and face, and essential substrate of all materialized memories are still measured by the scale of literacy. They are framed as the figures of the origin retrospectively. Archives in this regard hope to be preservers of the past presences.

The memory-traces and the reiterated learning that the Sanskrit tradition represents created a kind of 'textual' (from *textere* meaning weaving) tradition; this tradition is replete with citations, repetitions, condensations, and elaborations of what others have said, unravelling, supplementing, and recomposing the heard and the inexhaustible: an interminable response and rendering of one's duty (*vidhi*) to what is received.[12] It looks as if every composition is predominantly a recapitulation and re-citation (*smaraṇa/dhāraṇa*) of the inherited. In all this intense bodily activity, palpable indifference prevails towards scribal craft, the lithic technology, and the archival repository. In fact, a tenth-century composition on literary enquiry emphatically renders reading as an act of re-citation, and enumeratively specifies the varied effects of different 'readings' (as recitation). Further, the same composition, while acknowledging the prevalence of writing and writing material, identifies the poet as the one who does *not* (himself) write. The poet (kavi) is not the scribe.[13]

II

As is well known in the context of India, colonialism introduced the concept of the archive and inaugurated the practice of the centralized accumulation of documents. In a way colonialism can be described as initiating a colossal conflict of the archives. It is a conflict of two distinct modes of remembrance and articulation of heritages. It can be said that colonialism is a decisive encounter between an un-archival tradition and a mnemotechnical civilizational programme. Indeed it's a conflict between the scribal culture of monotheism (which began with Moses and the lithic script of the Commandments) and the dispersed enactments of mnemocultures. Colonialism (with its mnemotechnical–archival heritage) ruptures this mnemocultural performative ethos.

In the conflict of the archives, the civilizational pedagogic model accomplished its task by two powerful modes: (*a*) by displacing or reducing the prevailing immemorial traditions of speech and gesture; and (*b*) by instituting 'new' modes of teaching and 'new' materials for education. These new initiatives measured the tradition (or reduced it) in terms of scribal or print systems—systems that formed the bedrock of monotheism. (Translation and printed circulation of the Bible exceeded any single text in the history of human kind.) Retrieval and standardization of 'reliable' manuscriptural texts became the noblest vocation of the civilizational archival mission in the nineteenth century. A plethora of 'pandits' (among others), as will be shown below, serving as native informants functioned as scribes and lent themselves to the making of the colonial archive for inscribing and 'fixing' the tradition. (Initiated into the civilizational pedagogic programme, the 'new' pandits began to emerge since the second half of the nineteenth century.)

Almost every scholar/critic working in the field of Indic studies is aware of the alithic or mnemocultural system and substance of the Sanskrit heritage. Yet rarely (almost never) does the system and mode receive epistemological attention. The substance of the heritage often gets a historical/linearized treatment in the hands of Indological scholars. Often scholars like Bothlingk (to Olivelle), disregarding the proliferative force of the mnemic heritage, sought to squeeze out single 'critical' editions of specific texts. In such an enterprise, the pluridimentionally circulating texts first get reduced to the newly gathered scribal mode and substance, and then—after the 'correction'—they get subjected to the newly emergent print mode. Once the print mode makes over the routes of epistemic circulation, the proliferative mnemocultural force gets displaced.

For the mode brings forth an unforeseen category of addressees who begin to stake claims over the heritage. Indology as a print-dominated mode of enquiry remains a communicative network among the new inheritors. Their enquiry is conditioned by and functions as a response to the lithic/print mode of organizing/circulating inheritances. Once the print mode became the dominant vector for organizing and disseminating the past, even the heterogeneity of the scribal (manuscript) mode (later collected, preserved in centralized archives through systematic institutional and administrative channels) seldom receives attention.[14]

Archival impulse is the legacy of colonial modernity. Wherever colonial institutions took root, this impulse gripped all those who crossed their precincts. Thus we can broadly sketch, in the context of Andhra, at least five generations enveloped by the archival impulse. The archival–retrieval drive has captured five generations of learned men from coastal Andhra since the end of the eighteenth century. If Mackenzie and the Kavali brothers[15] begin the first period, Brown and his (lowly paid) team occupies the second generation; Manavalli Ramakrishna Kavi and Veturi Prabhakara Sastry[16] and such others' collections and classifications, their organization of manuscripts and corrected editions form the crucial third phase; in a modest but significant manner B. Ramaraju's contribution is also a noteworthy effort in this context.[17] We need to await the concrete outcomes, in the fifth phase, of the explorations of the Indira Gandhi National Centre for the Arts (IGNCA) and the National Mission for Manuscripts (NMM) in the coming years. These two organizations already indicate the challenges and the tasks awaiting a new generation of competent intellectual labour.[18]

When one looks at this entirely novel archival drive spanning more than two centuries (the period of colonial modernity and our contemporaneity), what strikes one is its resolute tone-deafness, its decisive separation of the scribal from the acoustic. Such a separation was unheard of in the entire stretch of Indic cultural formations. It is not just the question of practical limitations (lack of audio-recording facilities in the early phases) that is the issue here. What is at stake here is the decisive alteration of reflective practices through the new apparatuses (like the archive and museum) in the colonial civilizational programme.

What receives the centre of attention here is the centralized object called the 'text'—a scribal artefact resulting from sifting, filtering, and manipulative mechanisms of the expert reader or group of readers. Once such an object is brought forth into existence, it reduces all the multiple versions of the composition from circulation—if these versions have not already been captured in some prohibitive archive. Thus, for example, we barely get to know about the fifty odd manuscripts of Vemana once Brown's edition emerges.

Apart from this resolute birth of the text, the more decisive casualty of the archival imperative is the waning of the voice. None of the Vemana or Potana[19] editions can give us the experience of the immemorial acoustic reflective traditions that enabled these compositions. Colonial archives are deaf and dusty—for this institution emerged from a culture that for centuries silenced or broke away from the haunting melodies of immemorial voices and resonances. The point that needs emphasis here is not (just) about Indic indifference to writing, but the more specific colonial fabrication of the centralized archive, which wrenches the 'text' away from the voice and denigrates the latter (Max Müller's contempt for the 'babble of idiots', recitations of the Brahmins, is well known;[20] and Brown had no sympathetic ear for the metrical melodic compositions of the Telugus; he thought he could do away with the musical modes of reflection easily[21]).

Unlike the British colonial authorities, one wonders, what the foot soldiers of these new granaries of knowledge thought about what they were serving to consolidate; one wonders what someone like Veturi Prabhakara Sastry or Vedam Venkataraya Sastry,[22] with their gifted voice and celebrated teachers from the formidable tradition of acoustic reflective learning, thought of their work; what did Veturi think of his labour when he was so intensely, indeed feverishly, involved in collecting, classifying, and commenting on the manuscripts in Madras—when he was reduced to a mere copyist? Unlike Umakanta Vidyasekharulu or Sripada Subramania Sastry (formidable critics of colonial culture in the first half of twentieth century), Veturi may not have experienced any rupture between his archival passion and his traditional vocalic learning. (Ironically even the latter two learned Telugus were captured in colonial institutional structures—Umakanta in the Madras Government College and Sripada[23] with printing press.)

Veturi's gifted voice and learning remained with him even as he
worked on the manuscripts, with the voice probably guiding him;
he *listened* to what he read. But the archive would separate the voice
from the script unless the 'reader' is gifted with the voice and is
not ashamed of its call (for modernity muffles one's throat). But the
archive that these savants were pouring their life into has no space
for the reverberations of the voice that these foot soldiers nurtured.
Did this fate not bother them? Were they not disturbed by this
throttled destination of the recitational–performative mnemocultural heritage of which they were the worthy heirs? Were they not
sensitive to the colossal price that colonialism was squeezing out
from them even as they laboured indefatigably? The snares of scrip-
toria and its archival passion suddenly, in just a generation, seem to
have entrapped scores of Sastrys, Sarmas, Murthys, Acharyas and a
host of others nurtured in the mnemocultural *vāngmaya* (pervasive
utterance) traditions.

III

But surely colonialism did not initiate scribal collections? Indeed Jain
Bhandaras, sectarian *mathas*, temples and above all regional king-
doms did maintain personal, cult, or royal collections. Mongols were
said to have destroyed Nalanda 'libraries'; Bahamanis did this to the
Vijayanagara empire; Mughals are said to have burnt the libraries of
Chithodgarh; the British East India company took over Tipu Sultan's
acquisitions; the Nayakas and the Marathas are reputed to have maintained scribal collections. Even individuals like Kavichandracharya
of Kasi is said to have had a collection of 2,192 manuscripts in the
seventeenth century (and this collection is said to have moved into
Raja Anupasimha's repository in Bikaner). Yet the nature of these
collections in the first (mainly Buddhist and Jain) and the second
millennia (Persian, Islamic) is very different from the systematic
and institutionally expanding archivization drive of European
colonialism. In the new cultural politics of British rule, the archive is
the source of knowledge and power—it is the most powerful infor-
mational passage to grasp the native mind. The very concept of the
archive is deeply shaped by the conception of nation. On the other
hand, the precolonial scribal collections had no institutional status

nor were they conceived as sources of power and knowledge. Above all, no unifying conception of nation brought them forth.

The cherished pasts of the feudatory or princely estates, for example, of Telangana, appear to have little to do with the scribal accumulations of these regimes. Neither Gadwal, Jataprolu, Amarachinta, Papannapeta, nor Vanaparthy are remembered for their manuscript collections. Although Gadwal and Vanaparthy acquired printing presses (almost a century after Madras got them) and published books, their reputation has little to do with the print technology. Each of these modest estates (with a few hundred tiny villages in their regimes) has for centuries organized periodic *kavya* (poetic composition), *śāstra* (reflective composition) gatherings and contestations. These gatherings are essentially performative sites where the learned and the creative offer or perform their novel compositions. Such performative exposures are open to contestation and provocation.

Each such estate nurtured and sustained individual kavis, *gāyakas* (singers), *śāstrakāras*, and *vayyākaranis* (analysers of language formations). Although these estates were modest (Gadwal's value was about 12 lakhs by the end of nineteenth century), they were not only hospitable to savants from far-off centres of learning and creativity (such as Kashi, Jodhpur, Maharashtra, Bengal) but also sustained pandits who moved across the country to take part in agonal debates on kavyas, śāstras and *sangeeta* (musical performances). Celebrated pandits from Gadwal and Surapuram such as Bukkapattanam Srinivasacharyulu, Brahmatantra Parakala Yateendrulu, are reputed to have moved across various learned and contestatory arenas with accolades.[24] And, it must be emphasized here, none of these activities was driven by any literacy fever or archival passion. None of these estates appears to have either accumulated or organized surveys for manuscripts in their centuries-long existence. On the contrary, what gets emphasized is the fact that the entire literary agonal debates were essentially articulated in the sonic acoustic medium. Historians surmised that hundreds of thousands of on-the-spot (*ashu*) poems, poems composed in response to the situation at hand, were irretrievably lost.[25] The historian's lament has no matching sentiment in the poet's compositions, because the poet, unlike the historian, has no use for archived texts; he performs mnemoculturally.

There were about 400 such estates by the middle of the eighteenth century in Andhra, of which at least a hundred were actively involved in the literary cultural activities indicated earlier.[26] The story of such estates provides the essential clue to the heterogeneity of cultural creative and reflective formations of India. It is from one such modest Papannapet or Domakonda (Medak) estate that the celebrated Mallinathasuri received Kalidasa's work and responded to him singularly in the fifteenth century. The legacy of Mallinatha is warm in the memories of the (Telangana) region. Scores of such receptions, responses, and communications across millennia and from hundreds of miles of distance and difference can be grasped from such territorially small but culturally vibrant domains of this region. Manthena, Chennur, Dharmapuri, Domakonda, and Kaleshwaram[27] are just the hazy contours of this sprawling mountainous region. Despite political debacles of empires (Chalukyan, Kakatiya, Vijayanagara), the lively undercurrent of creative reflective force spreading across and refiguring its contours from time to time can be sensed here. Gadwal and Vanaparti sustained such currents until the formation of the Indian nation in the middle of twentieth century.

It is surely plausible to assume that the creative reflective life of these estates is not outside the literacy of scribal culture; surely the poets and śāstrakāras were familiar with scribes and palm leaves (let's recall Srinatha's contempt for scribes).[28] Some of them even might have had their own copies of various compositions of their interest. Yet nowhere do we come across any reference or sense of a common repository, a centralized archive under the control of any royal power which the kavi-pandits frequented. The scribal compositions were dispersed, individually received or circulated; we are yet to come across any reference to Rajarajanarendra acquiring any palm-leaf collections of the Mahabharata for Nannya for his Telugu translation in the eleventh century. Although, Kautilya refers to *akshapatala*, a repository of documents, these are apparently revenue records; curiously he does not refer to any 'department' that managed any of the literary reflective collections.[29] The routes through which these scribal artefacts circulated appear to be through the dispersed but connected nodal points of region- or princely state–specific and periodic literary reflective gatherings.

These gatherings enlivened, provoked, and recouped the savants. Such gatherings not only offered challenging occasions for creativity but they enabled critical reception and response to what one was exposed to. No wonder Gadwal received the celebrated appellation Vidvadgadwala, the learned or enlightened Gadwala (or the Gadwala of the learned or enlightened). Even after colonialism clamped its talons on cultural India (as archival work went on intensely) elsewhere, Gadwal was hosting its learned mnemocultural gatherings, with pandits and poets from various parts of India participating in them.

Colonial organizations such as the Asiatic Society, Oriental Institutions (Madras, Mysore, Maharashtra), Deccan College, Bhandarkar Institute and other archivally driven establishments began to displace the diversely interlaced circuits of performative learning and responsive receptions of the traditions. The scribal-philological identity of these institutions (as was the case elsewhere) is contingent upon their severance from mnemocultural performative sources. The Oriental Manuscript Library of Madras had no use for Veturi's metrical–tonal performative competence or his resonant acoustic memory. As foot soldiers of the archival empire, they were required to compile or 'correct' the anti-acoustic words on the page (at the rate of five rupees for copying one hundred *anushtup* (metrical quatrain) slokas/verses in the 1930s;[30] the copying did not require the copyists to know how to recite such slokas).

What we have elaborated so far can be formulated in a single sentence: despite the circulation of writing before colonialism, there is no simple continuity between Indic scribal cultures and the archival institutions of the colonial empire. Earlier, mnemocultural performativity structured the scribal cultures for millennia. Both the critical factors of embodied memory and lively performativity were either silenced or effaced in the imperium or the scriptorium of the archive. The question as to who possessed the manuscript does not appear to have had much significance earlier;[31] what mattered in the mnemocultural milieu was how one responded to the received in the acoustic–performative mode without the aid of memory surrogates (texts).

Many of the pandit–poets, śāstrakāras–vayyakarani–kavis, even when they had manuscripts or books, rarely referred to them in their dialogues and *goshtis* (gatherings). These 'texts' were of no use in their performatives. We can notice this even in contemporary performances of the Dakkali[32] *Jambapurana*. Although they bring forth their palm-leaf manuscript from time to time, nowhere does the performance get controlled or regulated by the reading from the text. The mnemocultural force brings the Purana to life. No wonder manuscripts in the earlier scribal cultures remained scattered and dispersed across individuals, families, mathas, and estates. Should it then surprise one that Ramaraju declared that 'the Telangana is a treasure trove of palm leaf manuscripts'?[33] With the famed Kakatiya empire and scores of cultural nodes spread out across Telangana, the dispersal of palm-leaf manuscripts in the region is certainly a plausible phenomenon. Even to this day, copies of unpublished manuscripts are said to survive among the descendants of the estates and families of poets and pandits.[34] Ramaraju's indefatigable searches yielded him rich rewards, and one among them was the famed stylus of Mallinathasuri in Medak.

IV

Whatever their existing conditions are, colonial institutions like the archive, museum, and the university are here to stay. One cannot, however, say that they have become worthy replacements for the earlier dispersed but connected networks of cultural nodes. This is because these institutions are transplants from a different cultural milieu. In Europe, where these institutions paved way for a whole range of activities (search for origins, originals, obsession with certainty and authenticity of the artefact, authorial identity, interpretative manoeuvres to establish the relation between the text, the author and the world, myth and history, possessive preservation of the relics of the past, professionalization and institutionalization of scribal practices and products, and so on), the church as the singular centralized institution oversaw and regulated them. As suggested earlier, these institutions are the calibrated vectors for initiating epistemic rupture in colonized cultures. Predictably these vectors have lured generations of eminent pandits to become foot soldiers or lowly paid coolies in consolidating those very structures that ruptured the cherished modes of responsive reception, modes that nurtured and enhanced variedly the cultural formations of India. These institutions turned mnemocultural acoustic performative energies into muffled voices condemned to dark and dusty shelves in barely accessed centralized repositories.

The cruel irony of the situation is that these institutions (especially, the archive and the museum [the latter received the name 'dead college' among some copyists])[35] devoted to archival passions should deploy those very heirs as these scribal coolies had no sense of an externalized retentional system (archive) in their immemorial past; and precisely these very mnemocultrually learned were drawn to embalm their lively heritage in the silent vaults of privileged possession (now designated with the lovingly repeated cliché 'wealth of India' on the NMM website).

Yet the colonial institutions cannot be wished away; at this stage there is no alternative to the continuity of these institutions. But we need to be sensitive, without succumbing to cynicism, to the fact that these institutions continue to perpetrate cultural violence—the violence of fundamental alteration of cultural orientation from outside with force, by which mnemocultural scribal modes are forced into anti-acoustic, non-performative institutions. The second major programmatic effect of this epistemic rupture is the foreclosure or even denigration of the *marked body* that invigorated and spread across heterogeneous cultural formations of India over millennia. As is well known, the creative and reflective forms and formations of India are entirely contingent upon the internally differentiated non-unifiable biocultural formation called the *jāti* (community).

In a word, in the 'Indian' context (although not limited to it), one cannot think of culture without the sense of the multiple singularities of community and their idiomatic articulations and inheritances. Neither these communities, which are themselves intricately differentiated internally and in relation to their counterparts, nor their articulations can be subsumed under a normative discursive order. No wonder that European human sciences could neither respond to the call of these deliriously varied singularities nor could they show any responsibility for them. With cultivated disregard for the unknown other, they violently imposed normative schemas on these formations. They fabricated a *system* of caste and erected a religion called Hinduism.

As a part of their protocols of representation, these human sciences tried to circumscribe the proliferating multiplicity of jātis by manuscripting, codifying, and recording them, centralizing their mnemocultural forms and formations by prosthetic means through primitive accumulation modes for archives and normed standards for them in forging 'critical editions'. It is impossible to think of the spread of the human sciences without the replication of the normative order and without the powerful reiterative techniques of scribal and print mechanisms globally.

'Caste' vindicates the limits of European sensitivity and responsibility to what does not conform to European cultural referents. Caste exposes the European failure to respond to the most unique opportunity it has had to overcome Eurocentrism; it is a colossal epistemic failure to respond to something radically different. Unfamiliar with and insensitive to profoundly heteronormative currents of life/living, European irresponsibility stigmatises what it dubbed as caste on the eve of colonialism. Colonial institutions aim at cleansing the Indian cultural heritage of its jāti springs that generate and disseminate it variedly. Alternatively, jāti is configured as a unified *system* of oppression.

Consequently, the constitutive relation between jāti and culture as productive and a singular source of Indic distinction and difference gets barely discussed. No wonder NMM (http://www.namami.org/index.htm) has no space for the newly emerged artisans of scribal culture: scribes, calligraphers, palm-leaf makers, and metal workers (surely, these *vruttikaras* (expositors) would have found differentiated but distinct space for them among the catalogue of the 64 'arts'—the *chatushshastikalas*).[36] Unlike in other cultural formations, in the Indian context artisans and 'service' groups are not merely anonymous workers or labourers as such. Each of these groups is a culturally configured and differentiated non-cohering collective. Jātis as distinct biocultural formations wove the varying hues and fibres of Indian reflective and creative traditions.

The archival catalogues, which are quintessentially the product of colonial institutions, stand eloquent testimony to the fact that they are cleansed of the jāti provenance of the material gathered. To put it more starkly—there is no jāti census of the catalogued material.[37] The fact that before scribal material was driven into centralized archives it was brought forth and circulated via the jāti circuits makes the epistemic rupture more palpable (that is precisely how a Savara elder or a Dakkali elder carries his palm-leaf inheritances intimately). Here once again the stark asymmetry between European and Indian entries into modern institutions can be pointed out. Almost every scholar who contributed or participated in the formation of modern scholarship and institutions in Europe was driven by a specific religious allegiance or antagonism (Catholic, Jew, Protestant [Lutheran, Calvinist], Jesuit, Renaissance, Restoration, Republic of Letters, Enlightenment). In other words, no epistemic rupture structures the transition from Christian (or Jewish) cultural ideational forms to modern institutional forms in Europe (though, ironically, 'epistemological break' and 'dissociation of sensibility' were hastily derived from the conflict between Catholics and Protestants).[38] On the other hand, these very institutions, wrenching and severing the material from practices, disregarding the relationship between jāti and heritage erupt an epistemic violence in the colonial context. If culture in the form of religion provides the dynamic in Europe,[39] the latter undermines and denigrates culture as jāti in our context. Today we continue to live this ruptured legacy even when we talk about our 'national wealth'.

V

The rupture between jāti and culture plays out most blatantly in the domain of ethnography and folklore; this throws into abyssal doubt the nature and purpose of these human sciences in our context. This is because the collectors and the custodians of these cultures in the newly emerged colonial institutions never had the privilege to receive those divergent cultures. Unlike in the case of scribal heritage, the radically heterogeneous mnemocultural inheritances of divergent jātis have never had (nor can they ever have one despite the catachrestic label of Hinduism) any single, unified cultural institutional space for their convergence or representation (there is no single temple that brings together all jātis and *janjati*s of India). The strength of their longevity and the source of their lively survival appear to be the result of the absence of any sovereign commanding and controlling institutional force. Jātis sustained and replenished their cultures autonomously. The immemorial guardians of cultural memories are

internally differentiated liminal figures—the excluded insider figures
of various jātis. They alone are the mnemocultural custodians and
innovative disseminators of the acoustic and performative idioms of
divergent singularities of jātis; they are the inheritors of the cherished
Suta–Bharata–Seer tradition, which opened up for the entirety of jāti
clusters the *itihasic–puranic*, performative and song-poetic cultural
forms. These lively heritages are unquantifiable and immeasurable.

Whereas ethnographic folklore, emerging from the devastating
disruptions of industrial onslaught (in Europe), is an urban vocation
about rural cultures; the addressees and agents of ethnographic folklore
(including ethnomusicology) remain, as in the case of Indology, urban
professionals of modern institutions. These emergent professionals
aimed at capturing and recording the mnemocutlural creations of communities that were vanishing rapidly into industrial urban complexes.
These communities were mainly identified as artisans, husbandmen,
servicemen, and peasants in European cultural history. As new professions and disciplines emerged, the immemorial custodians of mnemocultures disappeared in the European context.

The Indian scenario presents a fundamentally contrasting view to
that of Europe. As pointed out earlier, cultural forms and practices
of India are deeply filiated to the singularities of jāti. Despite radical
upheavals (Islamic invasions, British imperialism, Christian religious
and capitalist industrial onslaughts) the enigmatic cultural string
called jāti survived tenaciously (albeit with alterations) in the Indian
cultural formations. The divergent jāti strings wove the cultural fabric
of India. In response to the siren calls of colonial institutions, Indian
academics retrieved and recorded tonnes of 'folk' material and consolidated ill-thought disciplines called folklore studies. It is not just the
textualizing mnemocultures of divergent communities that one notices
here; these studies perpetrate the even more astonishing wrenching
apart of jāti and culture in a heritage that is essentially built on the
intricate weaving of jātis and cultures. Even today, it is impossible to
come across a narrative, song, or performatives of a community without becoming aware of the provenance of these forms in profoundly
differentiated jātis. Thus we know that the *Jambapuranamu* cannot
be associated with Kurmas and Madel cannot be reduced to Sugalis.
But this fundamental filiation between jāti and culture has not yet
received any serious theoretical–reflective attention.

It is impossible to believe that pioneers in Telugu folklore like Ramaraju, Donappa, Nayani Krishnakumari were unaware of the jāti provenance of the 'lore' they were passionately collecting and writing about. Their classifications, descriptions, thematizations, and commentaries (in short, their 'methodologies') have little to say about the relation between jāti and culture. Thus Ramaraju, for instance, proceeds to classify his 'data' in terms of singer (male, female, or child), themes (historical, mythological, otherworldly, and religious), and moods/motifs (heroic, ferocious, wondrous, humorous, erotic, and so on)—a classification without any source in Indian reflective creative traditions. Ramaraju devotes exactly 15 pages (Chapter 15) in a volume of 850 pages to give a descriptive list of some eight jātis. None of these cultural jātis and forms offers any insight to think about Indian cultural distinction or specificity in this work.[40] That is the measure of the disciplinary violence.

Similarly, Nayani Krishnakumari has exactly two pages of description about *kulas* (castes) in her *Janapada Geyalu–Samghika Charitra* (folk songs and social history), which she edited with Ramaraju.[41] This 400-page anthology (of about 19 recorded works) cleanses the song forms from their jāti provenances by default as it were. We never get to know which particular jāti or jātis weave and nurture the songs, ballads, or Puranas retrieved by the anthologists. Following colonial programming, these pioneers unify the heterogeneous jātis into 'folk', peasants, and beggars. Pathos and anxiety, typical of ethnographic folklore—a sense of remorse at the presumed loss of the lore of the folk—pervade the pioneers' work: 'It is worthy to uplift or retrieve and preserve all that orally available folk literary wealth.'[42] This is the ethnographer's credo.

VI

If culture is what we do and what we or others say about what we do, colonialism, through new discourses, modes, and institutions, ruptures the relationship between our experience and what we say about what we do. In privileging speech and gestural media, Indian cultural formations preferred embodied modes of articulation; they remained, despite the prevalence of scribal technologies, alithic in their orientation. Such an orientation remains indifferent to externalized storage of memory in surrogate bodies like archives and museums. This is because none of these can become effective substitutes for the materiality of the body. And existence requires that we grapple with and (at)tend (to) the body as such. From very early on one notices an intense engagement with the question of the body in Indian reflective traditions. Yet the body here is not seen as a mere physical entity; nor was the *human* body given any privilege in these reflections (human remained one manifestation of *pashu* [animal]). The body in these traditions appears to be a temporal-phenomenal entity composed of heterogeneous elements: physical and non-physical other (*para*). Indian mnemocultural formations can be explored on the basis of these fundamental or foundational reflections on the body complex.

Neither material nor immaterial but nestles in the material; neither physical nor substantial but circulates in the physical; neither temporal nor finite but woven into the temporal and finite; neither originary nor terminable but located in the circle of origin and cessation; neither destructible nor threatened but caught in the ephemeral and the vulnerable, para's non-relational intimacy with the *shareera* (the body) cannot be plotted either in exclusive or reductive terms. Temporally and spatially immeasurable, para lends itself to the temporal and phenomenal: that is the enigma of the embodied existence of the body complex.

> *Yatta dadreśya magrāhya magotra mavarṇa*
> *Machakśuh śrotram tadapāṇi pādam*
> *Nityam vibhum sarvagatam susūkśmam*
> *Tat avyayam yadbhūta yonim paripaśyanti dhīrah.*

(Para is ungraspable by the senses as it is without birth, has no *gotra* (clan epithets) or kula [home], has no properties, no colours, is without eyes and ears, without organs, and eternal; spreads everywhere, absolutely subtle, without end, source for all elements: that is the a-*kshara para* [the imperishable other] and thus the thoughtful sense it.)[43]

Yet one's presumptions about a conscious/cognitive apperception of what can be called para are discounted; one's presumed agentive, self-conscious command is undermined.

> *Yasyā matam tasya matam*

Matam yasya na veda sah
Avijñātam vijānatām
Vijñātam avijānatām.

(Those who learn that para [*brahma*] cannot be known are able to learn of para. Those who presume that they have known para know nothing of 'it'. Those who wish to know para are unable to learn about it. Those who have not learnt about para are alone able to learn of it.)[44]

Here experience or learning is distanced from perception and knowledge. No resolve of the will-to-know can be an effective mode of experiencing para. Experiential learning is in asymptotic relation with epistemophilia and conscious mastery. Para appears to force itself into and comes forth as the material and measurable entity, but cannot be reduced to or identified with calculable entities. Yet at the same time, all discussion or the entire reflective orientation concerning para is invariably articulated in the context of the shareera.

Ya deveha tad amutra
yadamutra tadanviha.

(Para that nestles among all the elements manifests in accord with the resources of the body that comes forth and appears as different para. This body that para turns into is itself the common one; and that common one is this very embodied para.)[45]

In short, the realm of para's circulation is the discrete and the phenomenal multitudes. In other words, para's non-relational relation to shareera, the force's relation to form, is based on a generative impulse that seems interminable and inexhaustible. Para appears to generate or morph itself into the phenomenal and dwells in the abode of the phenomenal, remaining irreducible to the latter. This morphing of para (*vivarta*) is co-emergent with time and space, and this sets in motion the machine of iteration. The coming forth of these complicit contraries must be seen as irreducible but intimately woven differences; they must be experienced as such in and as the body—the primordial spatio-temporal unit.[46] The body as such is at once immemorially durational and ephemerally instantial.

The instantial is the effect of the durational; the durational comes forth in the instantial. Neither the instantial nor the durational can be made sense of exclusively nor can they be opposed to each other.

The relation between the durational/instantial has an effect on the question of the agential. The instantial cannot sever itself from the durational and cannot claim absolute autonomy from it. Yet the instantial has to live on its own as it were, which is what ineluctably happens. When one forgets that the instantial, discrete existent is the effect of the immemorial durational and indulges the instantial as the absolutely autonomous, such existent condemns itself to machinic repetition; such existent equals death. This is bound to occur as the instantial (the individuated and discrete beings) and the durational (the immemorial and extensive) are seen as entirely exclusive.

Mrutyossa mrutyumāpnoti
Ya iha nāneva paśyati.

(Such a life/death [which disavows para and confuses it with a multiplicity of discrete beings] cannot move toward the path of emancipation.)[47]

The durational moves on as an immeasurable rhythm of varied repetitions. Para cannot be reduced to this repetitive rhythm. Yet, it must be pointed out, that the intimations of para can only be discerned in its (para's) generative effect—in its manifestation in the radical heterogeneity of the instantial.[48] In other words, the generative impulse sets in motion differential instantiations. The intimations of para and the work of the durational must be realized and responded to in the singularity of the instantial.[49] The call of para must be responded to only by putting to work the gift/curse of the singular instantial, the finitudinal existent. How to live the instantial/durational pulls in the double bind of shareera–para is an immensely important but tacitly and praxially reflected upon question in Sanskrit traditions.

Given that para's articulation of the temporal–phenomenal is an effect of a generative impulse, it has the immense power to multiply heterogeneous entities and their modes of being in existence. The *jana*s (people) or jātis/'communities' (without community) proliferate and along with these proliferate their modes of symbolization. In short, the generative impulse disseminates textual–sexual forms in time and space. Moving on with a differential impulse the jātis disseminate divergent narrative, performative, and visual genres of symbolization. All these formations—generic, jāti-generative—are essentially mnemocultural; and they embody these intimations and put to work the body as the most efficacious mode of living on. This mode of living on of the finitudinal existence and the mnemopraxial cultivation of response in the instance of being are common to every body. It is impossible to reduce the mnemocultural intimations of the double bind of existence to some unifying and totalizing categories. Yet, the response requires one—even as one praxially forges response in the singular context—to serve the passage beyond the singular, the differential, the generated, or the determined. The response will be ineffective, despite its actual emergence in an instance of being, if it is aimed at sublimating a particularity of mode or being. Mnemopraxial responsibility is enacted across the heterotopia of these jātis and genres.

Colonialism aimed at permanently altering the filiation between the modes of being and the paraxial accounts about modes and being, between what we do and what we say about what we do. Colonial institutions like the archive, the museum, and the university are the entrenched apparatuses of this epistemic rupture. We are all caught, in *different ways*, in the machinations of these apparatuses and their discourses.

While caught in these rupturing institutions and activities, we need to begin to learn that all the work of these discourses, archival accumulations (acquired through questionable means), and institutions are inversely related to the jātis and cultures. The more and more we possess them, the less and less we can sustain them and let them proliferate in their creative modes. This is because the essential generative impulse of these heterogeneous cultural forms is the immemorial gift of these divergent jātis. While jāti as a biocultural configuration enabled cultural generation here, our new institutions, as they foreclosed the jātis, make us turn cultural formations into museumized cultural wealth, a sort of frozen capital.

The diversely spread out cultural nodes and formations on the one hand and modestly established feudatory or princely estates on the other sustained and nurtured these cultural generative impulses. They affirm eloquently (without saying so) the fact that culture fundamentally is differential and local, whereas the modern colonial implants are by definition not oriented toward nurturing such cultural generativity. On the contrary, as they figure culture as a frozen past, they are yet to explore the ways of rekindling and reinvigorating the generative impulse of cultural formations of the jātis.

VII

Mnemocultural work involves precisely the living on, the embodied or enacted endurance of the idiomatic singularities of existence in speech and in gesture. The countless proliferations of the idioms of the domains of image, music, and text in the Indian context are a testimony to the circulation of the mnemopraxial impulse. The singular-plural living on of these idiomatic modes of survival—not as exemplary instantiations of any normative model, but as an interminable play of the figural and the empirical, the finite and the infinite—is the only absolute passage for each and every *genos* and species. None, not even gods, can escape these idiomatic workings of the home-dwelling-body complex. It is indeed this rigorous (im) possible, singular-plural structure of the idiomatic-bodies/*genos* that has brought forth the extraordinarily heterogeneous mnemocultural *vidyas* (verbal learning) and *kalas* (visual creations) of the Indic subcontinent.

The endurance, tenacity, and survival of the idiom depend on its paradoxical undecidable and indeterminable movements, its conservative and transgressive proliferations. Thus every genos that emerged from the infringement of the excluded insider Sudra and the disinherited woman forged a staggering range of verbal and visual idioms that remain hospitable to the figure-name configurations of the Sanskrit mnemotextual episteme. This remains the truly extraordinary phenomenon of Indian cultural formations.

It is precisely such contrapuntal impulses that turn the proliferating generations and their idiomatic mnemotexts into excluded insiders of the Indic mnemocultures. Otherwise, one cannot make sense of the most 'excluded' (insider) Dakkalis forging a Puranic idiom of distinction and rendering it with idiomatic visual scrolls forged by another distinguished genos, the Nakashis; one cannot make sense of the Muslim Manganiyars and Langas of Rajasthan and the Patuas of Bengal composing songs on the Ramayana and the Mahabharata for their proximate but distancing and differentiating communities. The proliferation of the idiomatic textual–generational complexes, it must be affirmed, are not governed by any common normative belief as such. This is dissemination without universalism, movement without normativity. Idiom and belief are not necessarily in continuity in these mnemocultural practices. Otherwise it would be impossible to think of the extraordinary range of the open-ended musical traditions (say that of the Hindustani) whose idiomatic singularities emerge from the vigour and sense of the bodies marked by Islam. Each of the excluded-inside communities (Sarada, Baindla, Chindu, Savara, Bhaat, Dakkali, Budagajangama,[50] and so on, the list can proliferate endlessly) has singular idiomatic mnemotexts of narrative, performative, and visual cultures across heterogeneous India. These n+1 communities continue to recite the immemorial mnemocultural imports in a million voices and gestures in idiomatic variations. The singular-multiple genre that crosses the borders and moves across in unforeseen ways is the mnemotextual composition ithiasa-purana.

The immeasurable proliferation of the Mahabharata, the Ramayana and the Puranas across a staggering variety of idioms and idiomatic genres (Telugu, Hindi, Kannada, Gondi, Tulu, Marathi, and so on; Yakshaganas, grinding-mill songs; pounding-rice songs, *geet-bol* [lyrical song-speech], lullaby songs, *pravachanas* [extempore commentary], and so on) is an obvious testimony to the textual-sexual dispersals. As the symbol survives in discontinuity with the body that brought it forth or circulated it, the idiom can remain in discontinuity with any norm or belief.

VIII

One can hint at the magnitude and sheer simulacral diversity of mnemocultures when one notices a certain textual demarcation of vidya and kala in the tradition. A Sanskrit text of rather disputed origin, *Śukranītisāra*, in a rather unusual definitional move pronounces the mnemocultural significance of vidya and kala with simplicity and clarity. It must be noted that this 'definition' and enumeration of vidya(s) and kala(s) take place here in a section that begins with the drift and proliferation of generations:

Vidyāhyanantāschakalāh sankhyātum naiva śakyate
Vidyāmukhyāscha dvatrinshachatushashti kalāh smrutāh

(It is impossible to count the vidyas and kalas as they are infinite. Yet it is remembered that the more significant vidyas number thirty-two and the kalas sixty-four.)[51]

Enumeration is a compositional strategy of mnemotexts. But nowhere is this technique used to totalize or norm any ideal injunction. Enumeration suggests the irreducible possibilities of differentiation without end; enumeration is one of the finite ways of hinting at the infinite and inexhaustible. No wonder the *Śukranītisāra*, in referring to incalculable proliferation of generations affirms

Jātyānantyam tu samprāptam tadvaktum naivaśakyate.

(Generations emerging from the sexually infringed relations result in infinite jātis. It is impossible to recount them.)[52]

After confirming the impossibility of exhausting the number of vidyas and kalas, the *Śukranītisāra* offers a figural–generative account ('definition') of vidya and kala that captures in an unprecedented way the mnemocultural work of the face and the hand, of speech and gesture:

Yadyatsvādvāchikam samyakkarma vidyābhisanjnakam
Shakto mūkopi yatkartum kalāsanjnam tatsmrutam.

(Anything that is properly, efficiently organized/composed by *vak* (speech) goes under the name of vidya. That which even the speechless (dumb) can perform without the use of the mouth goes under the name of kala).[53]

Through these enactments of the body, in speech and in gesture, mnemocultures proliferate. It is difficult to assume a rigorously conceptual definition of either vidya or kala in the Sanskrit traditions. Vidya, it is true, is learning but it cannot be easily assimilated to the concept of knowledge (episteme) that gets systematically theorized in Greek thought. A certain kind of meta-positional demonstrative deployment of reason aimed at building a normative system as the vocation of knowledge (in the West); in contrast, whatever may be the complexity of the domain explored, vidya seems to imply a learning that is entirely oriented toward mnemopraxial performativity, an embodied enactment in the form of speech and gesture. Vidya, unlike knowledge, is not oriented towards an epistemophilic end: vidyas and kalas are modes of liveable learning. The centrality of the body and the imperative of the body's transformation are absolutely critical in these mnemocultural practices and textualities. Living on with a doubly composed singular body, mnemopraxial textuality and responsibility are moved by the interminable, but variedly repeated *ālāp* (improvised musical prologue)—what do you do with what you have?

Caught in the disorienting colonial institutional structures that deny or efface our experiences but impel us to fabricate accounts of them, what can be done in our postcolonial situation? Most fundamentally we need to learn to see the disruptive asymmetry between what we do and what we say about our practices. Here it must be pointed out once again that the modern implants, while they wrenched culture from the jāti, have forged, as pointed out earlier, a dubious narrative about jāti 'system' as an oppressive structure (it is impossible to turn jātis into a *system*). This unexamined fabrication whips up communal animosities and chokes cultural generative impulses. Cowered either by unexamined guilt or armed with ill-thought rage, jātis are barely in a position to reconfigure their passages to their creative pasts beyond the disruptive colonial work for an unforeseen future.

The epistemic rupture (between our experience and what we/ others say about it) continues to entrench us within the derivative structures and discourses of colonial institutions. The disastrous consequences of this rupture are surging forth more and more stridently and genocidally (in the sense of erasing the genus) in the functioning of these colonially transplanted institutions today. This is because as 'new' cultural institutions they have barely any continuity with the mnemoculturally oriented heterogeneous cultures and jātis. Colonial institutions are yet to offer any innovative ways and modes of reorienting the generative impulses of our lasting biocultural formations. As the diversely spread sources that nurtured and sustained these jāti-cultural forms and formations have been liquidated, and as the colonially implanted new institutions have little comprehension or concern for these formations, the heirs of the jātis (distanced from creative impulses) see these institutions as only sources of upward mobility.

Yet, the disruptive institutions are here to stay. Political expediency ('democracy') has increasingly undermined the regulative procedures of access to these institutions. Predictably, public institutions witness mounting demands for access to whatever the dwindling resources that these institutions appear to promise. But these institutions are yet to be equipped to face the groundswell of demand from divergent jātis. What to teach, how to teach, what to archive, should one archive at all, how to train, what to impart to these new generations are the most challenging and grave questions; but they are barely confronted in the context of our colonially entrenched institutions today. In the absence of viable alternatives access to these alienating institutions cannot be denied to any.

IX

How can this aporetic predicament be negotiated? Can this situation of impossibility be turned into a situation of possibility? *Perhaps* it might be possible to turn this impossible impasse into a possible passageway to our varied pasts. In order to think through and move beyond (*via*) the violent colonial implants one needs to take radical risks. One such risk is to rearticulate the relation between jāti and culture as vigorously and openly as possible. This risk makes one notice the incongruity between the unified, centralized, top-down, normative colonial institutions and the radically heterogeneous, non-normative, differently dispersed jāti-cultural formations. We notice that no sovereign normative order oversees the emergence, continuity, and dispersal of these jātis and formations. These latter far exceed and go beyond the reach and grasp of the colonial institutions.

In this regard the radical contrast between the heteronormative, non-cohering cultural nodes and their networks in the precolonial cultural circuits and the colonial institutional structures is instructive. But today these institutions (mainly academic) are increasingly peopled by the distanced inheritors of the divergent communities. When we pay attention to the student composition of our classrooms, with a sense of the diverse genealogies of Indian cultural formation, we might become alert to the tasks we need to undertake. These first-generation entrants into the university must be exposed to the complex cultural fabric of India and the ways in which each of the jātis composing the class(room) has woven its strings and made its singular space in the texture of Indian formation.

This reorientation to cultural pasts may aim at affirming the jāti genealogies and their singular and incomparable cultural creations. In other words, one must aim at rekindling a sense of responsibility among the distanced inheritors towards their ruptured and denigrated inheritances. As jātis alone have access to the singularity of their generative impulse, jātis must be made responsible for resuscitating and transforming their cultural forms and formations. Although this might sound contradictory, the very colonial institutional site of the university must be made the venue or arena for this rethinking of jāti-culture filiation and their inter-animation; the university must be made the source for rekindling responsibility to cultural singularities and the general reorientation of cultural formations in the Indian context. For it is this rupturing institution that must itself be reoriented to suture the jāti-cultural fabric that it has violently torn apart. The university must enable the singularities to experience their generalizable potentiality and their relation to the cultural formations in general.

The university, while learning to be hospitable to the jāti-cultural filiation, will have the double task of nurturing cultural creative singularities and articulating the *generalizable force of the singular*. In order to render these tasks the university must immerse itself in the cultural formations of the region in which it is located. Depending on the number of universities and the jāti-cultural formations in the region the universities can form into clusters. While each of the universities attends to the jāti-cultural formations singularly and collectively (in the clusters), what will be common to the university in general is its task of articulating the general through the singular (where the relation between the singular and general is neither oppositional nor hierarchically sequential but supplemental). Practical and theoretical modules and tasks can be designed to be shared and tested across units, clusters, and constellations. Further the university must be made to play the catalytic role of initiating radical epistemic comparatological enquiries across singular Indian jāti-cultural formations and other European and non-European cultural formations.

However dangerous (risks must be taken!) and retrograde this might sound, in all the above activities jātis as the stakeholders of the region and cluster must be involved as role players in the common pursuit of cultural resuscitation in the Indian context. Given the formations of jāti and culture in the Indian context, the way to reorient and innovate cultural inheritances cannot ignore the critical space of jāti. Therefore, modern institutions must unlearn their colonial dogma about jāti as a *system* of pure oppression and learn to work with its cultural creative impulses and resources. Otherwise the colonial consciousness will aggravate the rupture between what we do and what we are programmed to say about what we do. Colonial institutions will continue to deprive us of our experience. It is against these paralyzing determinations that we must learn to strive and reinvigorate our heterogeneous mnemocultural, scribal, performative, and genealogical inheritances. Only through such a future anterior praxial mode can we hope to reconfigure a different future for our varied inheritances today. Such a task would perhaps enable us to reconfigure philosophical anthropology from outside the ipsocratic traditions of Europe and envisage a future anterior democracy to come.

Notes

This paper in its present form was first presented at the Backwaters Collective conference on Metaphysics and Politics, in Cochin in 2013. I wish to thank Vinay Lal and Roby Rajan for inviting me to the conference.

1. Jacques Derrida, 'The Other of Democracy', in *Rogues: Two Essays on Reason*, translated by Pascale-Anne Brault and Michael Naas (Stanford: Stanford University Press, 2005), 40–1.
2. Martin Heidegger, '"Only a God Can Save Us": The *Spiegel* Interview', translated by William J. Richardson, S.J., *Der Spiegel* (31 May 1976), 45–67, available at http://religiousstudies.stanford.edu/WWW/Sheehan/pdf/ heidegger_texts_online/1966%20ONLY%20A%20GOD%20CAN%20 SAVE%20US.pdf, accessed on 21 January 2014.
3. Therefore, the categories with which we think, say 'metaphysics and politics', themselves are part of the problem that one needs to think through.
4. Martin Heidegger, 'The Question Concerning Technology', in *The Question Concerning Technology and Other Essays*, translated by William Lovitt (New York: Harper Torchbooks, 1977), 35.
5. Rodolphe Gasche, *Europe, or the Infinite Task: A Study of a Philosophical Concept* (Stanford: Stanford University Press, 2009), 1–20.
6. Such differentiation is what Jan Meulenbeld, exploring the medicinal traditions of India, calls the 'demarcationist principle', which models scientific enquiry on European experience. Such an account contends

that 'Western science alone can be regarded as a system of knowledge based on rationality and directed at the structure of reality'. Meulenbeld, 'Reflections on the Basic Concepts of Indian Pharmacology', in *Studies in Indian Medical History*, edited by G. Jan Meulenbeld and Dominik Wujastyk (Delhi: Motilal Banarsidass, 2001), 1.

7. 'I beg, therefore, to submit to you that the future of philosophical anthropology does not lie in giving an Asian, African or an American-Indian answer to the western (religious) questions about man. Rather, the quest for man involves, in the first place, raising Asian, African, and American-Indian *questions* about "man". To do so, I suggest, is what makes philosophical anthropology "topical" ... Whether intellectuals from other cultures and groups are up to this task, however, is a totally different issue.' S. N. Balagangadhara, 'The Reality of Elusive Man?', available at http://www.hipkapi.com/2011/03/05/the-reality-of-elusive-man-s-n-balagangadhara/, accessed on 20 May 2013.

8. Richard Solomon, 'On the Origin of the Early Indian Scripts', *Journal of the American Oriental Society* 115, no. 2 (1995), 271–9.

9. This number is suggested by the Indira Gandhi National Centre for the Arts, whereas the National Mission for Manuscripts suggests about five million manuscripts as the extant Indian scribal collection. Sheldon Pollock, 'Literary Culture and Manuscript Culture in Precolonial India', in *Literary Cultures and the Material Book*, edited by Simon Eliot, Andrew Nash, and Ian Willson (London: The British Library, 2007), 87. Also see, Sudha Gopalakrishnan, 'Introduction', *Tattvabodha*, vol. 1, edited by Sudha Gopalakrishnan (Delhi: National Mission for Manuscripts and Munshiram Manoharlal Publishers, 2006), ix. David Pingree is said to have observed that the worldwide spread of Sanskrit manuscripts runs into thirty million. See, Mail from Dominik Wujastyk on 19 March 2009 available at http://list.indology.info/pipermail/indology_list.indology.info/.)

10. K. V. Sarma, a renowned scholar on Indian mathematics and astronomy, observed (in 2005) that 'a very large number of science manuscripts in Sanskrit' lay dispersed in manuscript libraries and in private possession and that 90–5 per cent of this scribal material is not available in print (and in translation). K. V. Sarma, 'Sanskrit and Science, A New Area of Study', in *Mathematics and Medicine in Sanskrit*, edited by Dominik Wujastyk (Delhi: Motilal Banarsidass, 2009), 16. A Japanese scholar has identified some eighteen manuscript libraries so far in India (including Nepal). See http://ricas.ioc.u-tokyo.ac.jp/eng/asj/html/guide/india/i_l1_f.html, accessed on 25 March 2013.

11. Sheldon Pollock's paper ('Literary Culture and Manuscript Culture in Precolonial India') mentioned in note 9 is mainly aimed at contending

that print, unlike in the case of Europe, has had no significant impact in Indian cultural history. Consequently, he emphasizes in this paper and elsewhere in his work, the predominance of the manuscript (or scribal) culture in India. However, when one examines this claim more closely in Pollock's paper, one cannot fail to notice that even manuscript culture could not undermine the power of the acoustic or recitational orientation of Indian cultural formations. Secondly, Pollock, while aiming at critiquing the universal claims of print culture pays no attention at all to the universalist claims made in European tradition regarding the impact of literacy or writing. If writing was such a crucial 'technological' development in the Indian context as Pollock claims, how do Indian scribal cultures differ from those of the West? Among the various works that deal with the impact of writing in Greek antiquity, see Eric Havelock, *Preface to Plato* (Cambridge, Massachusetts: Belknap Press, 1963). For a critique of Havelock, see G. R. F. Ferrari, 'Orality and Literacy in the Origin of Philosophy', *Ancient Philosophy* 4 (1984), 194–204.

12. Interestingly, Sankara, in his bhasya-response to the Bhagavad Gita differentiates between *vidhi* and *anuvāda*. Vidhi in this tradition of responsive reception brings forth something different and new; whereas anuvāda represents the already existent for a specific purpose. Commenting on the word *yuddhyasva*, Sankara points out that Krishna's counsel to Arjuna to commence the war was only a reminder of his pre-given activity and not an incitement to do something new. Krishna was only clearing the obstacle (formed by ignorance) coming in the way. '*Yuddhyasva iti anuvādamātram; na vidhih.*' *Srī Bhagavadgītā Śankarabhāṣyam: Āndhrabhāṣāsavyākhyāyā Bālānandinyā Samanchitam*, translated with a commentary by Pullela Srirama Chandrudu (Hyderabad: Arsha Vijnana Trust, 2001), 64. Viewed in this light, what Sankara does in his *bhāyaśyā*s is a vidhi (bringing forth something new) and not an anuvāda.

13. Rajasekhara, *Kāvyamīmāmsā*, translated by Pullela Srirama Chandrudu (Hyderabad: Sri Jayalakshmi Publications, 2003), 158.

14. For a symptomatic celebratory account of the arrival of print, which completely forgets or disavows the surviving acoustic cultures of memory in the provincial Indian context of Madras, see A. R. Venkatachalapathy, *The Province of the Book: Scholars, Scribes, and Scribblers in Colonial Tamilnadu* (Ranikhet: Permanent Black, 2012). The symptom of colonial–ideological frame can't be missed in the very opening sentence of this book: 'In the beginning was the word. And then came print, adding immensely to its fascination.' The book has little to offer in reflection on these crucial terms 'the word' and the 'the beginning' in the Indian cultural reflective context.

15. Colin Mackenzie as an engineer, surveyor, and, above all, collector of manuscripts of the East India Company meets two brothers (Borrayya and Lakshmaiha) in Andhra. These two brothers, as native informants, served Mackenzie in gathering, translating, and interpreting the local scribal output in the late eighteenth and early nineteenth centuries. See Arudra for a celebratory account of the trio in his 'Mackenzie and Kavali Brothers', in *Telugu Vaitalikulu* (collection of essays), vol. 3, edited by Devulapalli Ramanuja Rao (Hyderabad: AP Sahitya Akademi, 1979), 133–58.

16. Manavalli Ramakrishna Kavi (1866–1957) was a renowned scholar, collector, and curator of manuscripts in the first half of the twentieth century. He is known for his discovery of Abhinavagupta's *Abhinava Bharati*, which he edited. See P. S. R. Appa Rao's introduction to his translation (into Telugu) of Bharata's *Natya Sastra* (Secunderabad: Ajanta Printers, n.d.), 10–11. Veturi Prabhakara Sastry (1888–1950) too is well known for his work on manuscript collections and studies in folklore. He worked with Manavalli Ramakrishna Kavi at the Government Oriental Manuscript Library in Madras. See, *Veturi Prabhakara Sastry* by Pochiraju Seshagirirao (Delhi: Sahitya Akademi, 1999).

17. Biruduraju Ramaraju (1925–2010) is a pioneer in Telugu folklore studies. He has also extensively collected manuscripts of the Telugu (especially in Telangana) region. See, 'Telangana Talamanikam: Biruduraju Ramaraju' by Devulapalli Prabhakara Rao, *Prajatantra* (February–March, 2010), 8–9.

18. Here I have not included many Euro-American Indological archival projects. Among the most recent ones one can mention the grand project 'Sanskrit Knowledge Systems on the Eve of Colonialism'. This (now) Columbia University–based project aims at achieving 'four linked tasks: inventory the intellectual production in seven disciplines during this period; collect unpublished manuscripts and documents from archives in South Asia; create a bibliographical and prosopographical database derived from printed and manuscript sources; study selected Sanskrit works according to a uniform analytical matrix'. The project (spread over 2001–4) was funded by the National Endowment for the Humanities (NEH) and the National Science Foundation (NSF). See, http://www.columbia.edu/itc/mealac/pollock/sks/proposal.html#text8, accessed on 23 May 2013. A more recent one is the US (Columbia)–Germany (Heidelberg) bilateral project of SARIT, 'Search and Retrieval of Indic Texts' (sarit is a Sanskrit word for 'river'), that proposes to create a corpus of Sanskrit texts focused on three areas: 'Buddhist philosophy, Vedic hermeneutics, and literary theory'. This project integrates its archival initiative with the ongoing projects

of Heidelberg and Columbia (Sanskrit Knowledge Systems). See, the NEH site, http://www.neh.gov/divisions/odh/grant-news/announcing-4-nehdfg-bilateral-digital-humanities-program-awards, accessed on 6 June 2013.

19. Vemana is a seventeenth-century poet and Potana composed his Telugu rendering of the Bhagavata in the fifteenth century.

20. Max Müller cited in 'Neurobiology, Layered Texts and Correlative Cosmologies: A Cross Cultural Framework for Premodern History' by Steve Farmer, John Henderson, and Michael Witzel, in *Bulletin of the Museum of Far Eastern Antiquities* 72 (2000), 6.

21. When he was exposed to the traditional pandits, Brown's reaction was, 'Were we to submit entirely to their guidance we should learn little that is profitable. They [native pandits] exhort us to learn by rote long vocabularies framed in meter; but I rejected these, preferring the European method of study.' C. P. Brown quoted in *C.P. Brown*, by Kothapalli Veerabhadra Rao (first published in 1963; Hyderabad: Andhra Pradesh Sahitya Akademi, 1988), 133n2.

22. Well-known Sanskrit Telugu poet, playwright, translator, and critic (1853–1929).

23. Umakanta Vidyasekharulu was a Telugu-Sanskrit scholar and critic who collected folklore; Sripada Subrahmanya Sastry is a celebrated short-story writer. His autobiography, *Anubhavalu Jnapakalunu* (1955), is a milestone in modern Telugu literary history. They both belong to the early twentieth century.

24. In the Telangana context, the contribution of Srivaishnava pandits to Telugu and Sanskrit *vangmaya* in the second millennium is a worthwhile undertaking. See, Seshadri Ramana Kavulu, 'Purva Kavi Parichayamu', in *Golaconda Kavula Sanchika*, edited by Suravaram Pratapa Reddy (first published in 1934; Hyderabad: Telangana Jagruti, 2009), 389–93.

25. Keshavapantula Narasimha Sastry, *Samsthanamula Sahitya Seva* (Princely Estates and Their Literary Service) (Hyderabad: Andhra Pradesh Sahitya Akademi, 1975), 29.

26. Tumati Donappa, *Andhra Samsthanamulu Sahitya Poshanamu* (Princely Estates of Andhra and [Their] Nurture of Literature) (Hyderabad: Andhra Viswakala Parishattu, 1969), 17–18.

27. These are all bustling towns in Telangana.

28. On Srinatha's disparagement of scribes, see Thirumala Ramachandra, *Mana Lipi Puttu Purvottaralu* (Our Script–Its Genesis and Antecedents) (first published in 1957; Hyderabad: Vishalandhra Publishing House, 1993), 253.

29. Kautilya, *Arthaśāstramu*, translated into Telugu with commentary by Pullela Srirama Chandrudu, Section 2.7.1 (Hyderabad: Sri Jayalakshmi Publications), 132.

30. Thirumala Ramachandra, *Hampinunchi Harappadaaka* (from Hampi to Harappa), edited by A. Ramapati Rao (Hyderabad: Ajo-Vibho Prachurana, 1997), 296.

31. Lest one should presume that the epistemic conflict of memory and archive as a problem of 'Sanskrit Knowledge Systems', one must recount an anecdote from a Savara (aboriginal) mnemocultural experience. A Savara elder from the Araku valley (in Vizag), when compelled to part with his ancestrally inherited palm-leaf medicinal manuscript (for an English man), simply made yet another copy on palm-leaves with a stylus and kept the inherited one with himself and gave the copy to the Englishman. But when asked whether he was not losing his inherited medicinal learning and knowledge, the eighty-year-old Savara laughed and said, what is there in that book, if he needs herbs he will have to come to these mountains and slopes and recognize these leaves and roots. The Savara, who was rapidly losing his eyesight, identified his plants and roots with touch and smell, and not by turning the palm-leaves. See, Jayadheer Tirumal Rao, 'Arakulo Chillodi Kondappa', in *Tovva Muchchatlu* (Hyderabad: Spruha Sahiti Samstha, 2013), 44–8. Mnemocultural memories get articulated entirely through the medium of the (acoustic and gestural) body.

32. Dakkalis compose the community (jāti) called the Madigas (of the scheduled castes) among the Telugus.

33. B. Ramaraju, *The Contribution of Andhra to Sanskrit Literature* (Hyderabad, 2002), vi.

34. Ramaraju, *The Contribution of Andhra*, xiv–xv; and Reddy, *Golconda Kavula Sanchika*, XI–XXII, 350–1.

35. Ramachandra, *Hampinunchi Harappadaaka*, 294.

36. Here one must place on record the work of Jayadheer Thirumala Rao on the material culture of the Telugu scribal world. See, *Telugu Raatapratulu* (Telugu Manuscripts) (Hyderabad: Chelimi Foundation, 2012).

37. For the current modes of cataloguing manuscripts on the NMM site, see http://www.namami.org/catalog%20of%20manuscript.htm, accessed on 25 January 2012.

38. Here, among many other works, one can mention the rather celebratory work of Anthony Grafton. *Bring out Your Dead: The Past as Revelation* (Cambridge, Massachusetts: Harvard University Press, 2001), and *Worlds Made by Words: Scholarship and Community in the Modern West* (Cambridge, Massachusetts: Harvard University Press, 2009). As is well

known, the phrase 'epistemological break' is associated with Althusser (though he draws it from Bachelard); and the phrase 'dissociation of Sensibility' is T. S. Eliot's account of European modernity.

39. For an admirable work of critical insight, see Alasdair MacIntyre, *God, Philosophy, Universities: A Selective History of the Catholic Philosophical Tradition* (Lanham: Rowman & Littlefield, 2009).

40. B. Ramaraju, *Telugu Janapada Geya Sahityamu* (Telugu Folksong Literature) (first published in 1958; Hyderabad: Janapada Vijnana Prachuranalu, 1990), 791–807.

41. B. Ramaraju and Nayani Krishna Kumari, eds, *Janapada Geyalu – Samghika Charitra* (Hyderabad: Andhra Pradesh Sahitya Akademi, 1974), lx–lxi.

42. Ramaraju, *Telugu Janapada Geya Sahityamu*, 807.

43. *Mundakopaniṣad*, translated into Telugu with commentary by Brahmasri Kompella Dakshinamurthy, Section 1:6 (Hyderabad: Sri Sitarama Adi Sankara Trust, 2003), 50–4.

44. *Kenopaniśad*, translated with commentary into Telugu by Pullela Srirama Chandrudu, Section 2:3 (Hyderabad: Surabharati, 1984), 107–8.

45. *Kathopaniśad*, translated into Telugu with commentary by Kompella Dakshinamurthy, Section 2:4:10 (Hyderabad: Sri Sitarama Adi Sankara Trust, 2001), 266–70.

46. In the context of such a co-constitutive logic of the existent, casual declarations about inherent lacks in Indian thought seem absurd. Enquiring into Hegel's proclamation that 'man ... [as such] has not been posited' in India, Halbfass contends that one cannot find any anthropological reflection or universalistic thought concerning man/human as such in Indian traditions. Man as a 'master and owner of nature', an organizing and calculative being remains absent in India, argues Halbfass: 'No rigorous anthropocentrism or human self-elevation, even of a soteriological type, can develop' in Indian thought. Wilhelm Halbfass, *Tradition and Reflection: Explorations in Indian Thought* (Albany: State University of New York Press, 1991), 272–3. Indian thought lacks concern for the empirical, contends Agehananda Bharati: 'None of the scholastics of the Hindu tradition was concerned with the empirical self in any manner resembling that of psychologists, anthropologists, sociologists, and even poets in the West.' Agehananda Bharati, 'The Self in Hindu Thought and Action', in *Culture and Self: Asian and Western Perspectives*, edited by Anthony J. Marsella, George DeVos, and Fancis L. K. Hsu (New York: Tavistock Publications, 1985), 189. More surprisingly, even J. N. Mohanty has this to say: 'Just when philosophical interest in "man" was about to emerge, we find Indian thought displacing it by another powerful concept, the *ātman*.' J. N. Mohanty, *Reason and Tradition in*

Indian Thought: An Essay on the Nature of Indian Philosophical Thinking
(Oxford: Clarendon Press, 1992), 194. Consequently, India has developed
a transcendental notion of the subject on the one hand and a 'weak' concept of the person on the other (where the concept of person is related to
the 'mundane and empirical physical existent' [198]). How come such a
consensus about Indian thought persisted for two centuries (since Hegel
at least)? Should one look into Indian traditions more closely or should
one enquire into the presuppositions or frameworks that govern these
modern observers? Perhaps both these tasks must be undertaken. The
Christian–spiritualist–humanist framework that underlies the modern
critics' pronouncements has begun to receive critical interrogation. The
concept of spirit 'plays a major organizing role in the transcendental
teleology of reason as Eurocentric humanism'. Such an ethnocentrism
has grounded the discourse of the human sciences in the modern world.
'The history of modern metaphysics, which determines the essence of
man as animal rationale, divides as follows: There are two symmetrical
sides to understanding subjectivity: rationality of spirit on the one hand,
animality as body on the other.' Jacques Derrida, *Of Spirit: Heidegger
and the Question*, translated by Geoffrey Bennington and Rachel Bowlby
(Chicago: Chicago University Press, 1989), 73. This sovereign power
of human spirit, Derrida goes on to show elsewhere, is in the ultimate
analysis derivative of a theocratic source, which brings together force
and legitimacy ('ipsocracy' implicit even in democracy). Derrida, *Rogues*,
11–18. From a very different trajectory, Balagangadhara's critique of religion resonates deeply with this (Derrida's) account. In his discussion on
'moral domains', Balagangadhara explicitly questions the primacy of the
self/subject ('presence') in Western moral theory and exposes its human-
centric approach: 'That creatures other than human beings, under such a
view [where the self is not a sedimented and pre-given core but a hollow,
meaningless bundle of actions which only gain meaning contextually and
through others], end up having "selves" is not only not a problem, but
also a recognized consequence.' 'Comparative Anthropology and Moral
Domains: An Essay on Selfless Morality and the Moral Self', *Cultural
Dynamics* 1 (1988), 103. The template of animal rationale, as I have been
implicitly suggesting, is of no use in the thought of mnemocultures:
the para-shareera relationship cannot be subsumed under the human-
istic logic of the violent hierarchy, rationality versus animality. Sanskrit
traditions, it seems to me, repeatedly affirm the need to reflect on the
complicity of the heterogeneous only in the spatio-temporal formations
of the body complex. There can be no alternative to this rigorous practice
of moving and living on in the double bind of existence.

47. *Kathopaniṣad*, 266–8.

48. This is what Sankara in his poetic thinking composes as

> *Nānopādhivasādeva jātivarṇāśramādayaha*
> *Ātmanyāropitāstoye rasavarṇādi bhedavat.*

(Water in its original purity has neither colour, taste, nor odour. But as it draws in them we project such qualities on it. Similarly para's sheltering in name, jāti and the *ashrama* codes make us project them on to *atma*.)

See, Sankara, *Ātmabodha*, translated into Telugu by Jagannatha Swamy with a commentary, sl. 11 (Hyderabad: Ramakrishna Math, 2010), 9.

49. The arena of such a realization is none other than the body itself says Sankara:

> *Panchīkruta mahābhūta sambhavam karma sanchitam*
> *Śarīram sukhadukhānām bhogāyatana muchyate.*

(Based on the actions and the commingling of the five elements, the body gets formed. This body is said to be the space for experiencing pleasure and pain.)

Sankara, *Ātmabodha*, sl. 12, 10.

50. Various jātis from the Telugu regions.

51. *Śukranītisāramu*, translated into Telugu by Kandlakunta Alaha Singaracharyulu, 4:3:23 (Nalgonda: Sahiti Sanmana Samithi, 2002), 236.

52. The lines preceding the quoted one are more explicit about miscegenation:

> *Chaturthā bheditā jyātir brahmaṇā karmabhih purā*
> *Tattat sāmkaryasāmkaryāt pratilomānulomataha.*

Consequent upon the actions rendered previously, jātis are divided in four ways by Brahma. Due to mutual miscegenation among these jātis and further contamination among these mixed jātis result from *anuloma* (a particular type of marriage where male from any of the three jātis—Brahman, Kshatriya, and Vaisya—marries with a female from the Sudra jātis) and *pratiloma* (another type of marriage where a Sudra male marries a female from any of the other three jātis).

Śukranītisāramu, 4:3:11, 284.

53. *Śukranītisāramu*, 4:3:24, 286.

8

'UNARV'
The Poetic Factor in Metaphysics and Politics

M. C. DINAKARAN AND ANISH DAMODARAN

I

There is an anecdote, possibly apocryphal, from the early life of two mystics from the region of Travancore, which is today part of the southern state of Kerala. Chattampi Swamikal and Narayana Guru were in their early twenties and had developed a strong friendship. Being of different castes, this was not an easy matter; at a time when the practice of untouchability was the norm in that part of the country, any relationship that entailed physical proximity between a Nair and an Ezhava was a rarity.

The two itinerant friends had been wandering from place to place when late one evening they decided to sleep under a tree until dawn and then proceed to their next destination. They spread their *tortu* (coarse towels) on the ground and using their folded elbows as pillows, they lay down to sleep. A little while later, a few local villagers passed them by and looking at the two men sleeping peacefully on the rough earth, remarked, 'How happy these drunkards are, they sleep blissfully even on hard ground!' Hearing this, Chattampi Swamikal got up, and chuckling, immediately composed two lines in metrical Malayalam: '*Spashtam Nlavanguneengi, dinakaranudayamcheytu, chandranmaranju/Thattithattiperukkiperuveliyathilakkiduvanpinnayatte*' ('the clear moonlight has faded, the sun has risen, the moon has set/But enlarging it to encompass all of outer space?/Let that happen some other time!') to which Narayana Guru added, '*Kashtamdeenampidichomadirayatukudichokidakkunnalokarkku/ Utthishotthishtaseekhramnadiyilmuzhukuvankalamayivannitippol*' ('The sick, the addicted, the miserable!/It's time to get up and take a dip in the river!')[1]

It may be said without the slightest exaggeration that the Kerala Renaissance was set in motion at this precise instant. It was not any petition with tens of thousands of signatures,[2] nor any mass movement against oppression, nor the defiant consecration of temples on far away river banks[3] which inaugurated the Kerala Renaissance through which a metaphysics gave birth to a politics that transformed an entire society in crisis.

When the two wanderer friends composed these lines, they had not yet become the Chattampi Swamikal[4] or Narayana Guru[5] we know today. Both the mystics had undergone traditional Sanskrit education in schools run by *asans* (acknowledged masters). They had both learned Hatha Yoga from a teacher who made a living as a colonial bureaucrat; they had both drunk from the fount of ancient Tamil wisdom that preceded even the Vedas. Both had separately retreated to a mountain cave in Marutva Malai, close to the peninsular tip of Kanyakumari and were still young wanderers when they composed their impromptu stanzas. Chattampi Swamikal was known then as Kunjan Pillai, and Narayana Guru was just plain Nanu Asan at the time. However, the transformation of Kerala from an iniquitous and impoverished province given to the worst practices of an indigenously grown apartheid to its present status as one of India's most socially enlightened states has much to do with these two mystics.

II

What was the meaning of this spontaneous poetic dialogue between the two mystics? Both are said to have undergone their individual epiphanies while meditating in their hill caves. Both could have continued enflaming the spark of bliss within themselves to encompass their whole selves—*sahajabhava*—and lived until their karmic roles had been played out. But Chattampi Swamikal says, 'The *vrittis* [corrugations of the mind] have been smoothened out/the mind which causes restlessness has set with the moon/the brilliant sun of Knowledge has risen/But Wait!'[6]

'Wait!', he is instructing himself and his friend, 'Wait! Wait a while before immersing yourself deep into the bliss by enlarging your consciousness which has already risen inside the cave of your heart! Wait before expanding your *bodha* to encompass the whole of inner and outer space!'[7] And Narayana Guru in turn offers the precise reason to wait: the pull of compassion for other selves to help them on their way by mustering the courage to renounce one's own attainment, *prapti*, until that happens.

III

Poetry precedes politics here. But wasn't this true for all periods of human history? Weren't all great movements triggered by a flowering of an inner vision which then got relayed to the population at large through the medium of poetic language? Nagarjuna, Sankara, Kabir, Nanak, Hafiz, Rumi, Basho, had all turned to the language of poetry to communicate their message and set immense collective transformations in motion.

The two Kerala mystics were accomplished poets. Chattampi Swamikal composed numerous verses and prose pieces, but very few of these remain due to his total disregard for writing them down for posterity. Until his very late years, he did not even allow his disciples to be around him. He was an *avadhoota*—wanderer— but whatever is available as the corpus of Chattampi Swamikal is imbued with a rare poetry, whether written within metric rhythms or outside it. However, like a master ventriloquist, he often spoke through his friend's tongue: he had requested Narayana Guru to compose some poems to unravel complex metaphysical truths, as is explicitly acknowledged by the Guru in his nine-stanza poem, 'Navamanjari'. At the poetic plane, the two minds worked almost as one, and there is a congruence in the messages they gave to their respective followers.

Narayana Guru was fortunate to have attracted a few brilliant disciples early in his life as a *sanyasin* (renunciate) and they had taken down all that he had dictated as part of their training. Hence, we have more than sixty poems written by the Guru in Sanskrit, Malayalam, and Tamil, which give a true understanding of the mode these mystics had used to gently prod the sick, the addicted, and the miserable to take a dip in the river of their own consciousness, bodha, and emerge with all their faculties imbued with 'Unarv' (a Malayalam word used in common parlance to denote wakefulness).

IV

According to Buddhist legend, when the Buddha arrived at Sarnath from Gaya a few weeks after the night of Vaisakhi (the full moon night when Sidhartha Gautama attained enlightenment and became the Buddha), his companions are said to have asked him whether the strange aura enveloping him was because he had become a Deva, Gandharva, or some such ethereal being. Sakyamuni is believed to have replied that he had not become a Deva, Gandharva, or any ethereal being; he was just Awake. Narayana Guru's Unarv is also a waking up to a higher reality when even the last stains of ignorance, *avidya*, have been melted away by the rays of *vidya*, and all *triputis* (triads) such as knowledge, knower, and the known merge into a flowing river of self-effulgent consciousness.[8]

According to an old adage, what *rishis* (realized beings) say is poetry. Nanu Asan came down from the caves of Kanyakumari as a rishi and all his messages, until his Samadhi (demise) in 1928, were communicated primarily in two modes—poetry and silence. The Guru was deploying the power of poetry to indirectly fashion a politics in a scenario where multiple forms of oppression had devastated a whole population of farmers, artisans, fishermen, and tribes people. There is a common perception that it was only the untouchables in Kerala who were the victims of oppression. In fact, except for a few landed families who had access to large-scale rent-seeking within the feudal and colonial dispensations, most people had been living in conditions of near penury for hundreds of years. The prayers and spirituals they had inherited from their forefathers as well as some coarse forms of worship constituted the cultural life of the majority of the people. It was in transforming this dismal reality that the mystic duo of Kerala worked in unison. Their poems were written to stimulate an inner stirring within a people who had forgotten that they even possessed a self, slumbering somewhere deep under their surface awareness of being subjects to multiple masters. These poems were deceptively simple and were amenable to being sung or being set to music to be chanted in groups. Buried within them, however, were multiple levels of meanings that accomplished their work at an experiential level. Such stirrings within were the beginnings of Unarv, both at the individual and collective levels.

'Daiva Dasakam' is a unique prayer written by Narayana Guru that is chanted in hundreds of thousands of homes almost on a daily basis even today as dusk falls on Kerala villages and the family congregates in their prayer rooms before laying out the final meal of the day. Guru had written prayers hailing Vinayaka, Vasudeva, Bhadrakali, Subrahmanya, and so on, in Sanskrit and Malayalam, but 'Daiva Dasakam' stands apart as a prayer addressed to the universal God *Daivam*. Until then, it was the Malayali Christians whose antiquity is held to go all the way back to Didymus the apostle, who were using the word *Daivam* to denote the Biblical God. The 'Hindus' would pray to their personal deities or to the *Dharma Sastha* of the Sabari Hills. In one fell swoop, 'Daiva Dasakam' reduced this multiplicity of personal deities to one limitless flow of 'Light', for which the Guru created a metaphysical architecture in ten simple stanzas.

The poem starts with a plain appeal to God: pleading for the security of the devotee, comparing Him to the captain of a steam ship that crosses the sea of becoming. Then it reminds the devotee to examine the content of phenomenal bodies to uncover their emptiness and assists the devotee to become witness to his/her merging into an unpulsating consciousness called Daivam. The third stanza brings back the devotee to everyday reality and thanks God for providing food, clothes, and shelter as and when the need arises. From here, the prayer turns into an exercise in raising the consciousness of the devotee: examples are given of the transient human existence as a play of the self, the illusion and the substratum of all existence, and the limited levels through which we perceive Truth as the Glory of God. 'God' is defined here as nothing but what was, what is, and what will be—the Word and the remembrance of the Word. The world is God and vice versa, we are told, reminding one of Acharya Nagarjuna's[9] assertion of the complete identity of *samsara* (repeating cycles of birth, life, and death) and *nirvana* (liberation).

V

'Daiva Dasakam' is, on the surface, a poem written in very simple Malayalam designed to make it an ideal prayer for group chanting. It is possible that the philosophical insights that lie buried deep in the prayer may not consciously register in the minds of the devotees who chant it ritualistically. However, the politics that arose from this and other poetic interventions of the Guru cannot be missed by any observer of the last one hundred years of Kerala's socio-cultural life. The year 2011, when the followers of Narayana Guru were celebrating the centenary of the *Sarada Pratishta*,[10] the consecration of the Sarada temple at Sivagiri, was also the centenary year of another remarkable poem written by the Guru called 'Janani Navaratna Manjari' to commemorate the occasion.

It is interesting to note that accompanying each consecration (*pratishta*) that the Guru performed, he would also compose a poem to explain the metaphysical import of the pratishta. The famous '*Jaatibhedam, matadvesham ...*' stanza[11] composed at Aruvippuram would surely have become the national anthem of Kerala had it become a standalone republic in 1947! 'Subrahmanya Keerthanam' was composed at the Kunnumpara pratishta; 'Mannanthala Devi Stavam' was composed after consecrating the devi idol at Mannanthala; and 'Kolatesvara Stavam' was composed after the installation at Kulathur. The praxis of the Guru was simultaneously an attempt to recover the poetic life of a people and his poetry also a way to practise his Dharma.

This poetry set in motion the process of Unarv, first as a viewing of one's image in the mirror of self, then passing through a period of confusion as to the location of the self in an arena crowded with other selves equally confused about themselves, and eventually a slow process of resolution during which the chain of illusions binding the real self with the sensory organs are broken and a groundswell of the collective awareness of Unarv surges forth.

One arrives at a realm of consciousness in the objective world only after waking up from the Maya-induced sleep/forgetfulness of the inner subjective world.[12] In a vivid description of the relative soul (*jeevatma*) in his *Atmopadesa Satakam* (One hundred verses of Self-instruction), the Guru had a vision of an oil lamp with all its wicks burning furiously on its two tiers, rotating around its axis on a string tied at some point in infinity and casting a shadow under it. He then explains that the wicks are as functions of the mind, *vritti*; the self is the shadow; the oil in the tiers is prior habitual traits, *vasanas*. The two tiers represent the gross body, *sthulasarira*, and the subtle body, *sukshmasarira*, of the individual self. The fact that the lamp is anchored somewhere in infinity indicates that the self has no beginning as it had cyclically renewed itself into many life forms over cosmic time. Though the origin of the relative soul is in some infinite point in time, *anadi* (beginningless), its cyclical reincarnations can indeed be brought to an end if the self, the jeevatma, wishes to recover its true nature. It is not *ananta* (endless).[13]

It is here that the political erupts abruptly out of a seemingly harmless poetics. One has to discover the essence of one's existence through one's own effort, says the Guru, in order to walk the path towards one's liberation. The self that is unable to see its true inner substance is just as unaware as the moving shadow of a whirling lamp anchored in infinity. Both are unable to witness their real selves. Liberation is, therefore, Unarv, which is a natural consequence of the removal of the veil of Maya, which in turn allows the illumination to energize the collective to move to its own true rhythm. Narayana Guru calls truth variously in different poems—sometimes as *Jnanam-Anandam*; sometimes as *Arivu*, the proto-Dravidian word for knowledge. In the *Advaita Deepika*, he employs a double negation to indicate the Real by referring to it as *anritamalla*—meaning 'not out of alignment with the *ritam*[14] of universe'.

The Maya-governed material world is ever out of alignment with the cosmic ritam. It requires continuous individual and collective effort to restore it to its proper alignment. During periods in history when philosophy and poetry have been purged from a people's social and cultural life, a general enervation of the spirit is accompanied and followed by a crisis in material life at the individual and collective levels. These crises also trigger self-examination at both levels. Such an Unarv generates a politics that moves a collectivity towards a terrain of love and compassion, and away from a politics of counter-violence and resentment.

VI

The poetry and politics of the Travancore mystics triggered a wave of creativity throughout the coast of Kerala over a period of the last hundred years. Poetry, music, and literature flowed out of the crevices opened up by this great social churning. A new language was minted to articulate the new ideas, and a huge appetite for knowledge was created among ordinary men and women. Academics who catalogue the factors that gave rise to the 'Kerala Model' rarely mention the mushrooming of village libraries all over the state about sixty years ago at a time when the per capita income was abysmally low, the physical infrastructure was almost non-existent, and people had only the barest form of literacy. Even in such a scenario, every hamlet had a library with both Malayalam and English books and, more importantly, a room where newspapers were available for free reading. It is not accidental that Chattampi Swamikal spent his last days in a spartan reading room at Panmana, near Kollam.[15]

Chattampi Swamikal attained Samadhi (as Vedantins would call it) in the month of May in 1924. His companion Narayana Guru reached Samadhi in the month of September, 1928. Both had lived for more than seventy years at a critical time in the world's history. The American Civil War and the First War of Indian Independence raged when they were children; the British empire began displaying its colonial might in their boyhood; it was in their forties and fifties that the twentieth century had arrived bringing in its wake the first global war, technologically fine-tuned mass murders, and utopian visions of homogeneity.

The social innovations that were spawned from the orthodox doctrine of *Advaita* as taught by these masters were in complete contrast to the theology of industrial cornucopia. It was based on voluntarism, respect for the 'deviant', and permitting enough margins on the sidelines of individual and collective lives for a continuous rewriting of the script. Life for these two mystics was a search for an authentic existence, and their poetry was the language used to articulate the churning that occurred as a consequence of their interventions within the individual and in the collective at large.

VII

Advaita Vedanta defines *apara* as an incomparable entity that can exist with its own properties, without another substratum. The *aparaprakriti* as expounded by Narayana Guru in his writings belongs at this level. It is understood as the substratum on which the entire experience of the relative world rests. And it is through poetry that the truth about the self can be comprehended and experienced. At the conclusion of his *Atmopadesa Satakam* the Guru remarks:

> Knowledge and I are both one, for one divest of all veiling curtains;
> Another might have reason to argue still;
> If the 'I' could be taken as other than knowledge
> None there is to know knowledge here at all.[16]

The relativization of the self, according to the Guru, leads to segmentation into the knower, knowledge, and that which is known—the self, the consciousness of the object, and the object. The Guru remarks that the subtle experience of material objects can also open up a path to knowing ultimate reality: when individual parts are investigated one by one, they are seen to be consciousness alone.[17] Advaitins hold that the world of material objects also exists at its subtlest level as an unbroken flow of consciousness. Hence, the emergence of the Other arises due to a non-attunement of the self with the level of subtle experience. The distance between one's self and another's self emerges from the non-awareness of subtle experience. For the two Travancore mystics, poetry was the arena where a continuous re-articulation of de-reified notions of self and the other was possible.

Experience is but another manifestation of knowledge. When we experience a thing, we come to know of it from the inside. The fulcrum of experience is what Narayana Guru calls *Aham*—the I. Hence, I am nothing but a temporary embodiment of consciousness. Narayana Guru denies this property to material objects; they do not possess a sense of Aham. However, this is far different from the idealist view of life as defined by contemporary philosophy. In his hundred-verse Sanskrit composition *Darsana Mala*, the Guru observes:

> In spite of action becoming self-accomplished
> By the psychic dynamism and the senses
> The wise one thus knows—I am the
> Unattached Kutastha [firmly established like a rock].[18]

The poetry of Narayana Guru was a subversive engine that worked to de-stratify and dissolve the frozen social structure of Kerala. The social crust was dissolved by a reweaving of the new emerging selves into a web of fresh individual and collective experiences. In the 49th stanza of *Atmopadesa Satakam*, Narayana Guru observes that every congregation organized either for material or spiritual purposes works ultimately towards collective happiness.

For Narayana Guru, the material and spiritual are not two different worlds. The Guru says as much explicitly in one of his rare prose pieces: 'The human body feels happiness when all organs work in harmony. Similarly, if the human community has to achieve its ultimate goal of collective happiness, everything related to material and spiritual has to be integrated.'[19]

Through poetry, a balance is restored even when the world is tilted off its axis. Through his poetic interventions in metaphysics, Narayana Guru attempted to restore a balance in collective life by trying 'to change the life of his time to the life of his dream',[20] as one poet has said it. Through his poetry, Narayana Guru sought to transcend the human–ideal duality by humanizing the ideal and idealizing the human simultaneously.

VIII

At the centre of the poetic and the political there lies a deep silence—a silence which cancels out all orthodoxies and heterodoxies, a dimensionless depth of stillness. Narayana Guru calls this *mouna-ghana-amrita-abdhi*, silence-filled, frozen ocean of pure nectar. At that level, one does not need even the instrument of poetry—two realized souls can communicate perfectly through silence.

While travelling through Tamil Nadu in 1917, Narayana Guru's disciples requested him to visit Ramana Maharshi who was staying at Thiruvanna Malai. Pazhani Swami, a disciple of Maharshi, came to meet the Guru and formally invited him to visit the Ramana Ashram. 'Yes, yes; we should surely go and see the Maharshi. He never leaves his Ashram; so we should go to him.'[21]

When the Guru reached the Skanda Ashram where Ramana Maharshi was sitting, Guru watched him for some time and then sat under a mango tree. His disciples went inside the Ashram and sat near the Maharshi. When lunch was ready, the Maharshi came out and invited the Guru in chaste Malayalam. The Guru accepted the request in mellifluous Tamil. They had their lunch in silence and Ramana Maharshi went for his usual post-lunch walk. When he came back, the Guru asked his disciples, 'Don't we have to offer some donation to the Maharshi?'[22] And he took a paper and pencil and wrote five stanzas in Sanskrit. As a preamble he wrote:

> *Ityadivaadoparatammahantam*
> *Prasantagambhiranijasvabhavam*
> *Shonachale Sri Ramanamnirikshya*
> *Provacha Narayana Samyindrah*

(Dedicated to Sri Ramana, who after extinguishing all dualities, dwells in tranquil deep inherent *svabhava* [innate nature] in the Shonachala Hills, by Narayana, the one who has controlled all his sense organs.[23])

The five stanzas form part of his poem *Nirvriti Panchakam*.[24] When all plurality disappears from the consciousness and the bodha arrives at its own natural state of stillness, one attains the state of *nirvriti*, a word that can be loosely translated as inward release.

After composing the poem, the Guru sat close to the Maharshi, but there was no exchange of words. The disciples of both sages who had been holding their breath waiting for a grand philosophical dialogue were deeply disappointed. When they had finished sharing their silence, the Guru got up and declared, 'So be it!' and quietly left the Ashram.[25]

Notes

1. This poem is included as the 12th stanza of Narayana Guru's *Subrahmanya Stotram*. For a free translation, see the introduction by Scott Teitsworth in *The Psychology of Darsanamala* by Nitya Chaitanya Yati (New Delhi: D. K. Printworld, 2004), 12.

2. The Malayali Memorial and the Ezhava Memorial were mass petitions signed by coalitions of communities to highlight their need for greater inclusion in the state's power-sharing arrangements. For further details, see Robin Jeffrey, *The Decline of Nayar Dominance: Society and Politics in Travancore, 1847–1908* (New Delhi: Manohar, 2014), 142–94.

3. For an engaging analysis of one such consecration, see Roby Rajan and J. Reghu, 'Backwater Universalism', in *Political Hinduism: The Religious Imagination in Public Spheres*, edited by Vinay Lal (New Delhi: Oxford University Press, 2009), 58–95.

4. Chattampi Swamikal (1853–1924) was born Kunjan Pillai at Trivandrum, the capital of the princely state of Travancore and is said to have attained extraordinary yogic skills. He is considered to be the philosophical fount of the transformation of Kerala society in the last century. For more details on the life and times of this philosopher-mystic, see R. Raman Nair and L. Sulochana Devi, *Chattampi Swami: An Intellectual Biography* (Trivandrum: Centre for South Indian Studies, 2010).

5. Narayana Guru (1854–1928) was a philosopher-mystic who reinterpreted and renewed *Advaita Vedanta* in the last century and is considered the maker of modern Kerala. For more details on his life and times, see Nataraja Guru, *Life and Teachings of Narayana Guru* (Fernhill, Tamil Nadu and Bainbridge, USA: An East-West University Publication, 1990).

6. Narayana Guru, verse 12, 'Subrahamanya Keertanam', in *Complete Works of Narayana Guru*, edited by Muni Narayana Prasad, Malayalam edition (New Delhi: National Book Trust India, 2005), 219–20. Translated by the authors.

7. Narayana Guru, verse 12, 'Subrahamanya Keertanam', in *Complete Works of Narayana Guru*.

8. The penultimate stage of reaching one's true state is described in the 52nd stanza of Narayana Guru's *Atmopadesa Satakam*: 'Filled with word content, that day the firmament shall radiant blaze/And in it shall become extinct all the visionary magic/Then too, that small voice completing tribasic knowing/Shall cease and Self-radiance prevail.' in Guru, *Life and Teachings of Narayana Guru*, 608.

9. Nagarjuna (150–250 CE), the greatest exponent of Mahayana Buddhism and considered as the philosopher who gave the second turn to the Wheel of Dharma, defined *samsara* (the ever-changing world) as nothing other than *nirvana* (salvation, emancipation, extinction of relative existence). See David Snellgrove, *Indo-Tibetan Buddhism: Indian Buddhists and Their Tibetan Successors* (Boston: Shambhala, 2002), 123.

10. *Sarada Pratishta* refers to the consecration of the idol of goddess Sarada, the patron-deity of Knowledge.

11. This poem was inscribed on the walls of the temple that Narayana Guru had established after the consecration of the Siva Linga at Aruvippuram: 'This is the ideal place/Where everyone dwells in brotherhood/Without distinctions of caste/Or religious rivalry.' M Prabha, *The Guru* (Varkala, Kerala: Sree Narayana Dharma Sangham, 1954), 20.

12. Nitya Chaitanya Yati defines Maya as 'the force which gives rise to and sustains the nescience or ignorance that perpetuates the affectivity of the mind by attaching to it the seeming reality of names and forms'. Yati, *The Psychology of Darsanamala*, 196.

13. Narayana Guru describes it as follows: 'Suffering filled, with petals five and tiers two/Rotating beginningless, such a lamp hanging/The Self in shadow form, it burns, with prior habit traits/For oil, and function verily for wick.' Guru, *Life and Teachings of Narayana Guru*, 525.

14. *Ritam* is understood by Narayana Guru as the basic principle of the universe, the ultimate rhythm in which the cosmos exists. Sorrow in the relative world occurs as beings move out of alignment with ritam because of the illusory power of Maya.

15. Paravur K. Gopala Pillai, *Paramabhattarasri Chattampiswami Thiruvadikal Jeevacharitram* (Trichur, Kerala: Current Books, 2010), 149.

16. Guru, *Life and Teachings of Narayana Guru*, 709.

17. *Narayana Guru's Darsana Mala with commentary by Muni Narayana Prasad* (Varkala, Kerala: Narayana Gurukula Publication, 2004), 83.

18. Yati, *The Psychology of Darsanamala*, 318.

19. Quoted in B. Rajeevan, *Vaakkukalum Vasthukkalum* (Kottayam, Kerala: D. C. Books, 2009), 252.

20. Michael Schmidt, *Lives of Poets* (London: Orion Books, 1999), 623.

21. Nochoor N. S. Venkataraman, *Atmasakshatkaram* (Trichur, Kerala: Current Books, 2004), 122.

22. Venkataraman, *Atmasakshatkaram*, 123.

23. Venkataraman, *Atmasakshatkaram*, 123.

24. *Narayana Guru's Nirvriti Panchakam with commentary by Muni Narayana Prasad* (Varkala, Kerala: Narayana Gurukula Publications, 2004), 29–40.

25. Venkataraman, *Atmasakshatkaram*, 123.

NOTES ON CONTRIBUTORS

Udipi Rajagopalacharya Ananthamurthy (1932–2014) was one of India's most well-known writers and a widely respected public intellectual who played a major role in nurturing educational and artistic institutions. Born in Karnataka's Shimoga District, Ananthamurthy wrote largely in his native Kannada and left behind a corpus of works including five novels, nearly ten short-story collections, and many volumes of essays. Though his knowledge of Kannada and, more widely, Indian literature was breathtaking, he was also well-versed in English literature and he earned a doctorate from the University of Birmingham for a thesis on 'Politics and Fiction in the 1930s'. His most acclaimed work was the novel *Samskara* (1966), translated into English by his equally distinguished contemporary, the poet, translator, scholar, and literary critic A. K. Ramanujan. Ananthamurthy was honoured with the Jnanpith Award (1994), the highest literary recognition conferred by the Government of India.

Anish Damodaran is a Director with Shree Rajlaxmi Logistics Private Limited, Mumbai, and was instrumental in organizing the first meeting of the Backwaters Collective in Colombo, Sri Lanka in 2010. He has since been intimately involved in all the conferences of the Collective, and takes a deep interest in the life and thought of Narayana Guru.

Ashis Nandy is widely recognized as one of the leading and most creative intellectuals anywhere in the world. He has had a lifelong association with the Centre for the Study of Developing Societies, Delhi, as Fellow, Senior Fellow, Director, and now Distinguished Fellow. He is the author of over twenty books, most of them published by Oxford University Press, Delhi. His works include *The Intimate Enemy: Loss and Recovery of Self under Colonialism* (1983), *Tyranny, Traditions and Utopias: Essays in the Politics of Awareness* (1987), *The Tao of Cricket: On Games of Destiny and the Destiny of Games* (1989), *The Illegitimacy of Nationalism: Rabindranath Tagore and the Politics of Self* (1994), *The Savage Freud and Other Essays on Possible and Retrievable Selves* (1995), *Time Warps: The Insistent Politics of Silent and Evasive Pasts* (2002), and *The Romance of the State and the Fate of Dissent in the Tropics* (2008). Oxford University Press (India) has honoured him with a 3-volume Omnibus Edition, which reproduces nine of his books, and among his many accolades is the Grand Prize of the Fukuoka Asian Culture Prize (2007).

M. C. Dinakaran recently retired as a General Manager at the Board of Radiation and Isotope Technology, Department of Atomic Energy, Mumbai, and has maintained a keen interest in philosophy and politics throughout his professional career. He reads Sanskrit and Malayalam among other languages, and is particularly conversant with the thought of Shankaracharya and Narayana Guru. He is one of the founding members of the Backwaters Collective.

Julius Lipner, who is of Indo-Czech origin, has recently retired from the University of Cambridge as Professor of Hinduism and the Comparative Study of Religion. He was born and brought up in India, where he obtained a Licentiate in Theology (*summa cum laude*) in the Pontifical Athenaeum (now Jnana Deepa Vidyapith) in Poona and studied for an M. A. in Indian and Western philosophy at Jadavpur University in Calcutta. Lipner earned his PhD from the University of London in 1974. Among his special fields of study are Vedantic thought, nineteenth-century Bengal, and inter-cultural and inter-religious understanding, with special reference to Hindu and Christian traditions. Lipner is an Emeritus Fellow and former Vice-President of Clare Hall, a postgraduate College in the University of Cambridge, and in 2008 he became a Fellow of the British Academy. His dozen authored and edited books include *Hindus: Their Religious Beliefs and Practices* (2nd ed., 2010) and *Brahmabandhab Upadhyay:*

The Life and Thought of a Revolutionary (Oxford, 1999). He has also translated and edited for Oxford University Press two novels by Bankimcandra Chatterji, *Anandamath, or The Sacred Brotherhood* and *Debī Chaudhurānī, or The Wife Who Came Home*.

N. Manu Chakravarthy is Professor and Head of the Department of English at NMKRV College, Bangalore. He has taught literary criticism, literary theory, and cultural theory for the last thirty years. He received the *Swarna Kamal*, or the President of India's Gold Medal, for his contributions to film criticism and the V. M. Inamdar Award (2010) for his book, *Madhyama Marga*, on Kannada literature and culture. He writes extensively on cinema, music, literature, and culture and has had a long association as a permanent faculty member at the famous annual 'cultural workshop' at Heggodu, Shimoga District, Karnataka. He is the editor of several volumes of Ananthamurthy's work, including *Rujuvathu: Selected Essays* (2014), *Hunt Bangle Chameleon: Selected Short Stories* (2014), and the *U. R. Ananthamurthy Omnibus* (2007).

Roby Rajan is probably best described as an academic survivor who has managed to stay afloat on his flimsy non-affiliated raft for over three decades while being buffeted by fierce gale-force disciplinary winds from every direction. He now ploughs his lonely furrow at the provincial University of Wisconsin-Parkside, where as a Professor of Quantitative Methods, he often has to cut his way through a dense thicket of dispiriting words like 'excellence', 'assessment', and 'rubric'. He has a visceral aversion to trendy global ideas—especially those with the prefixes 'post' and 'sub'—and can't for the life of him figure out why the elites of the Third World are so intent on putting their societies on a course of self-destruction just so they can one day look into the mirror and recognize themselves as shoddy versions of (what they imagine to be) First World 'success'. When he surveys the contemporary landscape scarred by words like 'religion', 'secularism', 'sectarianism', and 'fundamentalism', what he finds missing is any serious grappling with the question of how the intercommunal relationality that is constitutive of most Third-World societies can be turned in a Utopian direction away from the thralldom to 'progress' and 'development'. He fears this fateful absence to be a symptom of the conceptual bankruptcy of the globalized Third-World intellectual who has become rather too adept at playing his/her designated role in producing sound and fury—while signifying little.

Sundar Sarukkai is Director of the Manipal Centre for Philosophy and Humanities, Manipal University. His research interests include philosophy of science and social science, and phenomenology and philosophy of language and art, drawing on both Indian and Western philosophical traditions. He has been a Homi Bhabha Fellow, Fellow of the Indian Institute of Advanced Study at Shimla, and a Fellow at the Advanced Institute of Study at Nantes. His books include *Translating the World: Science and Language*; *Philosophy of Symmetry*; *Indian Philosophy and Philosophy of Science*; and, with Gopal Guru, *The Cracked Mirror: An Indian Debate on Theory and Experience*. He is an Editorial Board member of MIT Press's Leonardo Book Series and Member of the Indian Council of Philosophical Research.

D. Venkat Rao is Professor at the English and Foreign Languages University, Hyderabad. He publishes widely in both Telugu and English. He has translated Ashis Nandy's *The Intimate Enemy* into Telugu as *Priya Shatruvu* (2009), and earlier translated into English the intellectual autobiography in Telugu of Rani Siva Sankara Sarma, which has appeared as *The Last Brahmin: Life and Reflections of a Modern-Day Sanskrit Pandit* (2007). His areas of interest include literary and cultural studies, image studies, comparative thought, and mnemocultures, and his most recent work that reflects some of these interests is *Cultures of Memory in South Asia: Orality, Literacy and the Problem of Inheritance* (2014).

Vinay Lal is Professor of History and Asian American Studies at the University of California, Los Angeles (UCLA). He has written widely on modern Indian history, colonialism, the worldwide Indian diaspora, the politics of knowledge systems, mainstream Indian cinema, and the life and work of Gandhi. His fourteen books include *Empire of Knowledge: Culture and Plurality in the Global Economy* (2002), *The History of History: Politics and Scholarship in Modern India* (2003), *The Future of Knowledge and Culture:*

A Dictionary for the 21st Century (2005, co-edited with Ashis Nandy), *Fingerprinting Popular Culture: The Mythic and the Iconic in Popular Indian Cinema* (2006, co-edited with Ashis Nandy), *Deewaar: The Footpath, the City, and the Angry Young Man* (2010), and the two-volume edited set entitled the *Oxford Anthology of the Modern Indian City* (2013).

INDEX